JUDGMENT CALLS

Making Good

Decisions in

Difficult Situations

John C. Mowen

A Fireside Book
Published by Simon & Schuster
New York London Toronto Sydney Tokyo Singapore

FIRESIDE
Rockefeller Center
1230 Avenue of the Americas
New York, New York 10020

First Fireside Edition 1994

FIRESIDE and colophon are registered trademarks
of Simon & Schuster Inc.

Designed by Liney Li
Manufactured in the United States of America

3   5   7   9   10   8   6   4   2

Library of Congress Cataloging-in-Publication Data
Mowen, John C.
Judgment calls : making good decisions in difficult situations / John C. Mowen.
p.   cm.
Includes index.
1. Decision-making.   2. Risk perception.   3. Risk management.   I. Title.
HD30.28.M69   1993
658.4'03—dc20   93-11011
CIP
ISBN: 0-671-72838-5
0-671-89883-3 (pbk)

The author acknowledges permission to reprint lyrics from "The
Gambler," by Don Schlitz. Copyright © 1977 Cross Keys Publish-
ing Co., Inc. All Rights administered by Sony Music Publishing,
8 Music Square West, Nashville, TN 37203. All rights reserved.
Reprinted by permission.

To those who have made good decisions that turned out poorly.

CONTENTS

PREFACE

Why did Drexel Burnham Lambert, Inc., a large, sophisticated Wall Street firm, go bankrupt while little Peoples Bancorp of Worcester, Massachusetts, continues to show profits year after year? Why did NASA succeed in putting a man on the Moon and then suffer the Challenger Space Shuttle disaster? Why was the United States victorious in the Persian Gulf war but failed so miserably in Vietnam?

The answers to these questions are found in the divergent judgment calls made by CEOs, politicians, and military commanders. A judgment call occurs when a decision maker must make a tough choice between two or more options based upon ambiguous information and conflicting goals. It is a high-stakes decision, which cannot be reached by computer simulations or with the help of mathematical equations. Bring in high-priced experts, and they will disagree. Possessing an MBA, a Ph.D. in economics, or the ability to read Tarot cards will not improve your ability to make such decisions.

Judgment Calls is a book about how *people* make decisions and about how choices made in a high-stakes environment can be improved. Over the past ten years, there have been countless books and articles arguing that management success depends upon creating "the learning organization" or "the total quality organization." But, of course, organizations do not learn—people learn. The great decision-making catastrophes of the last thirty years, such as the Space Shuttle Challenger explosion, the bankruptcy of Drexel Burnham Lambert, and the Vietnam War, resulted from the failures of *people* to make proper high-stakes decisions. Managers are also being urged to flatten their companies and empower employees. Indeed, employees do become more motivated when they are given greater decision-making autonomy. But in order to enhance productivity and achieve superior results, something more than motivated employees is required. They must work smarter as well as harder. With greater decision-making autonomy, employees and managers will be placed in the position of having to make high-stakes decisions. As a result, they need guidelines for making judgment calls.

The difficulty is that within the context of a world filled with risk and uncertainty, you can make the best possible decision, yet the outcome can still blow apart in your face. Chance, luck, happenstance—call it what you will—looms large in the real world. Because of the ambiguity and uncertainty of the high-stakes environment, cookbook-style recipes for success will not help you. High-stakes decisions cannot be approached from such a simplistic viewpoint.

However, guidelines for making judgment calls can be derived from the field of behavioral decision theory, on which the concepts in this book are based. I believe that *Judgment Calls* will help managers and employees to make successful choices and to minimize the chances of catastrophic errors. In writing this book for a general audience, my goals are to identify the types of judgment calls faced by high-stakes decision makers, to present new ways of thinking that can guide your problem-solving activities, and ultimately to improve your decision making. To this end, I will focus on eight fundamental judgment calls that take place when making high-stakes decisions: whether to shoot or not; whether to stay or quit; whether to emphasize the present or the future; whether to choose risk or security; how to find the cause; whether control or chance operates; which frame of reference to use; and when to employ reason versus emotion.

Along the way, I will describe the pitfalls of making high-stakes decisions through stories culled from numerous sources. Many come from the sixty-plus interviews that I conducted with individuals who have had to make high-level decisions; others are derived from my experiences in the military, business, financial investing, sports, and academia. Articles in the business and trade press, as well as newspapers and magazines, were gleaned for examples. I have also drawn brief illustrative stories from the works of a number of marvelous writers who have an uncanny way of vividly describing decision making at the highest level. These include David Halberstam, Tom Wolfe, Charles Murray and Catherine Cox, George Will, and Maryann Keller—to name just a few.

I have deliberately avoided narrowly typecasting *Judgment Calls*. The stories, cases, and examples are drawn from numerous contexts.

My goal has been to select the best stories possible to illustrate the concepts being developed. The principles of behavioral decision theory apply to all decision makers, whether in business, government, law, medicine, or the military. In addition, the ideas hold for judgment calls made at diverse levels of analysis—that is, to decision making at the individual level (should I quit my job?), the organizational level (should our firm attempt a takeover of a larger company?), and the governmental level (should the U.S. have taken Baghdad in the Persian Gulf war?). Harry Truman said that "the buck stops here." The concept that we are responsible for making our own decisions holds for us, just as it did for Truman. The ideas apply to all of us. Indeed, aren't we all the CEOs of our own lives?

Inevitably, authors who analyze major events risk oversimplification, and I too may be accused of that error. I have suggested reasons for why Saddam Hussein ordered the invasion of Kuwait, identified some causes for the savings and loan crisis threatening the finance industry, and analyzed why Soichiro Honda may be called a peerless decision maker. In each case, numerous factors combined to account for the effects found. Of necessity, my analysis will provide only partial answers. The goal is *not* to attempt to give the total story for why each of these events occurred; rather, the illustrations are used to depict behavioral decision theory principles in practice. In addition, my academic colleagues will find that I sometimes go beyond the empirical research findings in my analysis of judgment calls. I have attempted to found my story on the solid base of behavioral decision theory research, but in some instances I move beyond the data to offer explanations and suggestions for action.

On occasion, when I found myself writing critically of decisions made by individuals far more important and talented than I, the thought crossed my mind: "There but for the grace of God go I." How can I venture to criticize such people? Indeed, one of the topics I talk about is the "outcome bias." A pervasive demon, the outcome bias describes the tendency of people to base their evaluations of decision makers on the *results* of their decisions rather than upon the *quality* of the decisions. I do not mean to pass judgment on anyone in this book. In every instance the people described were attempting to make the best possible decision under the circumstances that they faced. Any criticisms here are of the decisions, not of the persons who made them. And of course, I take full responsibility for any errors that may occur in these pages. May they be few and far between.

JCM

1.

ON THE NATURE OF
JUDGMENT CALLS

In 1985, Bob Fildes, CEO of Cetus Corporation, was riding high. Cetus was making great strides in developing a promising anti-cancer drug, and Fildes appeared on the cover of *Fortune* for his bold "Assault on Cancer." The huge market potential of the drug and its early success in clinical trials led to a high-stakes decision: Fildes decided to bet the company on interleukin 2 (IL-2) by building an expensive production facility and developing an international sales force. According to one venture capitalist, "Cetus had a home-run strategy, with everything placed on IL-2 and oncology therapeutics."

Fildes made the judgment call of placing nearly all of his company's resources into the manufacturing and marketing of a single product. He ignored the old investment axiom to avoid putting all your eggs in one basket. Rather, he followed the equally valid, but higher risk, approach of putting all his eggs in one basket and then watching it very carefully. Unfortunately, Fildes's eggs cracked in 1990 when the Food and Drug Administration denied Cetus's request for approval to market IL-2. The high-stakes gamble failed and Fildes left the company.

A few years before Cetus embarked on its "all or nothing" IL-2 strategy, William Rutter, one of its original biotechnology pioneers, left the firm to start his own company—Chiron. From Chiron's beginning in 1981, Rutter began a diversification process in which scientists worked on several different products at the same time. Through hard work and good science, he and his colleagues discovered and successfully marketed a diagnostic test for the hepatitis C virus. Using recombinant biology, the company also developed a vaccine for hepatitis B and a human insulin. While some failures occurred, the company began to grow and become profitable.

Then, in 1991, something happened that would have been unthinkable ten years before: Chiron purchased the much larger, but weakened Cetus. Likened to a small fish eating a big fish, the bold move was applauded by many analysts. Meanwhile, Bob Fildes was exasperated by the turn of events and the 20/20 hindsight of analysts critical of his single-minded strategy. He argued that other biotech companies, such as Amgen and Biogen, succeeded by focusing on a single product. He said, "... some companies got dealt different cards than others from their research. No one knew in the early '80s what any of these products would do."

The decisions of William Rutter and Bob Fildes diverged, and in their high-stakes game only one company survived. The story of Chiron and Cetus illustrates just how closely the quality of decision making, the tenacity of the implementation effort, and the effects of luck can interact to influence results. It also portrays one of the key parameters of judgment calls—that is, the choice between risk and security.

We make hundreds of "routine" decisions a year. Do I exercise today? Do I purchase that great-looking sports coat? Do I have a piece of double Dutch chocolate mousse cake for dessert? Should I yell at my colleague who just screwed up? The sum of these decisions determines who we are and what we will become. They dictate our life patterns. If I stopped eating ice cream each night, over the course of a year I could lose those extra ten pounds that plague my midsection. I would like, however, to focus on decisions of a different kind —high-stakes decisions—similar to those faced by Bob Fildes and William Rutter. Such judgment calls are made rarely in our personal lives; for example, which house should I buy, should I splurge on an expensive sports car, do I allow myself to have an extramarital affair?

But high-stakes decisions must be made much more frequently in our professional lives. Put yourself in the shoes of a housing developer in California. By March of 1991, his firm had spent $70 million on a new subdivision, only to find that the great California drought caused the water district to place a moratorium on giving out water-meter permits. The water pipes had even been laid for two thousand homes, seventeen of which were ready for occupancy. Should he stop, or go ahead and hope for the best? His decision was to move forward. As the developer said, "What can I do now? What difference does it make now if I spend another $1 million? If it goes under, it goes under, and it doesn't matter whether we're buried under three feet of dirt or six feet." But of course it matters. One million dollars is one million dollars, no matter whether it is the first million lost or the last.

The developer was caught by the conflicting goals of wanting to complete the project and of wanting to avoid additional potential losses. Further, he was at the mercy of the weather. His case illustrates the extreme instance of a decision maker held hostage by conditions beyond his control. The dilemma that he faced involved the judgment call of whether to stay or quit. And his decision was that of an individual potentially trapped in a course of action from which he could not extricate himself. Such judgment calls are faced by decision makers in all of the major professions, whether in business, political, medical, legal, or technological settings. In some circumstances, a decision may influence the economic well-being of millions. In extreme cases, a judgment call results in life or death consequences.

On August 1, 1987, five prominent advertising executives drowned when their raft capsized in giant rapids in the Chilko River in British Columbia, Canada. The same year a Houston attorney, an ex-professional football player, was killed in Wyoming while rock climbing. His guide had anchored a belay and signaled the attorney to climb. He began climbing and fell once—his guide catching the fall with the safety ropes. Trying again, he fell a second time. This time, however, the guide felt the rope go limp. The attorney had slipped from his harness and fallen 135 feet to his death. In the United States on average twenty-six people a year die in mountaineering accidents, thirty die in parachuting accidents, and seventy die while exploring caves. In the judgment call of risk versus security, why do people choose danger over safety in their leisure activities?

High-stakes decisions involve trade-offs between important goals, and frequently no absolutely best choice exists. You can call in the most outstanding experts available and they will disagree on what to do. The use of complex computer programs results in confusion because completely different answers will be obtained simply by changing an assumption or an estimate of a key variable input into the program. In such instances, *you* must make a judgment call. The "right" answer will not be found in an expert system, the opinion of a guru, or the signs of an economist, astrologer, or soothsayer.

The Parameters of Judgment Calls

A judgment call occurs when a decision maker must make a tough choice between two or more options under ambiguous conditions. In business, CEOs make a judgment call when they must decide whether to continue or discontinue producing a faltering product. In the U.S. space program, Mission Control must decide whether to launch the Space Shuttle under marginal weather conditions. Similarly, in the political arena, the president must decide if he should attempt to strangle an aggressor with a blockade or if he should use maximum force to defeat enemy armies. In our own personal lives, we must decide if that nagging pain should be seen by a doctor.

While the circumstances may vary, in high-stakes decision making one or more of eight basic judgment calls can be made. The most fundamental judgment call of all is "Do you shoot or not?"

To Shoot or Not. Do you go for it? Do you take action or not? That's the fundamental question in high-stakes decision making. In each instance, one can either simply stand pat and do nothing, or take action.

All high-stakes decisions possess outcome uncertainty. As a result, you can make the "correct" decision, based upon the best information available, yet it may still fail. The environment in which the decision is made is so complex that precise cause-effect relationships simply do not exist. The situation is analogous to a radar operator working in the sands of Saudi Arabia. The operator must decide whether the blip on the radar screen is merely "noise" (e.g., a cloud) or a signal of an enemy aircraft. Because of the inaccuracy of the equipment, unfavorable atmospheric conditions, and other types of noise, radar operators cannot be absolutely sure of what they see on their screen. The decision whether to fire or not to fire the missile must be made under conditions of uncertainty.

The judgment call of whether to shoot or not is a metaphor for all decisions that involve the question of whether to take action or not. The issue pervades high-stakes decision making. Surgeons must decide whether or not to cut, lawyers choose whether or not to sue, and business executives determine whether or not to launch a new product. The ability to make such decisions depends upon one's competence in reading signals in the environment. The decision by Saddam Hussein to invade Kuwait in August 1990 provides fertile ground for illustrating the shoot/no shoot judgment call. Let us analyze the situation from Saddam Hussein's perspective in late July 1990, the days just prior to his invasion.

As part of his decision to invade Kuwait, Hussein attempted to read the signals of the United States in order to determine whether America would respond militarily to such an invasion. Was America signaling that it would ignore an invasion of Kuwait? Strong evidence exists that the Bush administration indicated the United States would not react militarily to such an attack. For example, when it became apparent that Iraq was massing troops along the Kuwait border in late July 1990, April Glaspie, the U.S. Ambassador to Iraq, met personally with Saddam Hussein. In that meeting, she said: "We have no opinion on the Arab-Arab conflict, like your border disagreement with Kuwait." Then she left the region to go on a vacation. To make matters worse, just prior to the invasion a State Department spokesperson said in public on orders from the White House, "We do not have any defense treaties with Kuwait, and there are no special defense or security commitments to Kuwait."

I spoke to a Middle East expert who argued that "anybody in his right mind would have perceived the U.S. response to the build-up on the Kuwait border to have been an open invitation to Iraq." He added, "Particularly when you consider that for ten years we gave them intelligence, satellite photos, and avoided criticizing them for human rights violations, Hussein had to conclude that the United States was either a patsy or simply ignoring Iraq."

The ability to make outstanding shoot/no shoot judgment calls depends in part upon the decision maker's expertise in detecting signals amidst all of the background noise. Thus, had Saddam Hussein been able accurately to decipher the mixed signals of the United States, perhaps he would have changed his strategy and avoided a massive military defeat.

In addition to improving their accuracy of signal detection, however, peerless decision makers recognize that they can make mistakes. As a result, when functioning in the zone of uncertainty in which the evidence for a signal is ambiguous, they seek to avoid making the worst of two potential mistakes; that is, they attempt to determine which is more negative, a false alarm or a miss. A false alarm occurs when a decision maker acts when he or she should do nothing. From Saddam Hussein's perspective, a false alarm would

occur if he invaded Kuwait only to find that the United States intervened with massive military force. A miss occurs when a decision
maker fails to act when he should; in this case, he or she fails to
perceive a signal when in fact it exists. Saddam Hussein had to ask,
"How bad would the error be if I decided *not* to invade Kuwait when
in fact the United States would *not* have intervened militarily?" The
error would have been extremely grievous from his perspective because he would have missed his chance to capture 20 percent of the
world's oil reserves.

In the zone of ambiguity over whether to shoot or not, the relative
risks of the false alarm and the miss must be weighed against each
other. How bad would it be for Saddam Hussein to miss an opportunity to annex Kuwait? In contrast, how negative would it be for him
to invade, only to face the full military power of the United States?

Hussein appears to have underestimated the negative consequences of a false alarm. Boasting that his struggle with the United
States "is going to be the mother of all battles," Hussein simply
failed to understand the forces that could be arrayed against him.
During the height of the diplomatic maneuvering prior to the initiation of the air war on January 15, 1991, Hussein said, "The Americans
will come here to perform acrobatics like *Rambo* movies. But they
will find here real people to fight them. We are a people who have
eight years of experience in war and combat." In his meeting with
April Glaspie just before invading Kuwait, Hussein told her, "Yours
is a society which cannot accept 10,000 dead in one battle." The
belief that the United States was a paper tiger extended to the people
of Iraq. An Iraqi university student who was interviewed just before
the war said, "We know America is very afraid of Iraq." Sitting in a
class with her peers, the student was asked if Iraq should not have
reason to fear the West's superior forces. Laughing, she responded,
"Vietnam is a very small country and look what it did."

Thus, a combination of events caused Saddam Hussein to make
the judgment call to shoot. He misperceived the weak signals given
by the United States, and he totally underestimated the military
potential that could be arrayed against him. Hussein should have
listened more carefully when Colin Powell, Chairman of the Joint
Chiefs of Staff, described the battle plan, saying of the Iraqi force,
"First we're going to cut it off, and then we're going to kill it." But,
in July 1990, it would have been difficult to imagine that the United
States could put together a coalition of 30-plus countries, coordinate
a force of over 700,000 troops, and keep Israel out of the fray while it
was being terrorized by Scud missiles.

Hussein's real mistake was to go too far. If he had merely seized Kuwait's oil fields, which lie on the border of the two countries and a couple of small islands, the United States and its allies would have been unhappy, but little concrete action would have taken place. His mistake was to take all of Kuwait and threaten the Saudi oil fields. The State Department spokesperson, Margaret Tutwiler, signaled this to Iraq in response to a reporter's question as to what the United States would do if Kuwait were invaded. After noting that the United States would not take sides in border disputes, she said: "We also remain strongly committed to supporting the individual and collective self-defense of our friends in the gulf with whom we have deep and longstanding ties." Saddam Hussein completely missed the message—"Don't threaten Saudi Arabia!"

To Stay or Quit. The second fundamental judgment call faced by decision makers is the question, "Do I stay with a course of action in the face of adversity, or should I quit?" American culture is full of "never say die" aphorisms. ("Winners never quit and quitters never win.") Yet numerous American corporations, indeed entire industries, have abandoned their technologies to the Japanese. For example, the fax machine is an American invention. It is omnipresent in the corporate environment. Our engineers designed and developed the device. Yet you cannot buy a fax machine made by an American company.

Similarly, robotics is an American innovation. In the early 1980s American companies, such as Unimation, dominated the field. Other American corporations jumped into the robotics revolution, including IBM, General Electric, Cincinnati Milacron, and United Technologies. By 1990, all had quit the competition. A past vice-president at Unimation described the situation as "absolutely sick." He said, "It breaks my heart to think of how we lost the industrial robot industry."

Like the question of "to shoot or not," the decision "to stay or quit" is made under conditions of uncertainty. While American corporations failed to stay the course in robotics and fax machines, in other instances incredible perseverance can be found in spite of almost extraordinary adversity. One of the best examples is the story of Chester F. Carlson. It begins in 1937 with the thirty-one-year-old Cal Tech–trained physicist working in the patent office of a New York City law firm. At that time the Great Depression still had America by the neck, and Carlson could not find work in his chosen field. One evening he faced the tedious task of copying a long patent application through the slow photostatic process used at the time.

He turned to an associate and said, "There must be a quicker, better way to make these copies!" "Sure," his colleague agreed, "but nobody has ever found it." Carlson responded, "Maybe nobody has ever tried."

The next year, when Carlson began studying law at night, copying problems again plagued him. He wanted to copy pages from the textbooks that he read at the public library and could not afford to buy. Gradually, the notion of developing a quicker way to make copies became an obsession. He began to read technical publications on printing, photography, and the chemical treatment of paper. The idea came to him of using photoconductivity for taking pictures. It would be done dry with electricity, and he called it "electrophotography."

Carlson turned his kitchen into a lab and began experimenting. Scraping together every extra penny, he hired a German immigrant, a physicist/engineer, to help him. In 1938 he successfully copied writing from a glass slide to a metal plate. He then transferred that image from the plate to paper. For Carlson, it was an emotional moment. To his German assistant, the words simply looked smudged, and he soon left to join a small company—named IBM.

Next, Carlson sent explanations of his process to IBM, A. B. Dick, RCA, and others. All turned him down. The years dragged by, but he continued working to perfect his copying device. He succeeded in developing something that he could take to companies for demonstrations. More frequently than not, it failed. All along he kept filing patents. Meanwhile, the arthritis that had plagued his father began to trouble him as well.

It was now 1944, and he was nearly ready to give up. But good fortune intervened. Dr. Russell Dayton, a representative of Battelle Memorial Institute—a privately endowed research organization—came to the law firm where Carlson was working to discuss some patent problems. Carlson mentioned the device and showed Dayton examples of some copies. Dayton was encouraging and invited him to visit Battelle's offices in Columbus, Ohio. After so many years of deprivation, Carlson expected nothing from the visit, but he went anyway.

When Carlson returned home, he told his wife that he had no idea how the meeting went. Unknown to him, the Battelle staff was looking hard at his invention. They were used to seeing research proposals at an early stage of development. They offered Carlson $3,000 to help in the research and development of his device; in addition, they began looking for corporate sponsors. Even Battelle, however, struck out. Quite simply, nobody wanted it. The lack of interest hit Carlson hard and his wife harder. She left him in 1945, but Carlson only threw himself into the project with more energy. Battelle encouraged him by adding $10,000 to the research budget.

Then, a writer visiting Battelle saw Carlson's device and wrote an article on it entitled "Radio-Electronic Engineering." It appeared in a Kodak research bulletin where John Dessauer, an engineer at Haloid, a small photo paper company, read it—the word "photography" had caught his attention. Haloid was small, but anxious to expand and looking for ideas.

From this point the story moves faster. In 1946, Haloid purchased the rights to Carlson's device from Battelle for $25,000 a year. At Haloid, highly talented people were attracted to work on the intriguing device. To find a name for it, they consulted a Greek scholar, who suggested "xerography," from *xeros* for "dry" and *graphein* for "writing." It perfectly described the dry writing process being developed.

On October 22, 1948, the device was demonstrated publicly to the Optical Society of America—ten years to the day after Carlson had made his first crude copy. Then came a big break when the Army Signal Corps gave Haloid $120,000 to produce a copier for their use. But Haloid shareholders were unimpressed; many went out and sold their shares. One investor would bemoan the fact that the shares he sold for $30,000 to buy a house were later worth $3 million.

The first commercial sales of a copier did not occur until 1951. In 1953, a research firm estimated that no more than five thousand copiers would be placed in American offices. (But remember also that in 1958 an IBM official estimated the world market for computers at five.) As xerography sales began to grow exponentially, Haloid realized that its business had changed. In 1958, the name of the company was changed to XEROX, and in 1961, twenty-three years after Chester F. Carlson's first experiment on the kitchen table, the firm was listed on the New York Stock Exchange.

To stay or quit? Carlson and Haloid persevered and were rewarded. On the other hand, stubbornly pursuing a course of action can result in calamity. For example, let's return to the actions by Saddam Hussein in the Persian Gulf war. By late December 1990, it was readily apparent that an overwhelming military force had been assembled that could be unleashed on Iraq. Saddam Hussein's failure to leave Kuwait when he was given the chance illustrates how obdurately staying with a losing course of action can lead to entrapment.

One irony of the Persian Gulf war is that Saddam Hussein's political power outlasted that of his conqueror, George Bush. But this Pyrrhic victory glosses over the inescapable conclusion that because of its entrapment, Iraq unnecessarily suffered enormous losses, both in human lives and in its infrastructure. In addition, the devastating loss strengthened the relative military and political power of its mortal enemy, Iran. The Bush administration left ample room for Iraq to maneuver out of the situation and "save face." By stubbornly staying when he should have quit, Saddam Hussein indefinitely set back his efforts to make his country an international power.

No decision maker would deliberately choose to fail. But when the stakes are high and the outcome is uncertain, the decision to stay or quit becomes a judgment call.

Present versus Future. When making a high-stakes choice, the decision maker must accept trade-offs. A common judgmental trade-off is between the present and the future. For example, when we make an investment, we exchange present consumption for potential future gains. The difficulty of this judgment call is illustrated by various aphorisms. The virtues of delaying gratification are exemplified by the axiom, "Good things come to those who wait." On the other hand, continually postponing pleasure can lead to an impoverished life, as suggested by the axiom, "In the end, we are all dead."

The choice between present and future is complicated by the outcomes of our decisions and when they occur in time. Any single decision is likely to have both good and bad outcomes, which can occur either together or separately, and either in the present or in the future. This juxtaposition of positive and negative outcomes in time strongly influences business decisions. When a company makes a decision to invest in research and development (R&D), both good and bad outcomes occur as a result. In the short term, profitability is decreased. Current U.S. tax regulations require R&D costs to be carried as expenses as they occur. Thus, in the quarter in which R&D costs are paid, they are subtracted directly from the bottom line. The positive effects of the investment, however, will not be felt for years. The negative effects on current balance sheets have resulted in American companies failing to invest sufficiently in R&D. In the late 1980s, the short-term focus of American business grew worse. R&D spending in the United States as a percentage of GNP declined to less than 30 percent of that spent in Japan and West Germany; spending growth on R&D fell from over a 6 percent growth rate (inflation-adjusted) in the early 1980s to less than a 2 percent rate in 1988 and 1989.

A grim example of such short-term thinking occurred at the Ford Motor Company. During the 1960s and 1970s, Ford was dominated by men trained in finance and operations management. They were the so-called whiz kids, brought into the company after World War II and exemplified by Robert McNamara. He and others helped to put into place the financial control systems that brought Ford out from under the primitive management style of Henry Ford; but they also nearly bankrupted the company with their focus on short-term profits and the neglect of marketing, manufacturing, and quality.

Perhaps the best illustration of the short-term focus of the whiz kids was the infamous E-coat affair. In 1958, researchers in Ford's manufacturing section invented a technique for improving the paint jobs and rust resistance of vehicles. The process involved dipping the entire frame in a vat of paint and giving it an electrical charge. The charge attracted the paint to the metal, allowing it to get into every nook and cranny. The process greatly improved the vehicles' rust resistance and became an instant success everywhere but Ford, U.S.A. Ford of Europe quickly adopted it because of the highly competitive market there. General Motors paid Ford a royalty and used the process. Even Japanese companies adopted it.

How quickly did Ford adopt the E-coat in its North American operations? By 1961, the company had installed it in the plant that produced its prestige Lincoln Continentals and Thunderbirds. However, getting it into the other plants became extremely difficult because the manufacturing people could not prove that the process would return the $4 to $5 million cost of installing it in a plant. In 1973 at a styling meeting, Lee Iacocca became enraged at the poor quality of Ford cars and particularly at the rust problems that were causing enormous warranty difficulties. But even though he was the president of the corporation, he could not turn around the short-term thinking of other executives. By 1975, the process was still in only half of the Ford plants; it was not until 1984 that the E-coat process was placed in all the plants. No wonder Ford's market share plummeted during this time span. The focus on short-term financial performance was one reason customers began saying FORD was an acronym for "Found On Road Dead."

In high-stakes decision making, the ultimate outcome of a choice can be measured at varying points in time. Because a time lag exists between when a decision is made and when its outcomes are felt, its results can be measured in the short term (one to two years), the midterm (two to five years), and the long term (more than five years). At Ford, the finance department wanted precise estimates of how many additional cars would be sold as a result of the E-coat process. This insistence that manufacturing *prove* the E-coat would produce a satisfactory return was simply not possible in the short or mid-term. Instead, the question that should have been asked was "How many cars over a ten-year period will *not* be sold if we fail to adopt the process?" The problems caused by the premature rusting of a brand of automobile can be expected to take several years to appear. And once problems concerning product quality and customer satisfaction have surfaced, a company is looking at a five- to ten-year horizon to regain lost ground. Indeed, once customer perceptions of poor quality begin to influence the bottom line, it will take another five to ten years to recover even if the problem is corrected immediately.

A fundamental element of the culture of the United States is its focus on the short term. Consider time capsules. How long do we plan to wait before opening a time capsule in the United States—fifty, maybe a hundred years? One American corporate executive on a visit to Japan toured a cultural center containing a sealed time capsule, which the curators planned not to open for another five thousand years. The divergence in time horizons reflects a fundamental difference in the cultures of the United States and Japan. It also explains, in part, the phenomenal success of this economic competitor across the Pacific. Japanese companies will wait longer for new product ideas to become profitable. Erroneously trading off the future for present consumption is the major corporate and governmental disease of the late twentieth century in the United States.

Risk versus Security. Another major judgment call involves the choice between security and risk. In 1979, religious conservatives in Iran overthrew the Shah and in the process took hostage American diplomats at the U.S. Embassy in Tehran. The shocking action broke the supposedly ironclad rules of diplomatic immunity of embassy personnel and created havoc within the Carter administration. Already reeling from the negative economic and psychological effects of the oil embargo and fuel crisis of the late 1970s, the administration faced major public criticism for its apparent weakness. The hostage crisis also threatened President Carter's reelection.

Against this backdrop, plans were developed to stage a dramatic rescue of the hostages. Helicopters were sent from ships stationed in the Persian Gulf on a long, circuitous route to a staging area in the Iranian desert. From there, they were to fly to Tehran, where they would land on the embassy grounds and rescue the hostages. But all did not go as planned. A sandstorm disrupted the flights from the staging area. One helicopter's engine malfunctioned and another collided with a transport plane that would have taken the prisoners back to safety. Eight would-be rescuers were killed. The mission was aborted and the surviving members of the team retreated to the carrier. Soon afterwards, Iranian pictures of the smoldering wreckage were played back to Americans on television news. Viewers saw Iranian "holymen" poking sticks at the dead bodies of U.S. servicemen.

Why would the Carter administration take such a huge risk to save the hostages? Many analysts argued that the mission was fatally flawed and doomed from the beginning. The American troops were lucky that they did not reach Tehran, because they almost certainly would have been captured. Admiral William J. Crowe, the head of the Joint Chiefs of Staff during President Reagan's administration, told me that the risks would certainly have been explained to President Carter by the military. He said that a likely explanation for the high-risk undertaking was that administration officials believed they were "up against the wall." They were so deep in a hole that they were willing to accept the risk. Individuals and organizations tend to take the greatest risks when they perceive themselves to be in a loss position. Ironically, the aborted rescue mission plunged the Carter administration into an even deeper dilemma.

Think back to the advertising executives who were killed while white-water rafting on the Chilko River. Consider the attorney who fell to his death rock climbing. Each of them made a judgment call: They selected risk over security. In making any judgment call, our goal should be to recognize and understand all the trade-offs. We must recognize that errors occur. Doubtless, the attorney knew the risks. But, unfortunately, the same may not have been true for the advertising executives on the Chilko River. As the lawsuits from the deceased families claimed, the pressures to conform to a corporate culture may have caused some of them to take risks for which they were unprepared. (In December 1990, in the first lawsuit to reach trial, the jury ordered the ad agency that had employed the deceased to pay $1.1 million to the plaintiff.) In order to make the judgment call, you must have free choice.

Finding the Cause. The need to pinpoint a cause for an event or situation strongly influences judgment calls. By finding causes for whatever has happened, we gain control, the world becomes more predictable, and we learn from our mistakes. Finding the cause, however, is a difficult task. High stakes can ride on identifying the "real" cause; all too often, we settle for convenient answers that minimize pain and/or preserve the status quo.

A recent illustration of organizational face saving can be found in the actions of the U.S. Navy. On April 19, 1989, the battleship U.S.S. *Iowa* was stationed northeast of Puerto Rico and engaged in practice firing its mammoth 16-inch guns. Without warning, the powder being stuffed into the guns of Turret 2 exploded. A videotape of the accident vividly showed the enormous size of the explosion. Forty-six men died inside the four-story turret. Immediately, the Navy, the press, and the American public wanted to know the cause of the explosion.

An investigation began, and it was quickly discovered that two of the sailors in the gun turret had had an unusually strong relationship. In fact, one of the crew, Clayton Hartwig, had purchased a life insurance policy and named the other sailor as its beneficiary. Hartwig was one of the forty-six men to die and Kendall Lee Truitt, the beneficiary, survived. Intimations of a homosexual relationship between the two were splashed across newspaper headlines. The theory that Truitt had killed Hartwig, however, was rapidly dropped because no proof of a homosexual relationship existed, because Truitt had recently married, and because he was stationed too far away from the point of the blast to have caused it. The Navy eventually apologized to Truitt.

Soon thereafter, leaks to the press revealed another theory held by the Navy: that the explosion was caused by Clayton Hartwig, who was in charge of a gun crew inside Turret 2. This theory held that Hartwig deliberately set off the explosion in order to commit suicide. Despondent over his close friend's forthcoming marriage, he decided to take his own life. Psychological profiles were created of Hartwig that portrayed him as a loner who was despondent and thinking of martyrdom. A few months later, the Navy officially concluded that the *Iowa* explosion "most probably" was caused by an intentional action by Clayton Hartwig.

From the beginning, it was clear that the Navy wanted to avoid calling the incident an accident. In this case, an "accident" would be defined as a situation in which all of the sailors performed appropriately, but that something about the powder or the gun itself caused the explosion. If the cause was in the powder or the gun, it would create major problems for the Navy. Indeed, early in the investigation suspicions existed that the powder had been stored improperly and had been exposed to very high heat; such conditions would make it unstable, and it could explode unexpectedly. If the powder was unstable, then the Navy itself could properly be held responsible for the explosion and the deaths of forty-six men.

After the Navy's conclusion that the blast was caused by Hartwig, red flags went up. Even the captain of the *Iowa* testified against the theory. While agreeing with the naval investigating team that the explosion was not accidental, he said that he could not come to the conclusion that Hartwig caused it. He could not, however, identify another cause for the explosion.

Indeed, psychologists who testified before the House Armed Services Subcommittee found little evidence that Hartwig was disturbed. A letter to his sister written three days before the incident revealed a person in good spirits, who had just signed up for four more years in the Navy and was looking forward to going to London to a new job working with the military police. Navy investigators had jumped on one letter, written by Hartwig, in which he had mentioned martyrdom and on another which he had signed "Love Always" rather than his usual "Love Clay." This was seen as evidence of instability and depression. The independent psychologists, however, pointed out that in the same letter Hartwig had written, "At sea, I spend a lot of time outside, thinking it's really quite beautiful out here if you stop to notice." Further, the sailor showed none of the classic signs of being suicidal. One psychologist noted that only evidence that supported their [the Navy's] assessment that Hartwig was suicidal was used in the analysis. Even when the Navy had asked the FBI to enter the case, the charge given to the agency was one-sided: the FBI was asked to determine whether the explosion was a suicide attempt by Hartwig, a suicide attempt by Truitt, or a homicide attempt by either. Having ruled out the possibility of an accident, the Navy had narrowed its investigation to blaming a person for the incident.

In March 1990, the House Armed Services Committee issued a report highly critical of the naval investigation. The report indicated that the Navy seemed to have been trying to force the technical analyses to fit the theory that Gunner's Mate Hartwig blew up the gun. At his retirement ceremony, the captain of the *Iowa*, Fred P. Moosally, said that the naval inquiry used "facts and opinions based on unsubstantiated third-party information, unsubstantiated reports, and supposition." Finally, a year after the blast, the Navy reopened the investigation when tests revealed that sparks could ignite the gunpowder bags if they were rammed into a gun barrel at high speed. Twenty-five million dollars had been spent on the investigation. On October 17, 1991, Admiral Frank B. Kelso, Chief of Naval Operations, briefed the press on the results: "Despite all the efforts that have gone into the *Iowa* investigation . . . my final conclusion is that there's no certain answer to the question of what caused the tragedy." He then apologized to the family of Clayton Hartwig as well as to the families of those on board the U.S.S. *Iowa*. One of the tough aspects of high-stakes decision making is that in some instances, the cause is difficult or impossible to identify.

The urge to sweep mistakes under the rug by placing blame external to yourself or to the organization for which you work is strong. But acting dispassionately to determine the real cause for both bad and good situations is imperative in making a judgment call. By finally admitting that an accident may have occurred, the Navy may well have saved many lives. As a result of the reopened investigation, procedures were changed in the operation of the 16-inch guns. During the Persian Gulf war, over one thousand 16-inch shells were fired without incident.

Chance versus Control. In high-stakes decisions, a critical issue is the extent to which outcomes occur as a result of chance, or whether they can be controlled through the application of diligent effort and intelligence. Overwhelming evidence suggests that people exhibit a kind of "creeping determinism"; that is, they will attempt to find logical explanations for events that are, in fact, controlled by chance.

A classic example of creeping determinism can be found in sports such as basketball, golf, or bowling. Anyone who has played a sport, or gambled for that matter, has felt it—the "hot hand." After you make a couple of long putts or a couple of baskets in succession, the feeling that you cannot miss takes hold. Some basketball players, like Vinnie Johnson when he played for the Detroit Pistons, are known as "streak shooters." (Johnson's nickname is "Microwave" for his instant offense.) Once streak shooters hit their first basket, so the theory goes, they become unstoppable. The problem is that absolutely no scientific evidence exists to support such a theory.

In a study of the "hot-hand" phenomenon, researchers asked basketball fans whether a player had a better or worse chance of making a second shot after having just made a first. Over 91 percent said that after making one shot, players had a better chance of making the next. That belief was even stronger after the player had made a series of shots. When the researchers interviewed professional basketball players, they expressed the same belief as the fans. People believe that hot streaks exist.

The researchers then looked at the shooting statistics for National Basketball Association players on the Philadelphia 76ers. Some of the players included in the study were Julius Erving, Lionel Hollins, Daryl Dawkins, and Andrew Toney (a well-known streak shooter).

They found that for eight of the nine players whose statistics were studied, the probability of making a basket actually decreased slightly after having just made a shot. In no cases were the results different from what you would expect from chance. When hot streaks were analyzed (defined as making three or more baskets in the last four shots), the probability of making the next shot was significantly lower than if the player had just experienced a cold streak.

How can so many players and fans be wrong? How can that hot feeling I have after sinking a couple of putts be misleading? The answer lies in how people perceive chance events. If you flip a coin over and over and record the pattern of heads and tails, it will be completely random. But people will not perceive it to be random. They will discern it to have too many runs of heads and/or tails. To the untrained eye, it will look as though a "streak coin flipper" has been at work. In other words, we have a built-in tendency to find a reason for the outcome and to ignore chance as the basis.

The gambler's fallacy is the opposite phenomenon to the "streak shooter" myth, but it also results from a misperception of chance events. According to this way of thinking, in a game of chance things always balance out. Thus, if you are throwing craps and "sevens" come up three times in a row, something magical will happen to change the odds so that the likelihood of their coming up again becomes lower.

Casey Stengel, the eccentric manager of the New York Yankees, provides a great story that illustrates the gambler's fallacy. In 1949, the Yankees and the Red Sox were locked in a tension-filled pennant race. During this period, Stengel brought many innovations to the game, including the platooning of his players. Previously, managers had never considered playing different players in the same position depending upon the ballpark and the opposing pitcher. In particular, Stengel platooned two players in right field—Gene Woodling and Hank Bauer. Between them that year, they batted .271, with 15 home runs and 99 RBIs. Both were great players, and they hated the strategy. Woodling called Stengel "that crooked-legged old bastard."

In one game the anger came to a head. A right-handed pitcher was on the mound, so Woodling was sure he would play because he was left-handed. Stengel, however, decided to play Bauer, and Woodling went crazy. Of course, Bauer egged him on by saying, "Hey, Gene, you caddy for me today." Bauer got hits his first three times at bat. The game was close, and in the late innings the opposing team brought in a left-handed pitcher. At this point Stengel completely violated the mythical "book" by bringing in Woodling (a left-handed batter) to hit. Now it was Bauer who became enraged, screaming at Stengel and throwing bats everywhere.

After the game, Stengel brought the two players into his office. "I don't give a good goddamn what you call me," he told Bauer. "You can call me a crazy old man, and maybe I am. But it's my team and I'm going to run it my way. Now I'm going to tell you why I pulled you. You got your three hits, right? So let me tell you something, Mr. Bauer. You're not a one-thousand hitter. And you're not even a three-thirty-three hitter. So you had your three hits for the day and that's all it was going to be. That was your quota."

Stengel didn't buy the "streak shooter" myth. Instead, he fell for the gambler's fallacy.

The problem of creeping determinism also relates to the age-old debate about ends versus means. Some decision makers assume that certain actions are necessary, even though they may be unethical, to achieve a certain goal which they perceive to be moral. In other words, the end justifies the means. That assumption can be dangerously wrong even in a culture where winning is everything. Decision making is a process in which means are more important than ends. As one observer put it: "People who make moral compromises in order to achieve good ends find that their compromises irrevocably alter the ends achieved. Thus they learn that, in a world of process, it is method rather than goal which carries the burden of moral value."

The means versus ends debate, however, goes beyond questions of morality to those who evaluate the competence of decision makers. Because the outcomes of high-stakes decisions are affected by luck and chance, as well as by good planning, accurate analysis, and sound judgment, evaluators must carefully attend to the process by which the decision was made—the means as well as the ends. Only by analyzing how the decision was made, what factors were considered, what planning took place, what information was available at the time, can you assess whether the decision itself was correct. More often, however, evaluators of decisions tend to focus largely on the outcome and to ignore the process used to reach the decision. As a result, those who make poor decisions, but are lucky enough to have chance intervene to yield a good outcome, will be rewarded. Conversely, those who make good decisions, only to have misfortune intervene to yield a bad outcome, will be punished.

A classic example of individuals being criticized for good decisions that turned out poorly (at least in the short run) occurred in

1988 during the massive Yellowstone National Park fires. In 1988, a severe drought struck the Midwest and Mountain states. Crops shriveled and timberlands turned to kindling. The National Park Service for several years had followed a policy of "natural burn," according to which fires caused by the whims of nature were allowed to burn as long as they did not threaten humans. This ecologically sound policy had resulted from years of study that achieved the desired result—until bad luck intervened.

A confluence of events in 1988 caused a situation in which the ability to control forest fires once they started was limited. The dry conditions, strong winds, and a build-up of fuel (which stemmed from an earlier policy of extinguishing forest fires) created a blaze at Yellowstone of a size and ferocity not seen previously. Those with economic interests in tourism became alarmed because visitors stopped coming to the park. Further, major resort complexes were threatened by the fires that burned largely out of control; the Old Faithful Inn was nearly consumed by flames.

Massive efforts to extinguish the fires were called "too little, too late." Congressmen from Wyoming and Montana launched investigations and demanded the firing of the head of the Park Service. Many articles highly critical of the Forest Service appeared in newspapers. In a retrospective look at the disaster, The Wall Street Journal called it the "Vietnam of forest fires." In general, the Park Service and those who ran it were beleaguered with criticism.

Fortunately, however, cooler heads eventually prevailed. No one was fired. The "natural burn" policy was deemed a sound one—except under extraordinary conditions. Indeed, the articles appearing a year later viewed the events at Yellowstone in a far different manner. Rather than focusing on the loss of timber, the threat to buildings and people, and the ferocity of the wild fires, they described the natural beauty released by the flames. The story became one of death, rebirth, and renewal. An article in The Wall Street Journal describing the park a year after the fire began:

> It is a new summer in Yellowstone Park. The meadows are deep green and rich and the high grass moves in the wind like water on a lake. On the burned forest floor, fuchsia fireweed, bright yellow arnica and 20 species of grass form gorgeous wild gardens. Even in the most intensely burned areas, where earth and trees are charred black, there are clumps of new grass and brilliantly colored flowers.
>
> I have come away in awe.

Because chance is omnipresent, in the short term we must look to process, not outcome, to evaluate decisions. Only in the long term can a decision be measured by its outcome, and even then evaluators must be wary of the effects of circumstances beyond the control of the decision maker causing poor results.

Choosing a Frame of Reference. When making high-stakes decisions, we have to consider the frame of reference from which we approach the decision. Completely different judgments can be made, depending upon the perspective we bring to the problem. The frame of reference you select can influence the amount of risk you deem acceptable. Frames of reference act as lenses to focus attention on particular decision elements and values. One source is a person's professional specialization, be it political, legal, military, scientific, marketing, or financial. Quite different choices may result, depending upon the frame of reference adopted.

The importance of properly framing a decision can be illustrated by the judgment calls made by Jim Webb, the first head of NASA. President John F. Kennedy appointed Webb as the administrator of NASA about four months prior to his "We Are Going to the Moon" speech in 1961. Numerous more qualified candidates had turned the job down. At the time of the appointment, no one, including John Kennedy, knew that he would soon set the Moon as our goal. Had the moon landing been announced prior to the appointment, dozens of more qualified engineer-scientists would have applied and been considered. But, as luck would have it, Jim Webb was the right person for the job.

Webb was a man who could wear many hats and handle the diverse pressures that NASA encountered. He left the technical judgments to the scientists and engineers, but he would override their assessments for non-technical, political reasons. For example, one high-stakes decision made by Webb early in the space program was to cancel a three-day flight by Alan Shepard, which would have been the seventh in the Mercury series. The engineers were furious. They argued that the flight was needed on technical grounds to prove out the systems. Webb's response was simple: "If you do it and it's successful, it doesn't mean a hell of a lot. If we were to have a failure, we couldn't recover. It might stop the manned space program." Webb framed his decision from a political as well as a technological perspective.

Frames of reference can also influence high-stakes decision making at a societal level, and in particular, the judgment call of choosing between the rights of the individual and the welfare of the group.

One such public policy problem concerns whether everyone should be given the "live" oral polio vaccine or the "dead" Salk vaccine. From a group welfare perspective, the clear choice is the live vaccine. It is highly effective, and because it is easily administered, more people will take it. The dead vaccine on the other hand must be injected, and the fear of needles deters many. As an added advantage, the live oral vaccine may act to inoculate other individuals against polio. Because it works by giving the recipient a very mild form of the disease, those who take it become carriers. Others who come into contact with them may also contract the mild form of the disease and develop an immunity. Statistical analysis has shown conclusively that the enforced administration of the oral vaccine would result in fewer cases of polio in the general population than if the dead vaccine were used. (Estimates are that 64 fewer cases per 3.5 million people would be found.) Thus, from a group welfare perspective the decision is clear: Force all citizens to take the oral vaccine.

When the choice is analyzed from the point of view of individual rights, however, one can reach the opposite conclusion. By taking the live vaccine, a person has an extremely small, but real, chance of contracting polio. In addition, a young unvaccinated child can contract polio from another child who has recently been given the live virus. Thus, while overall the live vaccine results in fewer cases of polio in the general population, it will cause more cases to occur either among those vaccinated or those unvaccinated children with whom they come in contact. Inoculations with the dead vaccine do not cause these difficulties. Is it ethical to place children in jeopardy by forcing them to take the oral vaccine when another alternative is available? Such judgment calls occur when individual rights and group welfare frames collide. The issues are contentious, and the decisions are difficult.

Reason versus Emotion. When high stakes are on the line, emotions are inevitably involved. In particular, decision makers experience fear because of the risk that is involved. Fear has both benefits and liabilities. On the one hand, fear is an adaptive response. It can save your life. Had the rock-climbing attorney shown more fear, perhaps he would have avoided the accident that caused his death. On the other hand, fear can inhibit high levels of performance. In baseball, for example, the more fearless the batter, the better his chance for a hit. In order to achieve an edge, pitchers will occasionally "brush back" batters. Their goal is to create fear, to cause the split-second hesitation that means the difference between a hit and an out. Some pitchers deliberately create fear through their wildness.

The Yankees once had a relief pitcher, Ryne Duren, who had a blazing fastball that was not quite under control. Duren could barely see through the bottom of the Coke bottles he used for glasses and was reputed to have a severe drinking problem. When he came into the game, his first warm-up pitch would be thrown ten feet over the catcher's head into the screen behind home plate. His next pitch would bounce ten feet in front of the plate. By the time the batter stepped up to the plate, he felt as though his life was on the line.

In response to intimidation, batters attempt to show no fear. If a batter fouls a ball off his foot, he will dance around on the good foot, grimace, and generally reveal immense pain. If the same batter is nailed by a fastball in the same location, he will drop his bat, stoically run to first base, and never reveal any signs of pain. The problem is that batters cannot be totally fearless, or they run the risk of seeing the world through only one eye. The same holds true in high-stakes decision making. There is an acceptable level of fear. If the fear—or any other emotion—rises above that acceptable level, actions will be taken to reduce it. In contrast, if the fear is below the acceptable level, actions may be taken to increase it to a higher, but still acceptable level, on the assumption that it will also increase performance.

This phenomenon has occurred in baseball. When batting helmets were made mandatory in 1971, the fear level went down because the risk of serious head injury was lowered. As a result, batters became more aggressive, and many hitters adopted the Charlie Lau approach in which they strode hard toward the plate in order to maximize their weight shift and add power to their swing. The tactic is a dangerous one. If you are striding into the plate and the ball zooms toward your head, you lose that split second of time required to avoid a wild pitch. Even with a helmet, a 90-mile-per-hour fastball crashing into the face can cause grievous harm. But the helmet decreased the perception of the costs of being hit, fear was lowered, and the Lau approach rapidly caught on.

The same effect was found among farmers after regulators decreed that tractors had to be equipped with roll cages. These devices dramatically decreased the risk from rollovers on farms and ranches. But when researchers analyzed the incidence of injuries, no change was found. Farmers merely began to plow on steeper hills. They had a greater comfort zone. When the fear of an accident was reduced by the roll cages, they compensated by taking greater risks.

In high-stakes decisions, one cannot eliminate emotion. The possibility of taking great losses or achieving major gains amplifies feelings of fear and hope. The ability to control emotion and to employ reason, despite emotion's inevitable presence, is one attribute of what I call the peerless decision maker. Rarely, however, does one find in one person the capability to use both reason and emotion effectively in decision making. According to Thomas Jefferson, George Washington possessed such abilities. Jefferson said of Washington:

> He was incapable of fear, meeting personal dangers with the calmest unconcern. . . . Perhaps the strongest feature in his character was prudence, never acting until every circumstance, every consideration, was maturely weighed; refraining if he saw a doubt, but, when once decided, going through with his purpose, whatever obstacles opposed.

When making reasoned decisions, peerless decision makers first identify all possible courses of action. They then exhaustively evaluate the benefits and liabilities of each. In this stage of decision making, when all the alternatives are being evaluated, the peerless decision maker must assess the positive or negative elements associated with every potential outcome. In addition, the probability of the occurrence of each of the outcomes must be identified. The decision maker then combines this information to make a choice, and then pursues that choice with vigor and diligence.

But such a reasoned approach can sometimes lead to paralysis. Emotions can help to break the impasse by pushing decision makers to action when optimism reigns or by pushing them to inaction when fear dominates. Because reason and emotion frequently conflict, one often finds symbiotic partnerships developing. The pattern was vividly portrayed in the television and movie series *Star Trek*. Part of the appeal of the series was the interplay between Mr. Spock (the logical Vulcan) and Dr. McCoy (the emotional earthling). Of course, Captain Kirk took the best features of each officer to develop his creative strategies.

Partnerships between more emotional and more reasoning individuals also occur quite frequently in the business world. Soichiro Honda was a carousing dreamer who longed to build motor vehicles. Hot-tempered (employees called him "Mr. Thunder") and emotional, he would impetuously initiate projects that seemingly possessed little chance of success. His company struggled until he joined forces with Takeo Fujisawa—a thoughtful investor with previous administrative experience. With Fugisawa in charge of finance and marketing and Honda devoting his prodigious energy to technology, Honda Motor Company became profitable. Honda said that he and Fugisawa shared the same goals. Using an assent to the top of Mount Fuji as a metaphor, Honda described each of them as taking different routes because of their personalities:

> Fugisawa would say to me, "I am at such and such a place, and I see a storm coming. So be careful!" Then I would be careful. We had heart-to-heart communications, although we were at different places and acted differently. Yet, we had the same goal of reaching the top of that mountain.

The Peerless Decision Maker

The person who can make successful high-stakes decisions over an extended period deserves the title of "peerless decision maker." Such individuals understand the nature of judgment calls and the trade-offs they produce, from the choice of whether to shoot or not to the decision of when to listen to the promptings of reason or emotion. Furthermore, peerless decision makers understand several additional issues. They recognize the importance of experience in decision making. They know that human beings have both physical and mental limitations and must be motivated properly. Finally, they don't underestimate the importance of planning. Among the many elements of planning is the fundamental concept of keeping things simple.

In this high-technology world, the acronym KISS, or "Keep It Simple Stupid," has much going for it. Consider the Warthog—a slow, ugly, plane that hot-shot Air Force fighter pilots have wanted to send to the scrapheap for years. Designed around the experiences of a famous World War II German pilot, the goal of the A-10 Warthog is to fly slowly enough and possess sufficient armor to absorb punishment while destroying enemy tanks. In the Persian Gulf war, it stole the show from the advanced Stealth fighters, the Tomahawk cruise missiles, and the Patriot anti-missile missiles. Flying between 150 and 300 miles an hour, it could linger over the terrain in order to find Iraqi tanks buried under the sand. As one pilot said, "Those tanks were sometimes buried up to the level of the turret. We knew that they had to be there, but we couldn't see them. It took a lot of looking, spending much more time in the target area to try to find them than we wanted to." And the planes were tough. Television cameras recorded the return of one Warthog that had helped rescue a Navy pilot: as it wobbled in for a landing, the entire world could see a gigantic hole in one wing. Upon landing, the pilot jumped out and kissed the Warthog.

Spending time over the target area was what the plane was designed to do. Ungainly, slow, and possessing lower technology than the sleek, fast jets that Air Force jockeys love to fly, the Warthog exemplifies the slogan, "Keep It Simple Stupid." While the expensive F-15s and F-16s used prodigious amounts of fuel as they sprinted to their targets, the Warthog moved slowly, with deadly results. Credited with destroying 1,000 Iraqi tanks and 1,200 artillery pieces, the mere sight of the plane brought panic to Iraqi troops, according to captured POWs. The slow speed was absolutely essential for it to fulfill its mission. The plane's secret, says its designer, was its ability to fly extremely slowly 30 feet off the ground so that it could pinpoint its target. It could then launch its Maverick missiles with deadly accuracy or fire its huge 30-caliber Gatling gun at 3,900 rounds a minute to annihilate the enemy. Those who fought for the Warthog recognized that complexity and high technology have their role, but they also understood that getting the job done efficiently is the most important criterion for success.

Even peerless decision makers, however, make mistakes. Because they have to make choices in an uncertain world, errors will inevitably occur. In order to improve the odds of making successful decisions, the peerless decision maker must be aware of all the factors that influence judgment calls. With that awareness comes the ability to identify and evaluate such factors. And with experience comes the ability, even under circumstances of extreme uncertainty and risk, to make high-stakes decisions in your personal and particularly in your professional life—judgment calls that will measure up to the highest standards of competence and withstand the test of time.

Now let us examine each of these factors more fully.

2.

TO SHOOT OR NOT

Edward John Phelps, an American diplomat to England, said in 1888 that "The man who makes no mistakes does not usually gain anything." Franklin Delano Roosevelt admonished, "But above all try something." An executive at Cadbury Corporation described his company's new approach as: "Ready. Fire. Aim." It has been put many ways. I call it the "Knox Ramsey rule." Knox Ramsey is an old family friend, ex-professional football player, and successful executive. His rule states: "If you don't try it, it won't happen."

Of course, the Knox Ramsey rule is an old one. Peters and Waterman in their book *In Search of Excellence* called it a "bias to action," citing numerous anecdotes that show how a bias to action leads to success. For example, a new product development manager at Cadbury Corporation found that several products had been languishing in the pipeline for years and never launched. He rolled out six new products in the next twelve months, and the result was three major successes, an extremely high hit rate.

A bias to action also describes the philosophy held by the president of Storage Technology in the early 1980s. The company was then selling a disk drive that was not making money because it cost $1,500 more to make than the price charged to customers. Recognizing the problem, the president's first action was to raise the price in order to increase profit levels. That strategy failed, however, because customers responded by switching to a competitor's product. The president responded by dropping the product. "I often believe," he said, "that making a decision, even a bad decision, is better than making no decision at all." Unfortunately, the "bias to action" philosophy at Storage Technology led to major problems. Throughout the mid-1980s the company experienced losses year after year, a low stock price, and generally low regard for its management. Perhaps the president could have taken other actions, such as cutting costs, rather than axing the product.

Do you shoot or not? Do you act or not? These questions address the same issue. When making high-stakes decisions, you have to consider the possibility of error and its implications. A bias to action, simply for action's sake, may in fact lead to egregious mistakes. Indeed, in some situations, a bias to *in*action may be the appropriate rule of thumb. Corporations launch thousands of products each year, yet 80 percent fail. DuPont spent millions developing Corfam, a leather substitute that never found a market. Actions can lead to success, but they also can lead to gigantic mistakes.

In some situations, a bias for inaction has proven far more effective. For example, the director of Flight Operations for the Apollo moon missions, Christopher Columbus Kraft, developed a set of precepts on how to run the risky and costly missions. His first precept was: "If you don't know what to do, don't do anything." One can say with some confidence that the Apollo program was run with more expertise than Storage Technology was in the early 1980s. So which is it to be when you are confronted with a high-stakes decision: a bias for action or inaction?

Two Types of "Shoot/No Shoot" Errors

Whenever an action is taken, two types of errors can result. If the action is taken and proves incorrect, the error of the false alarm occurs. If the decision maker fails to take an action when it should have been taken, the error of a miss occurs. When a "shoot/no shoot" judgment call is faced, decision makers must ask themselves which of the two erroneous outcomes would be worse. Then, when deciding whether to act or not, they should be biased away from the more negative outcome. Of course, if the choice is clear-cut and little doubt of the outcome exists, the decision maker should go with what his or her intelligence and experience indicate is the "correct" response.

However, if information is ambiguous and the correct response uncertain, as generally occurs in high-stakes decision making, the bias *away* from the action that will result in the more negative outcome should increasingly play a role.

Two recent and tragic military incidents illustrate the two types of shoot/no shoot errors. On July 3, 1988, Captain Will C. Rogers of the Aegis guided-missile cruiser U.S.S. *Vincennes* issued the order to fire the missiles that destroyed an Iranian passenger jet in the skies above, killing 290 civilian passengers. The *Vincennes* had just been engaged in a surface battle with high-speed Iranian attack boats when radar operators reported that an Iranian aircraft was descending from an altitude of 7,500 feet toward the ship. The crew construed the maneuver as a threatening dive. The aircraft did not respond to the three warnings from the *Vincennes* on civilian radio frequencies, or the four warnings on military frequencies. (Later information would show that the passenger airliner never descended toward the *Vincennes* and that Iranian pilots frequently did not respond to American radio calls, in part because of language problems.)

Captain Rogers made the decision to shoot down the aircraft, a decision that some have speculated contributed to the loss of 270 more passengers when Pan Am Flight 103 was blown from the skies over Lockerbie, Scotland, in possible retaliation for the catastrophe. His action vividly shows the crucial importance of judgment in decision making. Had he known that the aircraft was civilian, he would never have pulled the trigger. The problem, however, is that high-stakes decisions are made under conditions of uncertainty. The outcome cannot be known in advance. Technical systems may fail, human beings can make mistakes, and simple bad luck can intervene.

The *Vincennes* case illustrates a situation in which a decision to shoot ultimately resulted in hundreds of civilian deaths. In contrast, quite the opposite occurred with the destroyer U.S.S. *Stark*. Like the *Vincennes*, the *Stark* patrolled the Persian Gulf. In May 1987, its radar picked up the flight paths of two Iraqi F-1 Mirage fighter jets. Iraqi fighters frequently flew missions in the area, and at the time Saddam Hussein was not considered to be hostile to the United States. While the trigger-happy nature of the Iraqi pilots was well known, some of the *Stark*'s advanced defensive systems were turned off. In addition, a radar warning receiver that would have alerted the ship to incoming hostile missiles was not functioning. The Iraqis fired two French-made Exocet missiles at the *Stark*. An AWACs plane detected the firing of the missiles, but had to pass the message through the destroyer *Coontz*, which took several minutes. The first warning to the *Stark* of the impending attack came seconds before the first missile struck, when a lookout saw it boring toward the ship. The *Stark* nearly sank and thirty-seven sailors were killed.

The *Vincennes* and the *Stark* incidents illustrate two types of errors in shoot/no shoot decision making—false alarms and misses. A false alarm occurs when decision makers "shoot" when they should do nothing. A miss happens when decision makers do nothing, and they should have "shot." The *Vincennes* suffered a false alarm when it blew the passenger jet from the skies. The *Stark* suffered a miss when its lack of vigilance caused it not to detect the impending Iraqi attack. In both instances, the captains acted under uncertainty and made the wrong decision. To analyze the cases, we must ask what the cost of each type of error would have been. In the case of the *Stark*, the captain and crew knew that the two approaching aircraft were military, based upon the analysis of the jet aircrafts' radar by the *Stark*'s instruments. The shooting down of military jets could be justified due to the wartime setting in which the *Stark* was operating. In sum, the results of committing a false alarm in this instance were negative, but could be justified.

The false alarm error, however, must be compared to the negativity of committing a "miss." The cardinal rule of the Navy is to defend your ship, and in this instance the captain failed to do that by not firing at the approaching jets. In discussing the *Stark*'s lack of action, Admiral William J. Crowe, who was head of the Joint Chiefs of Staff at the time, told me that prior to the *Stark* and *Vincennes* incidents, a decision had been made to change the rules of engagement for our naval vessels in the Persian Gulf. While noting that the specific rules are classified, he said that they were "structured so that the commanding officer can shoot before being shot at." Earlier, the rules of engagement stated that ships and aircraft could fire only if they were in imminent danger, and what this effectively meant was that the United States could not fire unless fired upon. However, with Third World nations in possession of sophisticated missiles capable of sinking ships, a change was needed. Basically, naval officers had grown tired of placing U.S. ships and personnel in jeopardy. The changes in the rules of engagement made the lack of action by the *Stark* indefensible. "You sit in the Gulf for two years and nothing happens," as Admiral Crowe said. "After a while, you begin to believe that it's not a dangerous place." As a result of that kind of complacency, the *Stark* was attacked and nearly sunk.

While shooting down the military jets of a country with which you are not at war is bad, having your ship nearly sunk and taking numerous casualties because of a "miss" is clearly worse. Indeed, making a decision that would simply have minimized the number of casualties would have been justified. In sum, in this type of situation the cost of a miss was greater than the cost of a false alarm. Clearly, the military agreed with this assessment, because soon after the incident the captain of the *Stark* was retired from the Navy at a lower rank.

What about the *Vincennes*? The aircraft which the *Vincennes* crew perceived to be hostile had taken off from an airport used by civilian planes. It was well known that civilian planes frequently failed to respond to radio calls. It was also known that the cost of the false alarm of destroying a passenger jet would be extremely high—infinitely higher than that of shooting down a military jet. Undoubtedly, one factor contributing to the accident was the decision to change the rules of engagement. This decision was done only after much analysis at the highest levels of the government, and according to Admiral Crowe, "the greatest fear was accidentally shooting down a passenger jet." Killing innocent civilians in a jet liner was the worst-case scenario of what could go wrong. Indeed, the cost was so great that the captain of the *Vincennes* was obligated to place his ship at much greater risk than was the captain of the *Stark*. For the *Vincennes*, in terms of the trade-off of errors, committing a false alarm was clearly more egregious than allowing a miss to occur.

In addition to the new rules of engagement, a variety of other factors pushed the *Vincennes* toward the false alarm error. The near loss of the *Stark* was still crisply etched in the minds of ship commanders. The stress of battling hostile Iranian gunboats would make any decision maker more aggressive. The failure of the pilots to respond to radio calls created the appearance of hostility. The erroneous information that the aircraft had started to dive reinforced the conclusion. Finally, Captain Rogers and his crew on the *Vincennes* were known to be "trigger-happy" by naval officers. Indeed, based on the ship's previous highly aggressive behavior in the Gulf, sailors had dubbed the *Vincennes* "Robocruiser," according to *Newsweek* magazine. In sum, the entire force of the situation pressed the captain to shoot.

Although the loss of life was enormous on the Iranian passenger liner, interestingly, no reported punishment was inflicted on the captain of the *Vincennes*. He had followed the rules of engagement as specified by the Joint Chiefs of Staff. In fact, in 1990 the captain received a citation for his actions in the Persian Gulf. The different outcomes for the two captains of the *Vincennes* and the *Stark* dramatically depict the bias to action within the military. (We should note that revelations by *Newsweek* magazine in July 1992 of a cover-up of the *Vincennes* blunder may dramatically influence Captain Rogers's future in the Navy.) But is such a bias effective in other high-stakes arenas?

Punching Out a Dead Man and Other Shoot/No Shoot Decisions

In 1953, Don Cooper started his medical career as a young intern at St. Mary's Hospital in Kansas City, Missouri. Soon after Cooper arrived, a middle-aged Union Pacific Railway employee appeared, complaining that everything hurt. He was admitted to the general medicine ward, where he became increasingly belligerent. It was clear that the patient suffered from paranoia and needed psychiatric assistance. Cooper called the railroad surgeon, who told him to give the patient an intravenous sedative. After the patient was incapacitated by the sedative, he could then be moved to the psychiatric ward.

The first step in the procedure was to insert an IV into the man's arm, and with the assistance of the nurses, Cooper succeeded. But the patient was becoming increasingly suspicious; all he wanted to do was get out of the hospital. Further, he wanted nothing to do with the IV. The difficulty was that he was dangerous and had to be calmed down—somehow. Thinking quickly, Cooper decided to attempt to trick him. He told the man that he needed to have a shot of penicillin to take care of his mouth infection. The man seemed to fall for the ruse, and Cooper quickly inserted the needle in the IV device to give the patient the sodium amytal.

Cooper's intent was to follow proper medical procedures and slowly inject the tranquilizer. But just as he started the procedure, the railroad man changed his mind and grabbed at Cooper. Inadvertently, all 10 ccs of the tranquilizer were injected at once. Immediately, the man fell back, his eyes rolled up, he gurgled twice and died. Frantic, Cooper listened to his chest, but no heartbeat or respiratory sounds emerged.

Fear seized Cooper—one of his first patients dead from an overdose of tranquilizer! Again he put his stethoscope to the guy's chest and heard nothing. Cooper's next emotion was anger. How could a

paranoid railroad man ruin his career before it even started? He had
to act, but what could he do? Driven by his anger to do something,
he reared back and punched the dead man hard in the chest. Totally
unexpectedly, the guy coughed once. Cooper checked his heart and
heard an irregular beat. So he hit him in the chest a second time. He
checked again, and now the heart was beating normally.

The next day the man woke up feeling fine. His psychotic attack
had ended, and he was taken to the psychiatric ward puzzled by the
big bruise on his chest. A decade or so later, Cooper's crude attack
would be refined into cardiac resuscitation.

Don Cooper was lucky, and he knows it. But he was in a position
in which any action, even hitting a dead man, was better than none.
By having good fortune strike him square in his fist, Cooper's medical
career was extended for forty years beyond the railroad man's almost
last gasp. Cooper went on to become an internationally recognized
authority on sports medicine and a member of the President's Council on Physical Fitness and Sports. His experience with the railroad
man is a clear indication that in some cases action is paramount. In
addition, the incident reveals that luck, as well as skill and effort,
plays a major role in determining the outcome of judgment calls.
But chance favors no one. Bad luck influenced the outcomes of the
Stark and the *Vincennes* episodes. Cooper was blessed with good
fortune.

With good or bad luck as an omnipresent factor in high-stakes
choices, the decision to do nothing has just as much importance as
the decision to do something. Automobile executives must frequently
make such judgment calls when launching new models. Particularly
difficult is the decision whether to introduce a technological innovation. In his classic book on the auto industry, *The Reckoning*, David
Halberstam talks about General Motors' product innovation policy.
He describes a situation in which a senior manager, David Davis,
was sent to Europe in the early 1970s to check out the vehicles there.
Davis returned extremely impressed with the European cars and
highly concerned about GM's future competitiveness. According to
Halberstam, Davis's boss reacted to his report by saying: "When I
was at Oldsmobile, there was something I learned that I've never
forgotten. There was an old guy there who was an engineer, and he
had been at GM a long time, and he gave me some advice. 'Whatever
you do, don't let GM do it first.' "

Davis realized that this was the party line of a protected industry.
Let the other side make the mistake first; in other words, the error of
a miss was more acceptable to GM executives than a false alarm. It

was, as time would tell, a wrong judgment call. In the 1970s and 1980s, the auto industry would become highly competitive, a battle-field open to all players. The Japanese, Germans, and Swedes would take the initiative, and GM's market share would slide with each unanswered innovation. The introduction by German and Japanese companies of full-time four-wheel drive, four-wheel steering, anti-lock brakes, and four valves per cylinder wrested away from GM, Ford, and Chrysler any semblance of technological leadership.

The judgment call of whether to shoot or not pervades decision making whether one talks about military, medical, legal, or business problems. For example, individual investors, insurance companies, and banks must make the choice whether to lend money to firms. In this shoot/no shoot decision, the investor is looking for signals of the borrower's ability to succeed. Peerless investors have the competence to read the signals and to differentiate the good from the bad risks. In addition, they analyze the relative costs of the two types of mis-takes. Is it worse to have a miss and fail to make a loan to a company that will succeed? Or, is it worse to encounter a false alarm and make a loan to a company that will fail?

Historically, banks have focused on avoiding the false alarm of making bad loans. One individual who represents this conservatism is Woodbury C. Titcomb, chairman of Peoples Bancorp in Worcester, Massachusetts. During the roaring 1980s, many banks in New En-gland changed their practices in order to avoid the error of missing opportunities. Titcomb, however, stayed on a conservative course. According to one analyst, "When everybody was lending money like mad, they all laughed at crazy Woodie, the guy with the buggy whip being passed by all of those fast cars." When times were good in New England, Titcomb was pummeled for his stodginess by analysts and even by his own board of directors. One observer argued that Peoples Bancorp "missed the train" and that Titcomb falls into the category of "nothing ventured, nothing gained."

Going by the "banker's book," Peoples Bancorp made loans based only upon secured cash flow, not upon the inflated price of collateral. When people in the community were turned down for loans, his board members took the heat and passed it on to Titcomb. As he said, "It was a very tough time, but I said, 'No, no, no. We won't grow our loan portfolio the way others do—we just don't get paid to take those kinds of capital risks.' We stood alone—all alone." On one occasion, Peoples Bancorp was about to close a quarter with a nice profit. But while taking his early morning walk, Titcomb began worrying about "worst-case scenarios for the New England economy." As a result of his premonition, he nearly doubled the bank's loan loss reserve, and the bank showed its first quarterly loss since it went public.

Then came the great New England recession/depression, and Titcomb was vindicated. While the New England economy plunged to new depths during the winter of 1991 and most banks foundered, Peoples Bancorp prospered. Indeed, it grew by picking up the healthy pieces of the once popular go-go banks of the area, which were now in bankruptcy. As one analyst put it in February 1991, "Now he has one of the few healthy banks around, and they're calling him a genius."

Woodbury Titcomb and Peoples Bancorp prospered in part because he and his employees knew how to make shoot/no shoot judgment calls. They could read the signals of the environment and were skilled at discriminating good risks from bad. Furthermore, they understood that for bankers, the outcome of making a bad loan is worse than the outcome of failing to make a loan to a company that might succeed, because an accumulation of bad loans can sink the bank. As Titcomb said, the philosophy of "nothing ventured, nothing gained" is fine for businessmen, but not for bankers. The conservative philosophy is critical for bankers because signals can be illusory and because people can make mistakes. In the world of high-stakes decision making, we must always consider the possibility that the worst will in fact occur.

Separating Decision Making from Decision Implementation

The "shoot/no shoot" principle states that the decision maker, when uncertain, should select the action that, if wrong, will produce the least negative outcome. That principle, however, is criticized because it forces decision makers to consider the possibility of error. Business managers, military leaders, and other decision makers despise thoughts of failure. In order to achieve, you must be confident and eliminate all thoughts of losing. On the other hand, unjustified self-confidence in your ability to make a decision and evaluate its outcome can be equally dangerous. There is a solution to this dilemma: drawing a distinction between decision "making" and decision "implementation." The peerless decision maker is the person who is "a realist when making a decision but an optimist when implementing it."

Perhaps nowhere are thoughts of failure more lethal than in sports—and particularly in golf. What makes the sport so tough is that you must examine each shot and make a highly calculated decision about how to play it. You must consider the nature of the shot, your ability, and the odds that you can pull off the swing. You have to acknowledge and recognize the possibility of failure and then do your utmost to avoid it. After you make a decision, however, you must eliminate negative thoughts and visualize only the desired flight of the ball. Few can consistently accomplish these mental gymnastics.

High-stakes decisions are made every week in professional golf. One story with a happy ending involves Bob Tway. Tway played for Mike Holder at Oklahoma State University and was on one of Holder's three NCAA championship teams in the early 1980s. Tway has had a distinguished pro career, winning the PGA and numerous other tournaments. Yet he nearly failed to get his tour card. For four straight years he played well in the qualifying rounds until the last eighteen holes. Then his game would fall apart; he would shoot 80 and miss by a couple of strokes. He couldn't shake his negative thoughts.

On his fifth try, Tway's score beginning the last round was on the cusp of qualifying. On the front nine, however, he got hot, and he went to the 16th hole 7 under par. He could merely par in, and he would be in the top five overall. The 16th hole, a par 3, was 205 yards long. Earlier in the day, Tway had hit a four iron 205 yards, so he selected it in this situation—forgetting that he was now all charged up. He hit the ball right at the pin, but carried it twenty yards over the green. He made double bogey. Suddenly, negative thoughts again flooded Tway's thinking. He made a triple bogey on 17. On the last hole he 3-putted, and he was sure that he had blown it again. Fortunately, he was out of holes, and made the cut by a couple of strokes. Interestingly, once he cleared the qualifying hurdle and was on the tour, he relaxed and began to win on a regular basis.

I asked Mike Holder how golfers like Jack Nicklaus, and basketball players like Michael Jordan, seemed to be able to raise the level of their game a notch higher in the clutch. In his view, the key was experience. Players like Payne Stewart, Tom Watson, and Fred Couples all had reputations as chokers at one time. But as each gained experience, he learned to plan realistically and then execute the desired course of action under high-pressure conditions.

The "Can-Do" Syndrome. The tendency to plunge into action is frequently seen in people who confuse decision making with decision implementation. Often they act like "gung-ho" types who value action over reflection.

Long ago, I spent four years as a Regular Army Signal Corps officer. In 1970 I had the "opportunity" to go through the eight-week U.S. Army Ranger School. It was one of those experiences that a person never forgets. The first four weeks, I hoped I would break a leg in order to get out of that hellhole. The last four weeks, I would have kept going with a broken leg. On one simulated mission I was in a squad of ten: nine marines and myself. Our goal was to destroy a communications facility behind enemy lines. After accomplishing our goal we had to escape and evade the enemy, then travel some seven miles behind enemy lines back to friendly territory. Our attack would occur at dusk, so the escape-and-evade exercise was planned to last the entire night. That night, we quickly accomplished our mission and then regrouped to plan our way back. Basically, we had two options: Take the safe and slow way through the deep woods in the middle of the night, or take the fast and risky way down a road through the middle of enemy territory. The marines quickly agreed to the second course. The rationale was that if we ran the whole distance, we could get through before the enemy got organized. So we began to run in a gangly formation down a dirt road. Miraculously, it worked. For two hours we could hear firing and see the lights of flares behind us. We arrived at the base camp in record time and then froze all night waiting for the other teams to get back.

Marines are crazy. They have to be. In order to accomplish their mission of storming beaches and making first contact with an enemy, they cannot think about "false alarms" and "misses." I do not imply that marine commanders take unnecessary or uncalculated risks, but once the decision is made, the marines execute it without hesitation. However, the marine's gung-ho philosophy can apply in only a limited set of circumstances. Indeed, most business, personal, and governmental decisions are better served by maintaining an even balance between decision making and decision implementation. The "can-do" syndrome creates major problems when used inappropriately. Nowhere was this better demonstrated than in Vietnam.

Throughout the escalation of the Vietnam War, military and White House personnel revealed an incredible capacity for overoptimism and self-deception. It began in November 1961, when General Maxwell Taylor went on a fact-finding mission to Vietnam for President Kennedy and returned recommending an expansion of the advisory role of the military to 8,000 U.S. troops. Taylor argued that the advisers should allow the South Vietnamese government to build its army to 200,000; he estimated that for planning purposes the American advisers should be out of Vietnam by the end of 1962. At the time George Ball, Undersecretary of State for Economic Affairs, warned Kennedy that 300,000 American troops would be in Vietnam in a few short years. Kennedy laughed and said, "George, you're crazier than hell."

Early in the war, Taylor created an atmosphere in which the military was to exhibit confidence at all costs. He placed General Paul D. Harkins in charge of the Military Advisory Corps Vietnam (MACV) and gave him orders to create upbeat reports. Harkins responded by ensuring that documents were systematically rewritten as necessary to show that all was going well. In April 1963, Harkins told Robert McNamara, the Secretary of Defense, that it would all be over by Christmas.

In late 1964 and early 1965, the new president, Lyndon Johnson, was being pushed by the U.S. military to begin bombing North Vietnam in order to wear the enemy down and give a confidence booster to the South Vietnamese military and political leaders. Johnson was told that the bombing of the North should produce results in six months. Later in 1965, commanders realized that the bombing operation, called "Rolling Thunder," was having a minimal impact, and they began arguing for bringing in American combat troops. Again, the magic six-month figure was given. Eighty thousand troops would be placed in defensive enclaves to protect key airports and installations and be back home again in six months or so. Unfortunately, by the end of the year, 200,000 troops would be in Vietnam. In two more years, over 500,000 American troops would stand on Vietnamese soil.

Overconfidence continued to dog American predictions until the ultimate collapse of the South Vietnamese government in 1975. Back in early 1967, Walt Rostow, President Johnson's new National Security Adviser, talked about a Viet Cong defeat within weeks. Later in 1967, Ellsworth Bunker became the new Ambassador to South Vietnam. At a dinner party for journalists, he criticized them for being so pessimistic about how the war was going. He noted that he wanted to set the South Vietnamese army loose to go into Laos to pursue the North Vietnamese troops, who were using it as a sanctuary. A reporter sitting next to him began to laugh. Bunker became perplexed and asked why he was laughing. The reporter responded, "Because if you send them into Laos, they'll get their asses whipped, sir." The ambassador was offended, but four years later when ARVN troops went into Laos, they were mauled.

Unfortunately, the Nixon administration exhibited the same overoptimistic tendencies. Nixon ran for the presidency in 1968 on the pledge to end the war in six months. In 1969, Representative Pete McCloskey of California challenged Henry Kissinger, then Nixon's National Security Adviser, to end the war as promised. Kissinger told him to be patient and give them sixty to ninety more days. In fact, it would take four more years to arrange a truce and withdraw American troops.

In February 1973, I had been in Vietnam for seven months, and a cease-fire had at last been called. Civilians were supposed to display on the tin roofs of their small houses the flag of the country they supported. Our MACV team's commander, a full colonel, had the brilliant idea of flying the five remaining American advisers around in a helicopter (me included) in order to count the number of South and North Vietnamese flags we could find. To no one's surprise, no North Vietnamese flags were to be found in the coastal province of Binh Dinh where we were stationed, and I still remember to this day the colonel's self-satisfied statement: "We've done a good job, guys. ARVN can handle them now." Two years later, South Vietnam was overrun by the North Vietnamese.

The "can-do" syndrome can lead to overconfidence and get you into real trouble. In the Vietnam War, overconfident American decision makers pursued an unrealistic goal and tragically underestimated the determination of an enemy willing to achieve victory whatever the price.

The Overconfidence Bias. Problems of overconfidence can strike in the business community as well as in the military. A *Wall Street Journal* article reported the results of a study that found that the business plans of new computer software companies overestimated first-year sales by 28 percent. When asked to develop "optimistic," "expected," and "pessimistic" sales forecasts, the worst-case scenarios developed in their business plans proved to be the most accurate.

These findings are remarkably similar to the results of laboratory research on the overconfidence bias. In one study, people were asked to choose which of two causes of death is more frequent, citing a series of pairs of possibilities. For example, one question asked: "Is death by motor vehicle accident or death by stroke more likely?" After making a choice, the participants in the study were asked to express their confidence in their decision by giving the odds that they were correct. Odds of 2:1 meant that they thought they were twice as likely to be right as wrong; odds of 3:1 meant they thought they were three times as likely to be right as wrong; and so forth. The researchers then compared the odds given by the participants that they were right to the percentage of times that they were, in fact, correct. The results revealed that when the participants were uncertain, their calibrations were on target. Thus, when they gave odds of 1:1 (i.e., an estimation of a 50–50 chance of being right), they were correct 58 percent of the time. When they gave odds of 3:1, they were correct 71 percent of the time. However, as they became increasingly confident of their answers, their actual performance failed to improve. At 10:1 odds, they were correct only 66 percent of the time, and when they gave odds of 100:1, they were correct only 73 percent of the time. Thus, on an answer for which the participants thought they were 100 times more likely to be right than wrong, they were *actually* right only 73 percent of the time. When confidence increased dramatically (i.e., from 3:1 to 100:1), accuracy barely changed (i.e., from 71 percent to 73 percent correct).

The researchers tried several approaches to reduce this overconfidence. Paying the participants to increase their precision had little impact. Further, all types of people revealed overconfidence—it affected business people, physicists, doctors, and business professors alike. In one study, managers of a computer company were asked a series of company-specific factual questions and then told to give the ranges within which they were 95 percent confident that the correct answer would fall. (For example, suppose that you were asked to give the air distance between Tokyo and London. You would then give a range of miles within which you were 95 percent confident that the right answer would fall.) For managers of the computer company, in 58 percent of the cases the correct answer was outside of the range given. And remember, the questions pertained to matters that concerned their own company.

Do physicians do any better? When estimating the probability that patients had pneumonia, the range given by physicians proved wrong 82 percent of the time, when the ideal target was to be wrong less than 20 percent of the time. The overconfidence bias appears to strike all individuals regardless of occupation, intelligence, and experience.

The one factor that has been shown to reduce the overconfidence bias is feedback. Individuals whose jobs involve frequent feedback on the accuracy of their decisions—such as weather forecasters, for example—become more realistic in calibrating their own performance. Their self-confidence has a basis in fact.

Detecting Signals for Action

When making the judgment call to shoot or not shoot, the decision maker must look for a signal of action and evaluate its strength. If the signal is perceived as strong enough, the decision maker will tend to act. In the *Stark* case, for example, the officer in charge did not consider the signal representing the threat of the Iraqi aircraft to be strong enough to warrant action. In contrast, the captain of the *Vincennes* perceived a strong signal and blasted away.

One approach to understanding the nature of "shoot/no shoot" decisions is known as the signal detection theory. First developed to explain the detection of electronic signals, such as radio waves, the ideas were later expanded to explain why the performance of radar operators working on the DEW Line varied so much over time. (DEW stands for defense early warning—a radar system constructed after World War II to warn American military forces of a Russian bomber attack.) It was discovered that after an operator had worked on his shift for a few hours, he would tend to have more misses. Thus, when the simulated signal of an enemy plane was flashed on the radar screen, it would go undetected more frequently later in the shift. Were the operators becoming tired and making more errors, or were they simply shirking their duties? After a great deal of study, researchers found that the operators were making more mistakes, but they were also making different kinds of errors. The signal detection theory was developed to explain the phenomenon.

What signal detection theory says is that two factors influence the quality of judgments: accuracy and bias. "Accuracy" refers to how well a person can distinguish signal from noise. For example, to what extent can radar operators distinguish hostile from non-belligerent jets? A highly accurate decision maker will simply make fewer mistakes. The concept of "bias" refers to the types of errors made by the radar operators and whether they change over time. If a person is biased toward action and employs a "hair trigger," he or she will tend to shoot more frequently and commit the error of a false alarm. If a person is biased toward inaction and uses a "sticky trigger," he or she will tend to avoid shooting, causing the error of a miss to occur more frequently. The researchers found that when the radar operators first went on their shift, they employed a "hair trigger" and committed more false alarms. As time passed and nothing happened, their bias changed. The "hair trigger" gradually changed to a "sticky trigger." As a consequence, they committed fewer false alarms but had more misses.

The idea of establishing a criterion for action is extremely important. Set by the decision maker, it represents the amount of evidence required for the person to decide to "shoot." The criterion can be set at a neutral point at which false alarms and misses occur with equal frequency. If the criterion is set so that a large amount of evidence is required before a decision to shoot is made, a "sticky" trigger results. In contrast, a lenient criterion results in a "hair" trigger. Metaphorically, establishing a criterion is like setting the stickiness of a rifle trigger.

Setting the Trigger. A decision maker has to decide a priori whether to set a hair or a sticky trigger. When the officer in charge of the *Stark* found that military jets were approaching, he should have immediately adopted a "hair" trigger. In contrast, when the captain of the *Vincennes* learned that an unidentified jet had taken off from an airport used by civilian jets, he should have adopted a "sticky" trigger. Instead, a "hair" trigger was set, thereby paving the way for shooting a passenger jet out of the sky.

Under ambiguous circumstances, the peerless decision maker avoids making the worst error. He or she evaluates the relative costs of a miss or false alarm and sets the criterion so that the trigger has the appropriate "stickiness." Thus, the trigger setting is determined in part by the relative costs of the negative outcomes. However, a second factor may influence trigger setting: the decision maker's expectation that a signal will be encountered. If the expectation of a signal is high, a less sticky trigger is set. In contrast, if the expectation of a signal is low, a more sticky trigger is set. The expectation of a signal explains in part the actions of the *Vincennes* and the *Stark* crews respectively. After having just been in battle, the crew of the *Vincennes* was primed to expect trouble, and set a hair trigger. In contrast, the *Stark* hadn't been on alert for days. Problems were not expected, the trigger for action became sticky, and a miss resulted.

When Peters and Waterman called for a "bias to action," they argued that managers should set a "hair" trigger. When Chris Kraft developed his rule at NASA ("If you don't know what to do, don't do anything"), he was arguing for a "sticky" trigger that would result in more misses than false alarms. Remember, however, that the judgment of where to set the criterion has little to do with decision accuracy. The level of accuracy depends upon a person's ability to distinguish "signal" from "noise." Skilled decision makers make fewer errors simply because they can better distinguish signal from noise. Trigger setting merely influences the likelihood of which type of mistake will be made, if indeed one is made. It does little to affect the overall likelihood of a mistake occurring.

Trigger setting is also influenced by the overconfidence bias. Most people believe that they are better decision makers than they really are. As a result, they exaggerate their ability to detect signals and tend to set a hair trigger. In order to set the trigger appropriately, peerless decision makers must recognize that overconfidence can influence their expectations of whether or not a signal is present. It is difficult to gain sufficient self-insight to know our own expectations. This becomes particularly difficult when our expectations are built upon unchallenged assumptions.

Assumptions Are the Root of All . . .

Prior to the Persian Gulf war, Saddam Hussein assumed that America lacked the will to fight. His faulty assumption resulted in the needless loss of lives, infrastructure, and prestige. But American military planners have been known to base their strategy on erroneous assumptions as well. In 1940, U.S. cryptographers deciphered MAGIC, the top-secret Japanese diplomatic code. The United States was able to monitor Japanese military activity with complete confidence in the information gained. In November 1941, intercepted messages indicated that the Japanese had set a secret deadline of November 28 for concluding ongoing talks between Japan and the United States on avoiding a Pacific conflict. A series of at least nine messages was sent from Tokyo, and they revealed a sense of despair that the United States would refuse to cooperate. One message warned: "Should the negotiations collapse, the international situation in which the Empire will find herself will be one of tremendous crisis." By late November, the messages indicated that Japan was not going to resume negotiations, but that the United States should be made to believe that Japan wanted the negotiations to continue. Meanwhile, the American Ambassador to Japan was warning policy makers that U.S. economic sanctions were having a negative effect and increasing Japanese belligerence. Given this information and the ability to monitor military communications as well, how could Americans have been so totally surprised on the morning of December 7 when Pearl Harbor was attacked?

One can argue that faulty assumptions caused the failure to detect the surprise attack. American officials believed that Japan was more afraid of war than they were. The development of the B-17 bomber, which had the capability of bombing the Japanese mainland, reinforced the assumption that Japan would not attempt to wage war against the United States. American policy makers assumed that Japanese military leaders would not consider a military challenge. On the eve of Pearl Harbor, Secretary of War Henry Stimson said, "I entirely fail to see the dangers [involved in the application of economic sanctions] by a nation as powerful as ours against another nation as susceptible to them as Japan is in her present condition." In sum, decision makers in the Roosevelt administration simply assumed that Japan would not attack. The assumptions resulted in a failure to heed the clear warnings coming through intelligence and diplomatic sources. In effect, American officials had set an extremely "sticky" trigger when they assumed the non-belligerency of the Japanese. Evidence —a smoking gun—was needed. Unfortunately, we got it in the form of the carnage at Pearl Harbor.

Numerous other examples can be found of faulty assumptions that led to the success of surprise attacks. The sudden Chinese entry into the Korean War was totally unanticipated by General Douglas MacArthur. American decision makers assumed that because of their lack of military capability, Chinese leaders would act rationally and not enter the war. The thought never occurred to U.S. planners that the Chinese might rate their own capabilities higher than they (the Americans) did. Similarly, prior to Iraq's invasion of Kuwait, American officials suffered from what has been called "the mindset." Believing that the United States could offer "rewards" that could influence Hussein, American policy makers overlooked for almost two years his increasingly provocative signals in the region. Not his use of nerve gas on the Kurds, his summary executions of opposition leaders, his verbal attacks on his neighbors, nor the final troop build-up on the Kuwait border could trip the "sticky" trigger that resulted from the U.S. mindset. As a result, when his tanks moved on Kuwait, the attack was a surprise.

Evolving Surprises. In military campaigns, the element of surprise often results in quick victories and the immediate devastation of the loser. In personal, business, and political arenas, surprises tend to take longer to evolve. Evolving surprises, however, result from the same problem of faulty assumptions that cause a sticky trigger to be set. Therefore, decision makers ignore the accumulating evidence of a surprise action. A classic example was the 1973 Arab oil embargo. On October 21, 1973, the Organization of Petroleum Exporting

Countries (OPEC) announced an oil embargo. Focused primarily on the United States, it took Americans by surprise. Yet the embargo had been years in the making, and a series of factors placed America and the industrialized world in a poor power position. In 1970, American energy production began to decrease and the United States grew more dependent on imported oil. The need for imported oil by European Common Market countries also began to increase dramatically, while the growing Japanese economy had become totally dependent on foreign oil. In addition, tensions between Arab states and Israel were festering. The debacle of the Six Day War fought in 1967 still haunted the Arabs. In 1970, Muammar Qaddafi came to power and began to assert Libya's independence from the huge oil companies, pressuring others to raise prices. The tactic worked, and Arab confidence grew. Then, on October 6, 1973, Egypt and Syria invaded Israeli-occupied territory, and the stage was set for the embargo.

At that time, American political and business leaders still assumed that the Arab countries were backwater, Third World states that could be controlled. In fact, the Arab leaders and their advisers were highly intelligent and politically sophisticated men. Just after the October 6 invasion, four Arab foreign ministers flew to Washington to meet with President Richard Nixon. He refused to see them because his schedule was too busy. The ministers were angered—particularly the Saudi minister, Omar Saqquaf. At a press conference that day, Saqquaf revealed his annoyance when a pompous news reporter suggested that the Saudis might have to drink their oil. Saqquaf replied, "All right, we will!"

Meanwhile, OPEC was attempting to gain price concessions from the major international oil companies. OPEC was demanding $5 per barrel for oil, but management refused to go over about $3.75 a barrel. The oil companies and the governments of oil-consuming nations could not face the new realities of the marketplace. Their assumptions about the balance of power blinded them to the signals, and they failed to act. On October 21 the boycott began.

The effect was almost instantaneous. On December 16, 1973, the first auction for oil was held. The price jumped to $17 a barrel. In the United States the price of gasoline doubled, consumers had to wait in long lines for fuel, and people even began torching their gas-guzzling cars in order to get rid of them. While the gas crisis of 1973–74 was relatively short-lived, it did spark a major recession. It would be followed by another oil crisis in 1978, when prices again spiraled upward during the Iranian hostage crisis. In the 1980s, oil prices fell, and Americans grew complacent. We returned to driving muscle cars; domestic oil production decreased; oil output began to fall in the Soviet Union; programs to develop alternative fuel supplies were halted. We were ignoring the signals, such as our growing dependence on foreign oil. Then, in 1990, Iraq invaded Kuwait, and the price of oil soared once again. We failed to learn from our past mistakes, assumed stability in the Middle East, and again paid the price.

The Jury as a Detector of Guilt. While the average man or woman in the United States may feel far removed from such judgment calls, there is one place where the importance of high-stakes decision making is brought home: in jury duty. Such decisions must often be made under extraordinarily difficult conditions, as the late Federal Judge Jerome Frank noted:

> The surroundings of inquiry during a jury trial differ extraordinarily from those in which the juryman conducts his ordinary affairs. At a trial, the jurors hear evidence in a public place, under conditions of a kind to which they are unaccustomed: No juror is able to withdraw to his own room or office for private individual reflection. And at the close of the trial, the jurors are pressed for time in reaching their joint decision. Even twelve experienced judges, deliberating together, would probably not function well under the conditions we impose on the twelve inexperienced men.

In addition to the factors mentioned by Judge Frank, also consider that juries receive only the tough cases. Prosecutors avoid bringing weak cases to trial. Trials are costly and time-consuming, and the criminal justice system in the United States is already overloaded. Further, consider that defendants who face strong evidence of their guilt will seek plea bargains in order to obtain reduced sentences; prosecutors will frequently yield to the request in order to reduce their caseloads. Thus, the cases brought to a jury trial tend to be in that zone of ambiguity where enough evidence exists to bring the defendant to trial, but the evidence is not so overwhelming as to force the defendant to plea bargain.

Like radar operators searching for signals of enemy aircraft, juries seek to detect guilt. They attempt to find guilt signals amid the noise of the testimony given by witnesses and the arguments of the attorneys. How accurate are they in detecting guilt, and what factors will tend to bias their decisions? As it turns out, the American judicial system has created its own "bias to inaction" in jury decision making. The basic instruction to the jury, that "the defendant must be proven guilty beyond a reasonable doubt," acts to set a highly "sticky" trigger. The goal is to avoid the false alarm of convicting an innocent person. Of course, the trade-off is that more misses will occur. But in our system we seek to protect the rights of the individual, and we are comfortable with the trade-off—most of the time.

A number of additional factors, however, influence how juries set the trigger. The Algiers Motel trial provides one example. During the Detroit riots of 1967, three young blacks were killed in what became known as the Algiers Motel incident. One white policeman was brought to trial for the death of one of the men. The trial produced substantial evidence that the police had wrongfully killed the black men, and observers expected a guilty verdict. In his instructions to the members of the jury, the judge did something unusual but perfectly legal. He gave them only two verdict alternatives from which to choose: guilty of first-degree murder or not guilty. He omitted the possibilities of second-degree murder and manslaughter. The jury returned a verdict of not guilty, which incensed the black community. Could the jurors have been biased in favor of the white policeman? The judicial community immediately began to wonder if the judge's unusual instructions could have been a factor in the verdict.

My own research has shown that by reducing the number of decision alternatives to two, the judge dramatically increased the likelihood that the policeman would be set free. The guilty option of first-degree murder causes (and rightfully so) jurors to set a "sticky trigger," making it extremely difficult to convict.

More ominously, my research indicates that increasing the number of verdict options increases the likelihood of obtaining a guilty verdict. Compare the situation in which jurors must choose between the two verdict alternatives of guilty of manslaughter or not guilty to the situation in which four verdict alternatives are given: guilty of manslaughter, second-degree murder, first-degree murder, or not guilty. If a defendant is guilty of second-degree murder or first-degree murder, he or she is also guilty of manslaughter. In this case, regardless of whether two or four verdict alternatives are given, the number of not guilty verdicts should be the same. In mock trials, I found that on average jurors gave 31 percent innocent verdicts when the options were manslaughter versus not guilty. In contrast, when all three guilty options were available, the mock jurors found the defendant innocent only 17 percent of the time. Giving the juries all three verdict alternatives (in addition to not guilty) caused them to set a "hair trigger." They acted as though they reasoned: "We could have convicted the defendant of first-degree or second-degree murder, so convicting him of manslaughter gives him a break." In effect, adding additional verdict alternatives (i.e., first- and second-degree murder) reduced the amount of evidence required by the mock juries to convict the defendant of manslaughter.

In criminal trials, defense attorneys focus on changing the criterion for guilt set by juries. Their goal is to change the amount of evidence required by jurors to convict. Thus, the objective of bringing in character witnesses is to persuade the jury that the defendant could not have committed the crime and, thereby, raise the criterion for the amount of evidence required for a guilty verdict. Character witnesses have nothing to do with the evidence presented in the case. They are used merely to influence how much evidence is required to find guilt. Similarly, pretrial publicity acts to influence the trigger. When jurors learn about the case in the news media, their expectations of guilt are changed. The information influences the criterion for the amount of evidence needed to convict. That is why every effort is made, both in selecting a jury and in extreme cases in making a change of venue, to counteract the influence of pretrial publicity.

Another way to change the trigger is found in the selection of who is on the jury. During pretrial proceedings, the attorneys conduct "voir dire," the process in which potential jurors are questioned. If a juror can be shown to be biased in any way that could influence the outcome of the case, the judge will excuse him or her. In addition, attorneys are allowed a number of peremptory challenges. Through this procedure a juror can be dismissed for any reason. In high-stakes trials involving corporations or well-financed defendants, jury selection is considered so important that attorneys bring in consultants who specialize in the process. Indeed, the jury selection business is now booming as marketing professors, psychologists, and sociologists set up shop to help attorneys select juries.

Can the outcome of a trial be influenced by the characteristics of the individuals who make up the jury? Absolutely! Jury trials, whether criminal or civil, often occur in those cases in which the evidence against the defendant is in the zone of ambiguity. Such cases hinge on where the criterion for liability or guilt is set. Thus in a criminal trial, if jurors can be found who have a predisposition to believe that a person is guilty or innocent, it will influence the trigger's setting. Such individuals will not admit to a bias; they may even perceive the evidence in a manner similar to other jurors. However, they will require a different level of proof to convict. In a similar manner, the characteristics of the defendant will influence juries. Strong evidence indicates that the defendant's race, socioeconomic status, physical attractiveness, the heinousness of the crime, and a past criminal record all influence juries by changing the trigger's setting.

The American jury system illustrates many of the factors that influence shoot/no shoot decisions. Perhaps the most important lesson is that distinguishing between signal and noise can be extremely difficult in some situations. In a jury trial, the level of the signal of guilt received by the jury is the only indicator available for reaching a verdict. In some circumstances, the prosecution may be able to develop an extremely tight case and create a strong signal of guilt for a defendant who is actually innocent. Conversely, in other situations little evidence may exist against an otherwise guilty defendant. As a result, mistakes are made in the form of the false alarm of convicting an innocent person or the miss of failing to convict a guilty person. The same situation can occur in a business decision, such as the false alarm of firing an employee who has merely had a run of bad luck. In a medical setting, false alarms occur when physicians operate unnecessarily believing that a condition is present when in fact it does not exist. A miss occurs when a doctor fails to operate or to treat a condition that does exist.

The signal detection theory tells us that high levels of training are necessary for us to effectively distinguish signal from noise. It also tells us that mistakes will occur. For example, in the Persian Gulf hundred-hour ground war, despite the best efforts of the military, so-called friendly fire took the lives of at least 35 of the 148 Americans killed in the war. Because of the inevitability of error, peerless decision makers develop a sense of the most appropriate trigger-setting point. In the American jury system, judicial instructions result in a "sticky" trigger setting in order to avoid the false alarm of convicting innocent defendants. In a military setting, commanders are forced to set "hair" triggers because the consequences of missing the signal are so catastrophic, as illustrated by the U.S.S. *Stark* incident. Similarly, business managers must set a trigger for investment decisions. The CEO of Peoples Bancorp argued that for bankers, a sticky trigger is most appropriate. In contrast, a hair trigger that results in a bias to action is most appropriate for executives of firms operating in a highly competitive business environment. The same factors should influence surgeons. In deciding whether to operate, should a hair or a sticky trigger be set? Interestingly, buried within the Hippocratic

Oath is the concept "above all else, do no harm." This oath suggests that employing a "sticky" trigger is most appropriate in medical settings.

To Act or Not to Act, That Is Not the Only Question

A characteristic of peerless decision makers is their ability to avoid "shoot/no shoot" situations. They find new alternatives. Here is a classic example: A senior partner in a prestigious Denver law firm was also on the board of directors of a small college in Kansas. The president of the college suddenly died of a heart attack, and the partner soon found himself spending half his time in Kansas managing the college. He had to supervise hiring a new president, act to retain key faculty members, and ensure that the college continued its mission of educating students.

The problem was that he was not serving his law firm, and he knew it. One day he walked into the managing partner's office and said that he wanted to take a pay cut. While fair, the action would create major problems within the firm. It would set a poor precedent for other senior partners. Further, it would create problems when the attorney returned full time to the firm and wanted his old salary back. What mechanism should then be used to give him a raise when he came back to work full time? The "shoot/no shoot" decision was: Should the partner be allowed to take a pay cut or not?

The dilemma dragged on for a while with no one knowing what to do. Finally, the managing partner was able to find an entirely new option. Pregnant women attorneys went on part-time status at lower salaries just prior to giving birth. Why couldn't the same idea be applied to the male attorney? When suggested, the partner loved the idea. The other partners could buy it; it was the perfect solution. In hindsight, the solution appears obvious. At the time, however, it was viewed as brilliant.

It is extremely difficult to identify alternative solutions to shoot/no shoot situations. Sometimes there are, in fact, no alternatives. But even when they exist, people can become locked into known actions and reactions and can find it difficult to break new ground. Even worse, when asked if they have identified all of the possible solutions to the problem, decision makers will prove dramatically overconfident that they have done so.

Should you make that investment? Should you quit your safe job and start your own business? Should you fire an employee? Should you go to a doctor when you feel a small lump in your breast or testicle? Each time that you make the choice of whether to act or not, you are engaging in a shoot/no shoot judgment call. Some of the principles to consider when making such choices are:

- Think realistically when making the decision; act confidently when implementing the decision.

- In the zone of ambiguity, select the alternative that would result in the least negative outcome, should you happen to be wrong.

- Understand that the overconfidence bias causes people to believe that their decisions are better than they really are.

- Give decision makers frequent feedback on the accuracy of their predictions in order to reduce the overconfidence bias.

- Decide early in the decision process whether to set a "hair" or a "sticky" trigger, based upon the relative negativity of a miss or a false alarm.

- Know your expectations and balance their biasing effects by developing arguments against their occurrence.

- Avoid surprises by identifying all assumptions and checking their veracity.

- If known problem solutions are unpalatable, search for creative alternatives.

3.

TO STAY OR QUIT

In August 1979, Jose Gomez, an ambitious thirty-one-year-old accountant who had just made partner, was given responsibility for the audit of E.S.M. Government Securities, Inc., a relatively small Fort Lauderdale financial firm. A couple of days into the audit, two officers at E.S.M. told Gomez of a "crude" accounting ruse perpetrated in order to hide losses totaling several million dollars. According to Gomez, the officers pointedly noted that he had missed the irregularity in the audits in which he had previously participated. Feeling intimidated, Gomez agonized over what to do for a couple of days. He finally decided not to report the cover-up, because he felt that the E.S.M. managers could make up the $10 million easily in the loosely run savings and loan industry.

About a year after the initial incident, Gomez looked at the problem again. The deficit had grown to $100 million. At this point he reports feeling trapped. "I just totally felt that I'd lost control of it." After the new discovery, E.S.M. officers began giving Gomez loans that eventually totaled about $200,000. For five years Gomez helped to cover up the fraud being perpetrated. In 1985 the firm collapsed, at a cost of $320 million to investors, most of whom were municipalities and S&Ls across the country. In Ohio the collapse started a run on the state-insured thrifts, which the governor had to close for several days.

"It was a professional decision, a judgment decision that I was making that I felt would eventually work itself out," Gomez confided to *The Wall Street Journal* in 1987—a few days before going to prison for a minimum of four years. When asked if he viewed the loans from E.S.M. as a "quid pro quo" for his assistance, Gomez replied, ". . . it's hard for people to accept this . . . I didn't do it for money. I did it because I didn't want to have to face up that I had made a mistake. . . ."

This is an all too familiar dilemma in the world of high-stakes decision making. As Kenny Rogers sang in his song "The Gambler":

> You've got to know when to hold 'em,
> Know when to fold 'em,
> Know when to walk away, know when to run.

Knowing when to hold 'em and when to fold 'em perfectly describes the judgment call of whether to stay—or quit. Jose Gomez tried to hold on when he should have run. While the Gomez case illustrates how crimes can result from a person becoming entrapped by a bad decision, the problem goes beyond illegal activities. Business and political decision makers frequently face the dilemma: How long do you stay with a course of action that begins to show signs of failure? The error of quitting too soon means that all of your previous efforts are wasted. The error of staying too long and becoming entrapped, however, may be worse. Not only will more resources be wasted, but careers can be enslaved and reputations ruined through the attachment to a losing cause.

In her book *The March of Folly*, Barbara Tuchman called the problem of entrapment "wooden-headedness." She described it as a form of self-deception consisting of the assessment of a situation in terms of preconceived fixed notions while ignoring or rejecting any contrary signs. When entrapment occurs, the decision maker acts in a wooden-headed manner. He or she sticks to a course of action that has been shown to be a failure, being unwilling to take the consequences associated with admitting the failure.

Examples of entrapment are numerous. The Vietnam War is perhaps the best political case from recent times. The demise of Drexel Burnham Lambert shows the same problem on the business side.

The exact opposite of entrapment is abandonment, which occurs when the decision maker fails to stay with a course of action. What should decision makers do when they, or the organization they control, embark on a course of action that begins to encounter difficulties? As problems start to occur, it becomes difficult to stay the course. The question is asked, should the quest be continued? In too many cases, it is prematurely abandoned.

The problem for the analyst is that examples of quitting too soon are hard to find. Failures to stay the course are like ghosts—apparitions of what might have been. Lost opportunities lack the vividness of the death spiral of entrapment. Let us first, then, investigate the entrapment phenomenon.

Entrapment and Sunk Costs

Entrapment occurs when decision makers doggedly pursue a losing course of action. Rather than admit defeat, they escalate their commitment, throwing good money after bad. What causes entrapment to occur? The answer resides in the inability of people to understand the concept of "sunk costs." A sunk cost is the amount of investment in a course of action that cannot be recovered if the strategy is abandoned. Once an irrevocable payment has been made, it is gone. It cannot be recovered, and the fact that it is gone should have no impact on future decisions. The decision to move forward at any particular point in time with a decision strategy should be based upon a comparison of future costs and future benefits. Sunk costs should not be considered in the equation. Here is a simple illustration.

Brenda, aged fifty-five, opened a woman's apparel shop that specialized in designer labels. She and her retired husband Phillip worked six days a week in the store, and it was a smashing success. With all of the children gone, however, the couple became lonely, and so they purchased for $450 a cute, pure-bred Yorkshire terrier that they named Biscuit. But the dog had some health problems, and another $300 to $400 was spent on veterinary bills.

Within six months of the purchase, Brenda and Phillip were having second thoughts. Biscuit craved attention. With no one home for most of the day, he yipped and scrambled over them in the evening in his craving for petting. The couple was totally exhausted from working all day and had little energy left for the dog. To compound the problems, when let outside into the fenced backyard, Biscuit yipped and barked in response to any sound from the neighbors.

Because Phillip had previously sued a neighbor for letting his dog bark endlessly, Biscuit couldn't be let out unsupervised. The relationship with the dog simply was not working.

One evening Brenda and Phillip, who were friends of mine, were lamenting their situation. I casually suggested the obvious: "Why don't you sell Biscuit?" I was certain they could get $250 for the cute purebred. Their reaction was immediate and negative. They couldn't sell Biscuit for $250. They had invested too much in him. Why, they had bought him for $450; furthermore, they had spent over $300 on veterinary bills.

The situation lasted for two years. Brenda, Phillip, and Biscuit coexisted together—all perfectly miserable. Finally, a daughter-in-law couldn't stand the situation any longer and took Biscuit in. Her action broke the trap. Giving away the dog to a relative could be framed as a gift rather than a loss. Had the daughter-in-law not shown some compassion for the situation, I am certain Brenda and Phillip would still be entrapped.

To an outsider their unwillingness to sell the dog may seem ridiculous. Sunk costs, however, have great power over our actions. One study tested their impact on consumers' attendance at a university theater. In cooperation with the theater department, psychologists conducted an experiment in which they varied the cost of season tickets to the University of Ohio's theater. On a completely random basis, some people were given special discounts and others were not. The researchers then recorded how many people from each group actually went to the plays. They found that those who had paid the full price for the tickets went to significantly more plays than those who had received the discount. The money paid in advance was a sunk cost. Yet the ticket holders treated it as real. Those who had paid more for their tickets had more to lose, and in order to avoid taking the heavier losses, they showed up more frequently at the theater.

Pork Barrel Entrapment. The desire to avoid taking a loss, even if it is sunk, is extremely strong, and it can lead to irrational thinking —especially in making high-stakes decisions. Seemingly, few people are immune from letting sunk costs influence their judgment calls.

Water projects have long been a means for congressmen and senators to bring money into their states. Unfortunately, in too many cases one finds the familiar pattern in which past losses are used as a justification for continuing a money-losing project. For example, in 1981 a battle raged over whether to terminate the Tennessee-Tombigbee water project. Begun in 1972, the project consisted of building a set of locks to connect the Tennessee and the Tombigbee rivers in order to open the Tennessee directly to the Gulf of Mexico. The largest civil works project ever undertaken by the U.S. Army Corps of Engineers, the 234-mile-long waterway would dwarf the Panama Canal. Potentially, it would increase commerce in Alabama and Tennessee substantially by reducing the time required to move materials to the Gulf of Mexico. By 1981, the partially completed project had already cost over $1 billion. However, new estimates revealed that the cost of completing it from that point forward would be greater than the potential total benefits. Would you decide to abandon the project, or complete it?

How did the senators involved in the project react? Senator Jeremiah Denton (Republican from Alabama) said in November 1981: "To terminate a project in which $1.1 billion dollars has been invested represents an unconscionable mishandling of taxpayers' dollars." Senator James Sassar (Democrat from Tennessee) felt that: "Completing Tennessee-Tombigbee is not a waste of taxpayers' dollars. Terminating a project at this late stage of development would, however, represent a serious waste of funds already invested." Based upon the efforts of the senators, the Tenn-Tom Waterway was completed in 1985 and ranks among the world's largest navigational projects. Unfortunately, it will never pay back the costs incurred to complete building it. The judgment call of whether to stay or quit must be based solely upon expectations of what will happen in the future. The fact that money, time, energy, or even lives have already been spent should have no impact on whether to continue a course of action.

Financial Entrapment. In the 1980s, more bank and savings and loan failures occurred in the United States than at any time other than the Great Depression of the 1930s. Unfortunately, in Oklahoma we had more than our fair share. The failure of Penn Square Bank in 1982 created a financial crisis exacerbating the economic crisis that enveloped Oklahoma during the mid-1980s. Indeed, the failure of Penn Square rippled throughout the United States banking industry. A former chairman of the FDIC stated that "Penn Square permanently altered the public's perception of banker infallibility and the shape of banking and bank regulation in the United States."

In 1977, Penn Square was a $62 million bank. When it was closed in mid-1982, it was a $520 million bank collapsing under its own obesity. Many small companies in Oklahoma were damaged by the collapse, because they failed to get their deposits out before the bank was closed. Even more damaging was the fact that Penn Square had sold to other banks more than $2 billion in oil and gas exploration loans, extremely risky investments that were rapidly becoming worthless as the price of oil fell. Continental Illinois held about half of these loans; in 1984, Continental Illinois would have to be saved by the FDIC in the biggest bailout in banking history. Another large portion was held by Seattle First National Bank, which would fold under the weight of the loans and be purchased by BankAmerica Corporation.

Penn Square failed because its managers were unwilling to cut their losses. During the oil boom period of the 1970s and very early 1980s, the bank made large, risky loans to oil and gas drillers. The collateral for the loans was the oil and gas reserves that the drillers possessed. Unfortunately, these were valued on the basis of inflated oil prices prevalent at the time (i.e., $25 to $35 a barrel). Forecasters estimated that oil would reach $60 a barrel by the late 1980s. Thus, high-stakes decisions were made on the basis of unrealistic assumptions.

Penn Square made the loans at higher than market interest rates due to their risky nature. In the booming oil market of the late seventies, nobody was worried because they could foresee only growth in the price of oil. The bank would then sell a portion of the risky loans to other banks, which jumped at the chance to buy because of the high interest rates. Penn Square used the proceeds from the sale of these loans to fund other risky loans, which would in turn be sold to other banks, such as Continental Illinois. The Penn Square managers loved it. They created a gigantic pyramid scheme, and to celebrate they bought limousines, drank champagne from their boots, and generally had a good old time.

The whole process worked fine as long as the oil- and gas-drilling firms maintained their payments or as long as new money could be brought in. The bubble burst, however, in the early 1980s when two things happened. First, the Federal Reserve decided to fight inflation, and interest rates began to climb. With the interest rates of many loans tied to the prime rate, the cost of doing business soared. Shaky loans began to fall apart. The only thing that Penn Square could do to recoup its losses—or so the managers thought—was to fund ever shakier drilling ventures. If it failed to make loans and sell them, it would collapse. It became entrapped in a losing course of action.

The coffin was sealed when the price of oil began to fall. Suddenly, the collateral for the loans shrank in value. While the bankers who bought into the loans from Penn Square were easily duped, they were not total idiots. They became nervous and no longer bought the loans. As revenues from oil and gas plunged, due to the decline in the price of oil, more and more drillers began to miss payments. New money could not be found to fund new ventures. The combination led the bank into a death spiral that culminated in its collapse.

Penn Square Bank became entrapped because its managers were unwilling to cut the bank's losses by changing its loan practices and writing off the bad loans. Some of the highest stakes judgment calls require managers to accept small losses in order to fix problems before they become ruinous. As a rule, the earlier the loss is taken, the lower the overall costs of the course of action.

The Drexel Burnham Lambert Ponzi Scheme. Wall Street is also prone to entrapment, as the demise of Drexel Burnham Lambert illustrates. Created in the 1970s, Drexel grew rapidly and became Wall Street's most profitable company in the mid-1980s, the huge multi-million-dollar bonuses paid to its executives epitomizing the Wall Street greed of the time. The firm's enormous financial success was founded on the development of junk bonds, which financed corporate raiders, such as Boone Pickens and Carl Icahn. In February 1990, however, Drexel went into bankruptcy, leaving a host of companies holding largely worthless pieces of paper. What happened?

To understand the Drexel debacle, you have to know a little about junk bonds. Junk bonds are basically like any other bond—just riskier. When an organization needs money, it sells a bond. The buyer of the bond is in effect lending money to the seller, who agrees to pay the loan back at a specified time. In addition, the seller agrees to pay the buyer interest on the bond at a specified rate. A market exists for buying and selling bonds. Thus, the buyer of the bond can in turn sell it to someone else, and money can be made by adroitly buying and selling bonds. But therein lies the rub. Because a market exists, the price at which a bond can be sold will vary with interest rates. The price at which a bond can be sold moves in the opposite direction of interest rates. When interest rates go up, the value of bonds goes down. The reason is that in most instances the interest rate on the bond is fixed. If you are holding a fixed-rate bond and new bonds going on the market offer higher interest rates, they are worth more than yours. As a consequence, the price of your bond goes down. Of course, the opposite can happen as well. If interest rates go down, the price of your bond will go up.

Why are junk bonds riskier? The reason is that the companies that sell these bonds are in some way financially weak. Greater uncertainty than usual exists as to whether they will be able to pay the interest as it comes due. Further, a significant chance exists that the loan itself will never be paid off by the financially troubled company. In order to compensate the buyer for taking on these risks, the bond seller must pay a higher interest rate. Perversely, this makes the loan even riskier because the company must then pay out more in interest, which weakens it further.

Nevertheless, insurance companies, savings and loans, pension funds, banks, and even foreign countries were persuaded by Drexel to buy junk bonds, because of the extremely high interest rates. The theory propounded by Drexel was that if you bought lots of different junk bonds, you could lessen your risk. Across a portfolio of bonds, the cost of defaults was lower than the benefit gained from the high interest rates. Michael Milken, the mastermind of the scheme at Drexel, claimed that he had discovered a market anomaly. The market priced junk bonds too low. By diversifying your portfolio across numerous junk bonds, you could reap huge profits.

In addition to arguing persuasively that the firm had identified a market anomaly that could make investors rich, Drexel also carefully promoted the social virtues of its creation: junk bonds were helping America grow. Initially, Milken had discovered the anomaly among companies whose bonds had originally been investment grade. Corporate misfortunes, however, had caused the companies' bonds to be devalued to the "junk" category. Milken expanded the concept by beginning to offer subinvestment-grade bonds issued by businesses that had trouble finding financial support. For example, Golden Nugget casinos used junk to finance growth, and the results were highly favorable; Drexel trumpeted these successes in national advertisements.

The gold mine for Drexel occurred with the discovery that junk bonds could be used to finance hostile takeovers. By arranging for billions of dollars of financing for such takeovers as RJR Nabisco, TWA, and National Can, as well as for assorted other takeover attempts (e.g., Gulf Oil, Revlon, and Beatrice Foods), the firm raked in huge fees. Directed by Michael Milken, the Drexel strategy involved carefully selecting the companies that it financed through junk bonds. Risks appeared to be under control, and in 1986 the company had a pretax profit of nearly $1 billion.

What went wrong? Let me advance two theories. I will first describe the fraudulent Ponzi scheme theory, as propounded by a *Barron's* analyst. Then I will present my own entrapment hypothesis.

The Fraudulent Ponzi Scheme Theory. Writing in *Barron's*, Benjamin Stein argued that Drexel engineered nothing more than the biggest Ponzi scheme ever. A Ponzi scheme is based upon the "greater fool" theory. That is, I will purchase something at a low price and be able to sell it at a higher price to someone else more stupid than myself. The simplest Ponzi scheme is the chain letter: Early investors are paid off by later investors. The Ponzi theory states that from the first day the junk bonds were fraudulent and that they were sold by fraudulent people.

A number of pieces of evidence point to the deliberate creation of a Ponzi scheme. First, the scam was built upon the fiction that the default rate of junk bonds was about 2 percent. In the mid-1970s a then obscure, but now famous, economics professor at MIT, Paul Asquith, found that the default rate was more like 4 percent a year. In fact, his data showed that in an eight-year period, an investor could expect about one third of his bonds to go into default. Indeed, as the years went by, the default rates increased, reaching 10 percent a year in 1989.

Other evidence pointing to a Ponzi scam was available to regulators. First, how could Drexel get away with charging an outrageously high commission of 4 percent on the sale of the bonds if they were a good investment? Most bond commissions are less than 1 percent. Second, if junk bonds were really undervalued, why didn't the market bid them up? Milken had been trumpeting the strategy since 1974. If there really was an anomaly, the market would surely have corrected it within fifteen years. Third, why was it that Drexel was effectively the only company making the market for the bonds; why were many of the buyers' companies owned by Drexel; and why did the first trades in a bond usually come from within a select group of financial heavy hitters? The answer, according to the Ponzi theorists, was that Drexel was fixing the prices with a group of "good buddies," which gave the illusion of its being able to create huge profits. These good buddies would then bail out by selling the bonds to "greater fools." They were selling junk as if it were non-junk. Fourth, why were two former Securities and Exchange commissioners on the Drexel board? Answer: the SEC had oversight, and with ex-commissioners on its board, Drexel could avoid an investigation. Fifth, if the junk bond business was aboveboard, why did everything crumble when Michael Milken was fired? The answer is the same as for any embezzler. You get caught when you go on vacation and outsiders can look at the books. Finally, look at who was stuck with the bill—

for the most part a group of unsophisticated creditors. In fact, thirteen of the twenty-two largest creditors were foreign.

Stein's conclusion?

Drexel/Milkenism was largely a vast scam based upon myths about bond-valuing skills and bond value, kept going by a vast Ponzi controlling markets, prices, reputation and data about defaults, offering the kind of profits that a decade-long scam involving tens of billions of dollars of phony bonds would offer.

The Entrapment Hypothesis. My own entrapment hypothesis is that Michael Milken et al. did not deliberately set out to bilk institutions and regular investors out of hundreds of millions of dollars. They were not smart enough to create the huge scam. They were more like Jose Gomez. They started out with a good idea that gradually evolved into a scheme that they could not control. In the early stages it made them rich. However, when things began to go bad, greed got in the way. They could not retrench; they escalated their commitment to an idea that was going sour; and they slowly slipped into a death spiral.

The problems began in 1986—the year of the company's greatest profits. In May, an important Drexel executive was charged with insider-trading. This led to the indictment of Ivan Boesky, the famed arbitrager, and to rumors that Drexel itself was being investigated by the government. With the negative publicity, companies began to turn elsewhere for junk financing. In 1987 Drexel's earnings plunged, but the company still made over $100 million after taxes.

In 1988, however, stuff began to hit the proverbial fan. A two-year investigation by U.S. Attorney Rudolf Giuliani resulted in a guilty plea by Drexel to six counts of security violations. A fine of $650 million was levied. People became even more nervous about the company. The prices of junk bonds began to plummet, as some highly leveraged deals fell through. At this point, a prudent company would have furled its mainsails, battened down the hatches, and prepared to weather the storm. Instead, Drexel became entrapped. Rather than carefully analyzing proposed deals, executives would sell bonds for anything that moved. Bond traders were no longer consulted about their ability to sell the securities. As a result, Drexel was stuck with the bonds. The money that the company used to purchase the bonds had to be repaid, and Drexel rapidly became financially squeezed.

Other developments compounded the problem. Key employees started to leave. In order to retain these people, management promised huge bonuses at a time when the company was rapidly going insolvent. The bonuses were tied to the number of deals made, which resulted in the executives going after even more suspect transactions. Meanwhile, experienced members of the firm's bond review board departed, and the inexperienced new members lacked the expertise and seniority to handle the situation.

By September 1989, the death spiral was accelerating. The chairman of the company began calling other firms on Wall Street to inquire about the possibility of a merger. No one was interested. The legal problems of the company and the potential civil lawsuits had tarnished it—particularly for potential Japanese investors. Then, in late 1989, an important merger involving United Airlines fell through, and the company suffered $25 million in arbitrage losses. The blows intensified. *Standard & Poor's* lowered Drexel's credit rating, lenders began cutting it off, and the firm had to raid its profitable brokerage subsidiary to handle the cash flow squeeze. In February 1990, the Securities and Exchange Commission barred Drexel from borrowing from the brokerage subsidiary because it jeopardized its customers. The company had nowhere to turn. No one would buy it. The Federal Reserve refused to bail it out, and the company filed for bankruptcy.

A sideline to Drexel's entrapment was the company's build-up of psychological debits. The banks and securities firms that could have saved Drexel in its final days gloated over its demise. For years the company had stolen their clients and undermined their businesses. A story was told in *Fortune* magazine of one money manager's reaction to the meltdown of the firm. He recalled a time in 1982 when he had purchased some bonds from Drexel for 60 cents on the dollar. A few weeks later he wanted to sell them. Drexel was the only player in junk bonds and made the market for them. The Drexel traders told the money manager that they could only give him 50 cents on the dollar. The manager recalled, "I said that I could understand a haircut, maybe 58 cents or even 57 cents—but 50! I was told if I didn't like it, I could try selling the bonds through someone else. I won't miss Drexel."

Federal officials also showed little mercy. They viewed the firm's pleas for a bailout as ironic, because Drexel had always seen itself as the ultimate outsider. As one Treasury official said, "Drexel was a shark asking for mercy that it never gave anyone else." An old aphorism states that "What goes around, comes around." By alienating its customers, by acting as a predator in relations with competitors, and by fighting with government officials and covering up its misdeeds, the company had created enormous ill will. When its fortunes sagged, no one was there to offer any help.

One of the ultimate high-stakes decisions involves saving the life of a major corporation. Drexel Burnham Lambert was faced with the judgment call of "to stay or quit." It stayed too long, perpetuating a scheme that led to its demise. Many of its competitors were hurt by the scheme, and Drexel was caught in the predator's dilemma—when wounded, those playing by predatory rules can expect vulturous responses from their enemies. When the environment changed and things began going wrong, had Drexel's managers been willing to turn off the money machine and return to "by the book" lending procedures, the company would have survived. Instead, they could not forego the millions in profits. But, like the poisons that kill plants by causing them to grow so fast that their cells burst, the junk bond mania ruptured the moral fiber of the firm as it chased extravagant profits. In the end simple greed induced Drexel to hold its cards too long and defy a principal axiom of gambling: When your luck turns, get out of the game while you can. In the end Drexel couldn't run away; it couldn't even walk. It was carried off in pieces.

Political Entrapment and the Vietnam Debacle

As I have pointed out, entrapment results from the sunk cost snare and the desire to avoid a loss. In the financial world, the fear of losing money and reputation drove Drexel, Penn Square, and Jose Gomez into their respective death spirals. In the world of politics, power rather than money is the commodity on which reputations are based. Thus, entrapment rarely results from monetary greed. More often, it results from the desire to avoid the loss of power. Nowhere are the effects of escalation and commitment to a losing course of action better illustrated than in the Vietnam experience.

How did the United States become entrapped in the Vietnam quagmire? The hazards of becoming involved in an Asian land war were well known. The sobering experience of the Korean War could still be vividly recalled in the early 1960s when the Vietnam escalation began. Similarly, the French military defeat at Dien Bien Phu remained highly salient. However, the specter of a monolithic Communist empire enslaving Asia was readily imagined by politicians, generals, and the public. Halting the spread of communism formed the context within which the judgment calls were made that ultimately resulted in a debacle.

Two early fiascos in the Kennedy administration laid the groundwork for the fear of failure—the invasion of Cuba at the Bay of Pigs, and a meeting between President Kennedy and Soviet Premier Nikita Khrushchev in Vienna in 1961. The Vienna meeting was Kennedy's first encounter with Khrushchev. Later Kennedy described how the experience had shaken him in a private discussion with James Reston of *The New York Times*. Khrushchev had violently attacked the United States—particularly its presence in Berlin. He threatened to fire his missiles and roll tanks into the city. Kennedy interpreted Khrushchev's histrionics as an attempt to rattle a young, inexperienced president, who lacked guts and who had just emerged from the catastrophe of the Bay of Pigs. The bullying by Khrushchev forced Kennedy to increase troop strength in Europe. In addition, Reston believed that it was a major factor in influencing Kennedy to send 18,000 American advisers to Vietnam later in 1961. Thus, the Bay of Pigs represented a failure that loomed large in the eyes of the Kennedy administration. Khrushchev's antics exacerbated the trauma. The administration felt it had to stand up to communism, and a major hot spot at the time was Vietnam.

A year later, in 1962, the favorable outcome of the Cuban missile crisis would turn down the heat, but it was too late because the troops had already been sent to Vietnam. The entrapment had begun. Interestingly, Khrushchev would tell the American Ambassador to the Soviet Union that the United States was making a mistake in entering Vietnam. In a cable message, the ambassador quoted Khrushchev as saying, "In South Vietnam the U.S. has stumbled into a bog. It will be mired there for a long time."

An important aspect of entrapment is the idea that very small events can cause large outcomes. Physicists and mathematicians who do work on Chaos theory call the phenomenon the "butterfly effect." Thus, the beating of a butterfly's wings in China can cause hurricanes in the Atlantic. The gist of the butterfly effect is found in the old aphorism:

> For want of a nail, the shoe was lost;
> For want of a shoe, the horse was lost;
> For want of a horse, the rider was lost;
> For want of a rider, the battle was lost;
> For want of a battle, the kingdom was lost!

Small things can matter. However, people tend to believe that big events have big causes. One day in 1961 a Far Eastern correspondent talked to Robert Kennedy at the Justice Department about Vietnam. He expressed his belief that Vietnam posed a long-range potential for danger. Robert Kennedy responded, "Vietnam, we have thirty Vietnams a day here." Vietnam was too small a country in too remote a part of the world to matter to a nation worried about nuclear war and a Communist menace off the Florida shores. But once the decision makers were caught in the vortex of the fear of failure and the need to justify past actions, the lives and careers of hundreds of thousands of people would be affected.

In hindsight, the ever-widening spiral of escalation, failure, and increased commitment reads like a Greek tragedy. When American advisers were sent to Vietnam, they had to be protected. Thus, airpower would be introduced. The planes and their support personnel also had to be protected, so ground combat troops were introduced. To nullify each new American action, the North Vietnamese would counter with an action of their own. Every time we escalated our commitment, we had more to lose. If we failed, the loss was even larger. So, in order to avoid the loss, we had to commit even more resources.

The entrapment death spiral began in 1964. The military at the time was arguing that bombers needed to be based on South Vietnamese soil in order to support that country's ground troops. By chance a squadron of outmoded B-57 bombers was routed to the Bien Hoa air base in Vietnam, rather than back to the Philippines, because of bad weather. The generals argued that the planes were needed and that they should stay there. Others argued that they should be flown out immediately because they would offer a tempting target for the Viet Cong. The generals won. Several months later the planes were blown up by the Viet Cong. The event caused a cry for retaliation and an escalation of the war.

A rule of political life is that if you want to mobilize a country for war, exploit a situation in which an enemy has inflicted harm upon you to create a desire for vengeance. In that emotional atmosphere, Congress will meet the test with a declaration of war. Our history is filled with such events. In the Spanish American War it was "Remember the *Maine*"; in World War I, it was the sinking of the luxury liner *Lusitania;* in World War II, it was Pearl Harbor. And in Vietnam, it was a minor military incident in the Tonkin Gulf off the shores of North Vietnam that led to the congressional resolution giving President Johnson the ability to fight an undeclared war.

The Tonkin Gulf Resolution, while not an official act of war, allowed Lyndon Johnson to place combat troops in Vietnam. It was the single act that ensured entrapment. But like so many entrapment scenarios, the situation began with a seemingly innocent decision to initiate small-scale, covert military activities against North Vietnam. Code-named "Plan 34A," the idea was to respond to North Vietnam's subversive activities in the South by doing some "dirty tricks" of our own. Teams were dropped into North Vietnam by parachute and frogmen waded ashore to blow up bridges, explode oil depots, and generally harass the enemy.

Plan 34A operations were intensified in mid-1964 because things were going poorly in the South. As part of those operations, South Vietnamese PT boats under American orders engaged in hit-and-run raids on naval installations in North Vietnam. In late July, South Vietnamese PT boats raided two North Vietnamese bases. Concurrently, the American destroyer *Maddox* was on its way to the same area to play games with the North's radar defenses. The next day, the *Maddox* began probing the North's radar defenses with its own radar in an effort to simulate a full-scale attack. The goal was to get the North to turn on its radar so that positions would be recorded. The north, however, took the *Maddox* seriously and thought that it was part of the Plan 34A operation. As a result, the North Vietnamese attacked the *Maddox* with their own PT boats. The *Maddox* sank one of the boats and took no casualties itself.

President Johnson reacted with indignation. The *Maddox* had a right to be in international waters. (The ship, in fact, would at times move in close to the coast.) He ordered the *Maddox* and a second ship, the *C. Turner Joy*, to continue their activities. The *Maddox*'s captain cabled back, saying that staying in the area was an unacceptable risk. The North Vietnamese were highly sensitive to his ship because they thought it to be a part of the Plan 34A raid. However, as a sign that the United States would not back down, the *Maddox* and *C. Turner Joy* were ordered back into dangerous waters.

At this point everything became muddled and exactly what happened has never been determined. Some kind of incident occurred. The destroyers believed that they had come under attack from North Vietnam. (Some thought they were actually firing at each other.) Some months later, Johnson would quip about the difficulty of getting hard information about the incident. He jokingly said, "For all I know, our Navy was shooting at whales out there." Whatever the case, the immediate reaction in Washington was to retaliate, and the

Joint Chiefs of Staff identified a series of North Vietnam bases to attack.

President Johnson then went to congressional leaders and asked them to support a resolution that would allow for a limited retaliation. When he received the verbal support of key senators and congressmen, fighters were launched and hit four PT boat bases and an oil depot. Soon thereafter, Senator J. William Fulbright would return political favors to Johnson by successfully shepherding the Tonkin Gulf Resolution through the Senate—an act that he would rue to his grave.

Senator Fulbright knew that the resolution was ambiguously worded and could give the president the power to run a war without declaring it. A number of other senators were also extremely worried that the resolution would give the executive branch the power to wage war. When Fulbright went to Johnson with these concerns, Johnson assured him that a land war in Asia was the last thing that he or his administration wanted, and that any amendments to limit powers granted in the resolution would only attract numerous others. This was an emergency that had to be reacted to quickly. Only two senators voted against the resolution. One, Wayne Morse from Oregon, said that the resolution circumvented the Constitution and gave the president warmaking powers in the absence of a declaration of war. "I believe that to be a historic mistake," he declared.

Another key phase in the war escalation occurred in 1965. Operation "Rolling Thunder" was getting under way with the goal of bringing North Vietnam to its knees by bombing it to smithereens. At this point, the United States still did not have combat troops in Vietnam. The military wanted to station planes in Danang in order to place them closer to the enemy. To protect the planes, a couple of battalions of combat troops would be required. These battalions were the first real American combat troops introduced into Vietnam. Their presence increased U.S. exposure to losses, and when the massive bombing proved to be a failure, the way was paved for the large-scale introduction of additional soldiers.

Because of the increasing political opposition to the war, Lyndon Johnson stepped away from the presidency before the 1968 elections. Richard Nixon entered the race with a secret plan to the end the war with honor—it would later be euphemistically called "Vietnamization." But Nixon would also become entrapped. He could not face presiding over a defeat; the six months that he gave for getting out of the war lengthened to five years. While the Nixon administration eventually got the United States out of Vietnam, it must also be asked, at what cost? In the end South Vietnam fell anyway. In the meantime the United States had spent its financial, human, and moral capital on an unwinnable war. As early as 1966, General David M. Shoup, the recently retired Commandant of the Marine Corps, had called the contention that Vietnam was "vital" to American interests "poppycock—the whole of Southeast Asia was not worth a single American life. . . . Why can't we let people actually determine their own lives?"

In May 1991, Henry Kissinger spoke at the Tulsa Business Forum, an event sponsored by my college. He was asked what was the biggest mistake made in the Nixon administration. He replied that it was not forcing Congress to take a stand on Vietnam. He suggested that the Nixon administration officials should have done in 1969 what George Bush did in 1990 in the Persian Gulf crisis. They should have gone to Congress to obtain a commitment one way or another. They should not have waited until 1972 to act. Kissinger said, "If you are going to use military force, you go all the way and win. You get no rewards for losing with moderation."

Nixon and Kissinger never understood the principle of sunk costs. At the Tulsa Forum, Kissinger said that when Nixon went into office he felt that he owed it to the country to maintain continuity of policy. He could not just pull out the American troops and betray all 30,000 men who had already died in the cause. As a result, the administration upped the ante, hoping the North Vietnamese would fold. Under Nixon, over 15,000 more Americans died in Vietnam. Over the entire course of the war, 58,156 Americans were killed and 300,000 were wounded in Vietnam. The total financial cost was estimated at $150 billion. Such was the price of entrapment.

Avoiding Entrapment

How does a decision maker avoid entrapment? A glib response to the question is to recognize and avoid the sunk cost snare. But while absolutely correct, this answer fails to go far enough, because sunk costs are notoriously difficult to identify. In addition, social pressures to continue a course of action can be intense. The time to avoid entrapment is in the initial planning stages of a project. In all projects a plan should be developed describing the sequence of events that must take place and the milestones that must be reached in order for the project to be completed. Most importantly, contingencies should be specified for what happens if milestones are not reached. If the goals are not met by the date set and within the designated budget, an outside, autonomous team should be brought in to analyze the causes of the problem and make recommendations —one of which could be the termination of the project. As an old Chinese proverb states, "If you must play, decide upon three things at the start: The rules of the game, the stakes, and the quitting time."

Knowledge of when to quit is one of the hallmarks of the peerless decision maker. Nowhere is the skill better illustrated than in financial investing. Long ago this important idea was vividly demonstrated to me. In the early 1970s, my wife Maryanne and I were newlyweds. I was stationed at Fort Carson, in Colorado, and she was teaching history in an inner-city high school in Colorado Springs. We were living frugally on two incomes and had some extra cash. We wanted to begin doing some investing so that we could accumulate savings for graduate school. Through one of her teaching friends, Maryanne found a broker with a regional brokerage firm. I no longer remember his name, so I will call him Al. To a couple of novices, Al impressed us as knowledgeable, smooth, and patient. He got us into a new stock issue that his firm had underwritten—F&B Trucklines— which went absolutely nowhere but down.

One day my wife and I went in to see Al to talk about F&B Trucklines. We could see that he had a worried look on his face. In a moment of weakness, he began to confide in us. A couple of years earlier he had started investing in Levitz Furniture for his own account, as well as his grandmother's. At the time everything looked great. The company had a whole new concept—distribute furniture out of highly mechanized warehouses and sell a high volume at extremely low prices. The approach worked, and the company took off.

The problems began when the company overexpanded and took on too much debt. Add in a mild recession and suddenly the high-flying stock price headed south. Al was caught in a bind. He was buying on margin (i.e., borrowed money) for both accounts. Covering the margin calls was a highly unpleasant experience. Yet to sell out would mean that he would have to face his grandmother. The stock fell from the mid-50s to the mid-30s; so, operating on the old adage to "buy low and sell high," he doubled up and purchased more stock. Then it fell to the low 20s, and he doubled up again. When we saw him, the stock was trading at about 5. He was still agonizing over what to do. Learning from his experience, we decided it was about time for us to get out of the stock market for a while. We sold our F&B stock and took a loss.

Benjamin Graham, regarded by many financial writers as this century's most important thinker in applied portfolio theory, developed a series of rules for buying *and selling* stocks. His three selling rules were:

1. Sell after your stock has gone up 50 percent; or
2. Sell after two years, whichever comes first.
3. Sell if the dividend is omitted.

While other investment gurus may disagree with these particular rules, the point is that rules exist. By following the rules, the investor can avoid entrapment.

Entrapment can occur any time high-stakes decisions are made to take a course of action that fails to pay off. At that point, the peerless decision maker will realistically reevaluate the situation. If future benefits do not outweigh future costs, it is time to quit.

No one likes to be known as a quitter. It's an insult. But knowing *when* to quit is a compliment.

The Other Error—Quitting Too Soon

Which occurs more frequently—entrapment or failure to carry through a course of action? Certainly, the consequences of entrapment can be extremely dangerous. On the other hand, quitting too soon can result in the crime of lost opportunity. I have little evidence for this statement, but my belief is that quitting too soon is the more prevalent malady. Look at high school dropout rates of over 50 percent in some areas of the country. At major state universities, 40 percent of those who enter have not received a degree within a six-year time span.

In American culture, staying the course is highly valued and quitting is viewed with disdain. We have aphorisms, such as: "Quitters never win, and winners never quit." In children's literature we have *The Little Engine Who Could.* Americans are suckers for the story of the person who stays with a course of action and wins against long odds, as exemplified by the popularity of Sylvester Stallone's *Rocky* movies. There are even programs that exist to teach people how to avoid quitting. One of the purposes of U.S. Army Ranger School is to demonstrate to soldiers that they can endure more hardship, stress, pain, and fatigue than they realize. I still remember the sergeant yelling at me: "Reach in and pull out a handful of gut, and drive on, wimp!"

Knowing whether to stay or quit is one of the toughest judgment calls faced by decision makers. On the one hand, if you stay too long, entrapment results. On the other hand, if you quit too soon, opportunities are missed, and you may be labeled a quitter. Several principles to consider when making the "stay or quit" judgment call are:

- Avoid entrapment by being willing to take a loss.

- The first loss is usually the best loss.

- Losses occurring in the past are "sunk" and should have no impact on current decisions.

- Weigh future benefits against future liabilities when making a judgment call.

- If you play by predatory rules, your opponents will answer with vulturous responses if you are wounded.

- In order to avoid entrapment, create milestones in the initial plan of action, which if not reached will result in the cancellation of the project.

These principles for making the stay/quit judgment call are not foolproof. In the risky world of high-stakes decision making, even peerless decision makers can and do make errors. When making the judgment call of whether to stay or quit, peerless decision makers analyze the goals they are trying to reach, their value and importance, and how determined they are to achieve them. The high-stakes decision maker has to take a realistic look at the situation at varying times and act on the accumulated evidence. But time itself can influence the stay/quit judgment call. In particular, the relative impact of present versus future outcomes may dramatically affect the ability of decision makers to stay with a winning course of action—one of the key topics of the next chapter.

4.

PRESENT VERSUS FUTURE

The Arizona State University All-American linebacker took the news hard. He had a congenital narrowing of the spinal canal, and two orthopedic surgeons advised him to quit playing football. Not satisfied with their opinion, he went to a third orthopedist, who had previously counseled professional basketball and hockey players on health matters. The doctor made the judgment call that the athlete could play and not risk permanent injury because of his spinal cord problem, although he warned the linebacker that he could have an "episode of transient paralysis." Reluctantly, the Arizona State University medical staff let the player return to action.

Then, in a fateful moment in a game against the University of Washington, the linebacker collided with the opposing team's quarterback, and his body went numb. Watching from the stands, his mother could see her son's motionless body on the ground, and she ran onto the field. She held a crucifix as the team physician carefully rolled her son over to examine him. Fortunately the consulting physician had been right, and the paralysis would be brief. Within hours of the injury, the player was walking again. But Mark Tingstad quit playing the bone-jarring sport. Later, he remarked of the incident, "When you're an athlete and you're involved in sports with physical activity, you think you're impervious. You're talented and you think nothing can happen to you. It goes to prove how fragile life is."

A recurring high-stakes decision made by athletes, their coaches, and their families concerns whether to halt a promising career after an injury is sustained or a serious health problem emerges. This "stay or quit" judgment call illustrates the difficult problem of deciding when the pain outweighs the gain. Like Al the stockbroker, the Drexel Ponzi scheme, and the Penn Square Bank failure discussed in the last chapter, athletes can become entrapped in a losing course of action. The causes of the calamity for injured athletes who fail to quit are different, however, from those found for the other illustrations of entrapment. Al, Drexel, and Penn Square officials were trapped by the sunk cost bias of letting past losses influence current thinking. As a result, they were unwilling to cut their losses and get out. In contrast, Mark Tingstad failed to quit because he wanted to maintain the glory of the present and was unwilling to acknowledge the dire future possibilities of his condition until he actually experienced the paralysis.

Present versus Future: A Special Case of Stay/Quit Decisions

The choice between present and future is one of the hardest judgment calls. The decision influences whether a person will stay or quit, whether he or she will endure or become entrapped. For an accomplished athlete, giving up a sport is extremely difficult. In the present, hopes and dreams are dashed; a lifestyle and adulation are lost. Long term, however, the decision to continue playing can lead to a life of pain, or the ultimate long-term outcome—death. Too frequently, the short-term positives of continuing to play overwhelm the potential long-term negatives that could result, and the player is trapped in a calamitous course of action. Marc Buoniconti, who played football for the Citadel in the mid-1980s, observed, "What I've always said is that a young college player will always want to play. It's up to the doctors and trainers to stand between the athlete and the field." Buoniconti understands this fact all too well because in 1985 he became a quadriplegic after he made a tackle that broke his neck.

The tragedy of Hank Gathers also illustrates the difficulty of choosing between the present and the future. An All-American basketball player, Gathers played for Loyola Marymount in the late

1980s. In March 1989, he became only the second player in history to lead NCAA Division 1 teams in both scoring and rebounding. In practice sessions he would frequently yell, "I'm the strongest man alive!" as he swooped in for a monster dunk. The perception of invulnerability was shattered, however, when on December 9, 1989, Gathers collapsed while shooting free throws during a game. After lying unconscious for three minutes, he recovered rapidly and walked off the court. In the locker room, a friend attempted to console him. Weeping, Gathers said to him, "You don't understand. I just blew the NBA." Gathers's life was built around basketball. If he had to quit the sport, what would he do?

Tests were run immediately, and they uncovered a heart-muscle disease that produced a potentially fatal irregular heart rhythm. However, the judgment call was made that the condition could be controlled. Placed on the drug Inderal, Gathers was cleared to resume basketball. Perhaps he could still play as a professional. Other players, such as All-Star forward Terry Cummings, had been able to play in the NBA with heart arrhythmias.

But a problem soon emerged with the treatment program. While Gathers could feel no symptoms from his heart condition, the drug made him drowsy and hurt his basketball performance. Yet within about three weeks of the fainting spell, Gathers returned to competitive action. On December 30, he scored 22 points against Niagara. His game quickly began to improve, and in February he scored 48 points against Louisiana State. His pro career looked to be back on track. Then, on March 4, 1990, Loyola Marymount played Portland State. Early in the first half, Gathers made one of his patented dunks. He ran back up the court to begin playing defense, and suddenly collapsed. He died shortly thereafter.

Gathers's untimely death shocked the sports world. Charges and countercharges filled the news headlines. Had Gathers stopped taking his heart medication? Did his coach push him too hard to play? Regardless of the outcome of the multiple lawsuits winding their way through the court system, in the final analysis Hank Gathers took a calculated risk and paid the ultimate price. He could not imagine life without basketball, and as a result, he continued to play—choosing the present over an uncertain future in another field.

A vast array of behavioral science literature supports the principle that people act as though they are biased to value the present more than the future in their decision making. While our intellect tells us to delay gratification, we behave as though we want to have our rewards right now while simultaneously postponing the payment of our debts. The resulting myopic decision making affects individuals, corporations, and governments alike.

Two researchers at the University of Arizona Medical College have described a problem frequently faced by patients. The pattern goes like this: A patient, perhaps a busy, overweight executive, is diagnosed as having high blood pressure. He understands the dire consequences of not controlling the problem—a heart attack down the road—and he promises to begin a program in which he wakes up thirty minutes early each morning to exercise. Promising to change one's lifestyle is easy when the torment of feeling the burn of calisthenics is far away in time. Then, the first morning comes. The pain of waking up early and exercising is now in the present; it weighs heavily, counteracting the distant goal of losing weight and reducing the chances of heart disease. As a result, the executive turns over and goes back to sleep.

We also act as though we can discount gains and losses over time. We reason that receiving $10,000 will mean less five years from now than it means today, and we apply the same reasoning to outcomes harder to quantify than money, such as feeling physically good or having a winning professional sports team. But according to economists and psychologists, the implicit discount rate that people use to lower future valuations is much higher than that suggested by interest rates. Long-term interest rates in the United States have consistently hovered between 7 and 14 percent during the last decade. In contrast, people's implicit interest rate ranges widely, but on average hovers at about 30 percent. (This means that investments must be recouped within about three years for Americans, or they will not make them.) The net effect is a systematic bias toward overweighting outcomes that will occur in the present and toward underweighting outcomes expected to happen in the future.

Ford Quits the Mini-Max. A classic example of preference for the present over the future was the decision of Ford Motor Company to discontinue its mini-van project in the 1970s. The original idea for an all-purpose vehicle, a combination car-van, emerged in the late 1960s in the Ford design shop. The concept was to produce a vehicle, called the mini-max, that handled more like a car than a van, that would be attractive, that would get good gas mileage, and that would be perfect for suburban driving in which lots of people have to be transported short distances. The head of the design team, Gene Bordinat, knew that this was one of those rare, once-in-a-lifetime ideas that had to be pursued.

The problem was Henry Ford II and the finance people in the company. Producing the vehicle entailed risk, since it would require the creation of expensive new technology. In order to combine the features of a car and a van, the vehicle would have to have front-wheel drive. Front-wheel drive, in turn, would eliminate the need for a drive train to connect the engine to the rear wheels. Thus, the mini-max could be made lower, which would allow people to walk through it, and it would also be lighter and more user-friendly. In the late 1960s and early 1970s, however, front-wheel drive was considered exotic by American auto manufacturers. The judgment call at Ford involved deciding whether the short-term costs of designing the vehicle could be offset by future benefits in sales.

During the early 1970s, the designers would periodically bring out the plan, and the finance department and Henry Ford would shoot it down. The finance people insisted that because the technology was unproven, it involved too much risk. Market research studies were commissioned. A study performed in 1976 revealed that in fact the possibilities were enormous. The data indicated the company could sell more than 800,000 units a year. These estimates were far higher than those for the wildly successful Mustang. Even if the estimates were off by a factor of 3, the project would still be successful. The research also showed that the vehicle could be priced so as to achieve high profit margins—a major problem with the smaller vehicles that the company would soon have to produce. The results of the research were so wildly optimistic that a second study was performed—with the same result.

But nothing happened on the project at Ford. Norman Krandall, the head of marketing research, brought up the question again two years later, in 1978. At the time Ford had $3 billion in its coffers. However, management also had to make a decision on whether to go with another front-wheel-drive project—the Escort. Krandall wanted to do both. The head of the finance area, Ed Lundy, stated that the company did not have the cash to do both. Krandall suggested that the company borrow money, to which Lundy responded, "If we go out to borrow money, we'll lose our triple-A rating." Krandall countered, "If we don't borrow it and don't follow the market with cars like this, we may lose it anyway." Krandall had pushed hard—too hard within the Ford corporate culture. Within a few months he was forced to retire. Lundy won, but Krandall was right —the company did lose its triple-A bond rating in 1980. Indeed, by 1982 the company's bond rating had dropped entirely out of the A-rating category.

Ford quit on the mini-max, but the project continued—at Chrysler. This story began in the 1970s, when key managers at Ford were fired. The two vital figures were Lee Iacocca and Hal Sperlich, called by some the best product man of his generation. Both had been involved in the push for the mini-max project, and both lobbied hard for Ford to produce a small car that used an engine and transmission manufactured by Honda. Ford Corporation desperately needed a small car, and going the Honda route would save time and money. Soichiro Honda loved the idea, but when Iacocca took the concept to Henry Ford, he responded, "No Jap engine is going under the hood of a car with my name on it." Sperlich was fired in 1976 for insubordination when he continued to argue for the car; he was then rehired by Chrysler. When Iacocca was pushed out of Ford in 1978, Sperlich helped persuade him to come aboard.

The decision by Iacocca to produce the mini-van was made in the fall of 1980. Times were desperate for Chrysler, with the company close to bankruptcy. The United States was entering a major recession. Gasoline prices and interest rates were exploding. Some years later, Iacocca was asked how he could have made such a risky decision when times were so bad. He responded, "When you're already losing your ass, what's another billion among friends?"

The decision to produce the mini-van saved Chrysler. The market research predictions were accurate. The vans came out in 1984 and immediately created a new product category. *Time* magazine wrote a story on the phenomenon, entitled "A Maxirush to Chrysler's Minivans: Suburbia Piles into the Latest Hot Ticket from Detroit." At the annual auto show in New York City, the mini-vans stole the show from the new Corvettes, Porsches, and other exotics. Dealerships quickly sold their allotments, but production limitations held first-year sales to only 170,000 units. Both Ford and Chevrolet were caught asleep at the wheel, and they rushed to launch their own versions of the vehicles.

Sometimes people become more aggressive, creative, and take greater risks when their backs are to the wall. Chrysler took the gamble of creating a new automobile category because the company had little choice. A few years later the same phenomenon occurred at Ford. In the early 1980s, the company was in perilous shape as the recession and surging oil prices caused auto sales to plummet. Only under these conditions was the company finally able to find a renewed entrepreneurial spirit. Design teams were given the go-ahead to create an entirely new passenger car that could go against the best in the world. The Taurus was the result, and it was quickly embraced by the automotive press and consumers. I asked Tom Gorcyca, manager of customer quality at Ford, what caused the turnaround in the company's thinking. His answer was simple: "Impending disaster. We had to change, or the company would have died."

Changing Strategy versus Quitting. Individuals, corporations, and governments rarely stand up and say, "I quit. Things are just too tough for me." Instead, they mask the decision by proclaiming a change in strategy. For example, in April 1990, Eastman Kodak announced that it would stop production of its highly touted Ultralife lithium battery. A technological breakthrough, the industry's first mass-market lithium battery was originally expected to have a ten-year shelf life. Kodak, however, ran into a series of problems. The battery's shelf life was shorter than expected, and there were early production problems. The size (9 volts) was also an obstacle because these batteries accounted for only 15 percent of battery sales, being useful mostly in home smoke detectors and garage door openers.

The question that might be asked is whether Kodak gave the product sufficient time to bring an adequate return on investment. Introduced in 1987, the Ultralife had only three years in the marketplace. When one recognizes that the Japanese frequently give new products seven or more years to break even, the situation at Kodak looked suspiciously like yet another case in which an American company had a short time horizon. But Kodak would never admit that it simply gave up on the product. It phrased the decision in terms of "strategy." In the official announcement, company officials said: "The investment necessary to grow the [Ultralife] market just wasn't consistent with our financial objectives."

Changing strategy can be just as bad as quitting. A classic example took place in the 1990 Masters golf tournament. With just six holes to go, the old warhorse, Raymond Floyd, was leading the tournament by four shots over the closest competitor. At forty-seven, Floyd was the sentimental favorite of millions of forty-plus golfers. With a seemingly insurmountable lead, he changed his usual aggressive strategy and began playing conservatively. Rather than going for the green in two on the short par-5s, he played it safe. As a result, he made routine pars while his challenger from England, Nick Faldo, birdied both. The challenger then made a long putt to birdie the par-3 16th hole. When Floyd three-putted from 50 feet away on the 17th hole, the match was tied. In the playoff, on the first hole, Floyd had a 15-foot putt for the win, but it died just an inch in front of the hole. On the next hole, catastrophe struck Floyd, when he pulled a seven iron into the water beside the green.

Floyd didn't lose the match in the playoff—anything can happen in sudden-death circumstances. He lost the match when he changed the aggressive strategy that had been successful throughout the tournament and began playing it safe. Floyd said, "When nobody ran at me early today . . . I started playing for pars. On the [par-5] 13th and 15th holes, I didn't go for the green in two like I might have. I don't know if I did it purposely—it's a natural thing to do in the situation. But I did it, and it cost me. It was devastating. I never felt like that before, ever. At this stage in my career, I have to wonder how many more chances I'll have." Floyd didn't quit, he changed strategy, which was disastrous.

Creating the Conditions for Endurance. People, companies, and governments quit or change strategy prematurely when the perceived costs of action in the present overwhelm the perceived future benefits. So, how does one keep from quitting? One answer lies in reversing the sunk cost equation that causes entrapment. In order to avoid quitting, increase the costs of abandoning a course of action. How can you increase the costs of quitting? First, commit yourself to the action publicly: Tell friends, acquaintances, the press. If you quit, you will be publicly humiliated. The strategy is used frequently. Indeed, a fundamental part of the Alcoholics Anonymous (AA) program is for people openly to pronounce their addiction and to vow to eliminate alcohol completely from their lives.

Another method is to increase your monetary investment in the course of action. This approach is sometimes used by people attempting to increase their exercise regimen. One woman paid $900 for an exercise bike with a timer and other assorted bells and whistles, which allowed her to monitor her physiological functioning. Asked how much she used the device, she replied, "I'm using it a lot. I spent so much money that if I look at it, and I'm not on it, I feel guilty."

Lee Iacocca recognized intuitively the effects of creating penalties for quitting. When he arrived at Chrysler in 1978, he was totally disgusted by the ravaged state of the company. He asked where he could find the person in charge of quality control. The response was that everybody was in charge of quality. Right then, he realized that the company was in worse shape than he expected. Shortly thereafter, he asked the board of directors to approve a five-year, 50,000 mile warranty package. Everyone was aghast. It could cost $100 million a year. Iacocca responded, ". . . if we have the five-fifty, if we have to live up to it, then I know damn well that finance is going to give us the money for plants, and I know the marketing people will really use it in their ads, and I know that manufacturing, if it's a question of doing a thousand new pieces or doing a smaller number right, will do it right." The program worked because Chrysler openly committed itself to quality and because the cost of failure was so high.

Endurance versus "Woodenheadedness"

Weighing the present versus the future is central to the dilemma of knowing when to endure or when to quit. How can we avoid the woodenheadedness that results from the entrapment perils discussed in the last chapter, without becoming a quitter? One means of approaching that dilemma is to look at examples in which endurance brought success. The story of Thomas Edison's accomplishments is a case study of endurance in creating new technologies. Edison spent years in laborious experimentation before he finally found solutions to the multiple problems of creating an incandescent light bulb. At one point, he worked for forty consecutive hours with only three hours of sleep. Weeks went by in which he never went home but simply slept in his lab in his clothes.

Because others were working on an electric light bulb simultaneously with Edison, in some respects his real contribution was the idea that an electrical distribution system could be developed on which many different devices (e.g., sewing machines as well as light bulbs) could be run by electricity. In an article in *Scientific American* in 1879, one scientist stated that it would be "almost a public calamity if Mr. Edison should employ his great talent on such a puerility." Even after Edison developed a working system, the scientific world scoffed at him and viewed his demonstrations as hoaxes. One scientist felt compelled to "protest in behalf of true science . . . ," claiming that the experiments were "a conspicuous failure, trumpeted as a wonderful success. A fraud upon the public."

One of Edison's characteristics was his penchant for making outlandish promises. A terrific marketer, he would fill investors' heads with visions of schemes that would make them rich. (Indeed, in many cases they did.) In most instances the invention had not been perfected when the promises were made. In April 1878, Edison promised to place an incandescent lighting system on board a passenger ship —the S.S. *Columbia*—that would set sail from New York City at Christmas. The vacuum bulb had not yet been considered by Edison, and he had not yet developed a filament that would last even an hour. Indeed, even the electric generator had not been developed. The deadline was missed. But through hard work and some good luck, the ship was outfitted by May 1879 and sailed from New York around South America to San Francisco. Edison endured because he committed himself to a course of action both publicly and financially.

Robert W. Kearns, who invented the first practical, electronic, intermittent windshield wiper, provides another example of endurance. In 1962, Kearns was looking for a dissertation topic to complete his degree in engineering at Case Western Reserve University in Cleveland, Ohio. On his wedding night he had been hit by the cork of a champagne bottle, which nearly blinded him in one eye. As a result, he learned a lot about how the eyes work and how they clean themselves when we blink. He began to envisage the windshield as an eye that had to be cleaned periodically, and the idea emerged to create windshield wipers that "blinked." Kearns tinkered with transistors and Ford windshield wiper motors that his brother, who worked at the auto company, supplied him. In a few months he had developed the prototype for a "blinking wiper"—that moved intermittently, regulated by an electronic device that could be mounted under the hood and attached to a control apparatus in the car. Late in 1963, he took the idea to Ford. As it happened, Ford had been working unsuccessfully on an intermittent windshield wiper for some time, using a complicated mechanical approach. Over the next six months after that first meeting with Ford, Kearns perfected his method and took out several patents on the device. Between 1966 and 1969, he worked with Ford to perfect the mechanism further. Ford even gave him an award (oddly, in the form of an old-fashioned two-speed wiper motor), but no contract.

Then, in 1969, Ford came out with its own electronically controlled, intermittent windshield wiper. When Kearns looked at it, he found that it was based on his ideas. Ford argued that Kearns's patents were based on common knowledge. Some years later, in 1976, Kearns learned that Mercedes had introduced a wiper whose electronic circuits also matched his design. He suffered an emotional collapse, and it was not until 1978 that he began filing lawsuits. By 1985, he had charged most of the major auto manufacturers with patent infringement. Meanwhile, Kearns had gone through three law firms. One quit because of his tendency to reprimand the attorneys verbally for not working hard enough. In 1980, he turned down a settlement of $150,000 from Porsche-Audi, and a second set of attorneys bailed out. Another firm quit when his son allegedly seduced a secretary in the defendant's firm in order to get crucial information and arrived at one meeting armed with a loaded pistol. Finally, a fourth law firm got the case into court. The trial lasted three weeks, and the jury ruled that Ford had stolen Kearns's idea. In November 1990, Ford settled with Kearns for $10.2 million. After twelve years of fighting, Kearns's perseverance finally paid off.

I believe that Kearns persevered because something had been taken from him that went beyond mere money. Ford and other auto manufacturers had ripped off an idea that formed part of his most important possession—his honor.

A historical parallel can be found in the actions of Finns during World War II. Called the "bastard children of Europe," the Finns are neither Scandinavians nor Russians, but have been frequently invaded by both. Most recently, during World War II, Finland was attacked by the Soviet Union. Making the most of their ability to mount guerrilla warfare in snow-covered, densely forested terrain, the Finns battled Russian forces ten times larger than their own. Owning no anti-tank weapons, they threw bottles filled with kerosene and sprouting a wick at the tanks; they named this concoction the Molotov cocktail, after the Russian foreign minister, whom they despised. The Finns lost 60,000 lives, but they saved their country. The defense of something extraordinary—such as one's honor or homeland—can account for extraordinary perseverance.

The decision to persevere in a course of action toward some future but uncertain goal can also be reinforced by achieving lesser goals along the way. In April 1990, I had lunch with a colleague, Bob Weber, who was writing a book about creativity and invention. We were talking about Edison's comment that creativity is 1 percent inspiration and 99 percent sweat. My question was, how did people know when all that sweat was going to be worth it? Can you predict whether a set of actions done over a long period of time will result in entrapment in a losing course of action or success?

I asked Bob what kept him going in his study of creativity. He had been struggling for over four years, and he told me that he began the book by writing a series of short essays—150 or so—that he used in his classes. The completion of each essay represented a small victory that reinforced his efforts to complete the book. If he had focused only on the enormity of his task and its uncertain rewards, he might have been intimidated. In his case, as in many others, endurance resulted from the enjoyment of many small victories along the road, rather than from the hope of achieving a huge victory far into the future.

How is it that many business entrepreneurs, athletes, composers, musicians, painters, and writers can endure for years with little success or recognition? The answer is that they have both a psychic and a tangible foundation for perseverance. Their psychic base is their love, enjoyment, and total commitment to what they are doing. Psychic resources arise from the instinct to avoid a loss (e.g., one's honor, homeland, or possessions), from a strong desire to fulfill a dream or goal, or from a passion for a certain activity. Their tangible base consists of the support system that enables them to pursue their quest—jobs, scholarships, grants, awards, family, friends, associates. Tangible resources are those physical or financial assets that permit you to absorb at least a certain degree of loss and still continue to pursue your goal. Without some kind of support system, few athletes, artists, or business entrepreneurs would be able to endure for very long.

Time Traps

Time does not stand still. Both positive and negative change inevitably occurs. And it is logical to assume that decision makers would seek to pursue positive change. But a person's ability to effect positive change can be clouded when the relationship between time, pleasure, and pain intervenes. An individual can become trapped in time when an action leads to pleasurable outcomes in the present, but harmful outcomes in the future. Similarly, he can become trapped in time when he gives up a positive course of action for the future because it causes short-term negatives to occur in the present.

Time traps are set when good and bad outcomes occur at different points in time. On a personal level, the executive who chose not to get up early to exercise was experiencing the "bad" outcomes in the short term. Only much further ahead in time would the "good" outcomes be felt as a result of his regimen. The negative response to getting up early stopped an action that would create future benefits. In the same way, addiction to drugs and irresponsible sexual behavior are examples of an apparent preference for present pleasure over the risk of great future pain.

The same time traps affect decision making in business organizations. Few American executives are willing to take a cut in their salaries or in the perquisites of their positions to benefit the long-term growth of their companies. Indeed, in recent years, some executives have seen their companies destroyed, while they landed safely with the massive bonuses and benefits of their "golden parachutes." Similarly, many American companies fail to invest sufficiently in research and development, in part because of a time trap. When a U.S. company makes an investment in R&D, the costs are incurred in the present (R&D expenses must be written off as they occur); but the profits from the new products will accrue only far into the future.

Another example of choosing an action that leads to short-term gain, but also to long-term pain, can be seen in the heavy use by auto makers of sales promotions. In the long term the auto industry has been hurt by the reliance on short-term rebates and other sales promotions to bring customers into showrooms. As Peter Drucker, the management guru, describes the situation: "The offers attracted few, if any new buyers; customers who already decided to buy a domestic car simply waited for the next special offer to come along. Potential customers, however, were turned off. 'If they can sell cars only by giving them away,' was the reaction, 'they can't be much good.' " In the short term, sales promotions may sell more product. However, they borrow sales from the future. In 1989, General Motors' auto divisions in the United States lost money, as well as market share, in part because of the high cost of the rebates it had offered to consumers.

Time traps may also occur when companies compensate sales personnel through a straight commission system that pays them a percentage of their sales. Such a system rewards activities that lead to short-term gains. In the short run, the salesperson can earn more by minimizing service (because it takes time) and by selling to regular accounts. The future rewards of the hard work of prospecting for new clients and providing excellent service are discounted, and the consequent lack of new clients and reputation for poor service results in stagnation for the firm. In extreme cases, a short-term orientation can lead to unethical or illegal actions. The revelations in 1992 that Sears automotive mechanics charged customers falsely for unneeded repairs is one example. As a result of those revelations, Sears changed its policy of using a straight commission system to pay its mechanics.

On the other side of the coin, because they perceive a short-term negative, decision makers may fail to take actions that would benefit themselves and their companies. The "no pain, no gain" aphorism does contain a kernel of truth.

Don Cooper, the team sports physician at Oklahoma State University, told me the following story that perfectly illustrates this time trap. In the early 1970s, Cooper was on the NCAA national executive committee trying hard to get the football coaches to require their players to use protective mouthpieces. The coaches, however, were against it, and year after year voted down the recommendation. The "big-time" coaches, like Darrell Royal at Texas, led the group, arguing that if the players wore mouthpieces, they would be unable to communicate clearly with each other; in particular, the quarterback and defensive players who called signals would not be understandable.

A colorful character, Cooper knew this was nonsense. So, he had a local dentist make up a translucent plastic mouthpiece for him. At the national meetings in 1973, he wore it while he gave his ten-minute talk on preventing athletic injuries. At the end of the speech, he asked the coaches if they could understand him. They all said, "Yeah," puzzled as to why he would even ask the question. To their utter astonishment, Cooper then triumphantly pulled the plastic device from his mouth and held it in the air. Later that day, the coaches passed the rule change unanimously.

In this case, the coaches' perception of the negative outcome of making a rule change was purely imaginary. The presence of imaginary short-term costs also influences business decisions. The sentiment of some of today's CEOs is that if their companies' profits sag for just one quarter, the stock price will plummet and the company will be perceived as a loser. Interestingly, studies fail to support this contention. The data indicate that investors in the stock market value highly those companies that do invest for the long term. Indeed, the companies with some of the highest price-earnings ratios (e.g., Genentech, Boeing, and General Electric in the early 1990s) are the ones which tend to invest significantly in long-term projects.

Investing for the future can require some very real short-term sacrifice—both for the individual and for business organizations. Strikingly few Americans are willing to endure the short-term costs in order to send their kids to college or even to create their own retirement plans. In 1987, the overall U.S. savings rate hit a forty-year low at 3.2 percent. Since then, it has bounced back, but was still less than 6 percent in 1992.

American corporations also have problems investing for the future. They expend substantially less on research and development than do companies in either Germany or Japan. One reason is that the short-term costs of investment are higher in the United States. The Center for Economic Research estimated that throughout the 1980s, the costs of capital in the United States were the highest of any industrialized nation—nearly twice as high as in Japan. As a result of those high capital costs, fixed investment as a percent of GNP was half of that in Japan. Even worse, 60 percent of investment in the United States was financed from abroad.

Some companies have taken internal steps to avoid the natural reluctance of people to make short-term sacrifices. For example, managers of the 3M Corporation developed a number of rules designed to increase R&D spending. One is the 25 percent rule, which states that 25 percent of a division's sales must be from products produced within the last five years. When this norm is broken, managers are penalized at "bonus time." To encourage individual innovation, the company also offers $50,000 grants to employees and allows them to use as much as 15 percent of their time to prove an idea workable. In essence, the company is creating side bets that rearrange the timing of the rewards and the cost of actions that can lead to product innovation.

Future Optimism

Future optimism is the pervasive tendency for people to believe that the future will somehow be better than the present. A Lou Harris Poll taken in 1989 asked a sample of Americans how their present standard of living compared to what they had thought it would be when they were younger. Only 36 percent said it was better. They were also asked what they expected their children's standard of living to be. In this case, 59 percent said it would be better than their own. When one considers that the standard of living in the United States has been slowly slipping over the past two decades, such optimism for the future would seem to be unjustified.

Nevertheless, future optimism has had a major effect on decision making throughout history. In 1865, an English court ruled against an action to stop an industry from polluting the Thames River because the plaintiff had not established the existence of an actual and immediate nuisance. It also argued that establishing injury due to events that may occur a hundred years hence was unreasonable because science would probably have solved any such problems. In sum, prevailing opinion held that "the future would have better solutions for its problems than the present generation could devise." Despite some improvements, over a hundred years later, the Thames remains a polluted river.

Another river, the Mississippi—third largest waterway on earth and the sewer of North America—illustrates how future optimism can influence high-stakes decision making. Its story is vividly told in John McPhee's book *The Control of Nature*. For eons the Mississippi has drained the Great Plains of North America, picking up earth in its fast-moving currents and then dumping it when the water slows at sea level, thus slowly building a gigantic delta in the Gulf of Mexico. Physics provides the reason for this phenomenon. Periodically, the river floods. When the water spills over its banks, it slows down and deposits a new layer of silt. Slowly, the river builds its own levee as its banks grow higher. As it nears sea level, at low-water periods, it also deposits silt at the bottom. Eventually, the river actually rises above the surrounding landscape.

For over a hundred years the Mississippi has wanted to change its course. The Atchafalaya River, which passes close to the Mississippi, has since the 1860s been siphoning off more and more water via a channel that connects the two rivers. In the late 1940s, the Atchafalaya was taking fully one third of the volume of water. From where the two rivers graze each other, if you follow the Atchafalaya to the west, the distance to the Gulf of Mexico is 140 miles. In contrast, if you follow the Mississippi, the distance to the Gulf is 280 miles. The shorter distance of the Atchafalaya means that the slope is steeper—and that is the direction in which the Mississippi wants to go. The shifting of the flow of the river into new channels has taken place about once every three thousand years, and now is the time for it to occur again.

Think for a minute about what would happen to New Orleans and Baton Rouge if the Atchafalaya swallowed the Mississippi. Calamity. The old Mississippi channel would become a bayou, the cities would lose their water supply, salt water would intrude, and the area that has become known as the "American Ruhr," with hundreds of industrial companies attracted to its plentiful water supply, would be in deep trouble. Thus, as far back as 1950 decision makers concluded that it was imperative that the Atchafalaya not be allowed to capture the Mississippi. Too much was at stake. The solution devised by the U.S. Army Corps of Engineers was to put a lock in the connection—called "Old River"—between the Mississippi and the Atchafalaya. In 1963, the Corps completed the decade-plus project in which they built a dam with 5 million tons of earth to block Old River, created a new "Old River" some ten miles away, inserted a lock, and regained control of the Mississippi—for a while.

At the lock, the Mississippi is some 13 feet higher above sea level than the Atchafalaya. Because rivers tend to follow the steepest incline, during a major flood the Mississippi could jump its bank and carve a new channel to the Atchafalaya at countless places. A study completed in 1980 at Louisiana State University maintained that despite all of the construction, the Mississippi would win its battle with the Corps of Engineers: "Just when this will occur cannot be predicted. It could happen next year, during the next decade, or sometime in the next thirty or forty years. But the final outcome is simply a matter of time and it is only prudent to prepare for it." Nevertheless, in its official pronouncements, the Corps of Engineers insists that "Man is directing the maturing process of the Atchafalaya and the lower Mississippi." Some have called this attitude the epitome of arrogance. Clearly, it represents the same future optimism that so strongly influences high-stakes decision making.

Here is a judgment call of gigantic proportion. It is absolutely certain that the Atchafalaya will capture the Mississippi and that New Orleans, Baton Rouge, and billions of dollars of industry will sink in the muck. Should we give in to the inevitable and abandon the effort to stop it? Giving up and quitting would ruin Louisiana. The only sensible alternative would seem to be continuing the effort to contain the Mississippi while simultaneously planning what to do when the event occurs so as to minimize the effects of the catastrophe. Future optimism can be a great strength in decision making because it helps us both to innovate and to take risks. It can also be a fatal weakness if we ignore future realities.

When the Future Is Now

While we know that we should consider the future impact of our decisions, an important question is just how far into the future we should look. Winston Churchill once said, "It is a mistake to look too far ahead. Only one link in the chain of destiny can be handled at a time." My interpretation of Churchill's quote is that "sometimes, the future is now." Sometimes, we must shift our focus from the long term to the short term and enjoy the fruits of our labors. We cannot perpetually endure pain in the present in the hopes of obtaining future positive outcomes. While most of us are biased to emphasize the present over the future, on occasion the reverse error is made. People can become so engrossed in creating a better future that they forget to live in the present. The choice between present and future is, indeed, a judgment call.

Earlier, I cited the mini-max project at Ford and Kodak's lithium battery as instances in which companies revealed the bias of failing to take the long view. On the other hand, at some point an investment must begin to show tangible results. The problem is particularly acute when investing in new start-up companies. How long should investors wait before they should expect the company to begin showing a profit? According to one old-line Boston venture capitalist, investors should expect to see a profit within two to three years. The reasoning is that if you start a new company in a growth industry, you should be able to make money quickly, or you are not going to make money at all.

A dilemma frequently encountered by venture capitalists and bankers is the case in which a loan is made to a new firm, and six months later the company comes back and asks for more cash. Not only is the company not becoming profitable, but also it is asking for additional financial assistance. This is where the sunk cost trap can ensnare an unwary investor. In order to avoid taking a loss by writing off the initial investment and letting the company die, the venture capitalist makes the loan. Six months later, management comes back with another horror story, asking for more money. Of course, they are absolutely confident that with one more loan, the company will prosper. Letting a company die is one of the toughest decisions that a venture capitalist can make. But in these instances, an old Wall Street rule should probably be followed—"Your first loss is always your best loss."

Martin Mayer, one of the foremost authorities on the savings and loan and banking industries, told me that the government's reluctance to let S&Ls die is one of the causes of the crisis in the savings and loan industry. After noting that the S&L bailout will cost taxpayers at least $200 billion, Mayer argued that a similar, but larger, bank bailout is forthcoming. One of the reasons for both the S&L and banking problems is that the government attempts to save ailing institutions rather than letting market forces eliminate them. Mayer maintained that an imbalance between supply and demand exists. Quite simply, in many parts of the country too many S&Ls and banks are competing for business. The market tells us this fact each time one begins to fail. In the United Kingdom, there are 63,000 people per financial institution; in Japan, 18,000. In the United States, the figure is 7,300 citizens per financial institution. Instead of letting nature take its course, however, the government steps in to try to save the institution, and the American taxpayer is stuck with the tab. According to Mayer, a situation has been created in which institutions "have ease of entry and no possibility of exit." To make matters worse, once a bank or S&L is saved, the underlying problem remains, and competing financial institutions are subsequently placed under increased financial pressure. John Maynard Keynes once pointed out, "In the long run, we are all dead." In the case of some failing S&Ls and banks, it is best for their demise to occur sooner rather than later.

In order to build a winning team, sports coaches must think ahead by making wise draft selections and by slowly developing their players. The first thing that a new coach says when hired is "I will need time to develop the team." Of course, the problem is that in the meantime victories are required in order to sustain fan interest. In addition, fans and management expect that at some point the planning for and investing in the future should result in a championship.

Prior to the 1990–91 basketball season, the Chicago Bulls decided that the future is now. Jerry Krause, the Bulls' general manager, said: "Everything we've done for the last six years has been designed to win the world championship." What he did was build a cohesive team around Michael Jordan, the Bulls' superstar. But as Krause said, building a championship team around a shooting guard is the "hardest thing to do in our game. Nobody has ever done it before and won a championship." After making Jordan a first-round draft selection in 1984, Krause attempted the impossible and began to build for the future by putting together a balanced team around his superstar. In the 1990–91 season, Jordan had been with the club longer than any other player. Six of the remaining eleven players were first-round draft selections. The remaining players were veterans selected for their ability to complement Jordan.

When the Detroit Pistons beat the Bulls in the deciding game of their championship series in 1990, management knew that the Bulls were close to being a championship team; but something was lacking. As a result, a decision was made to stop investing in the future and take concrete steps to bring a championship to Chicago the next season. A series of actions followed. A future first-round draft selection was traded to New Jersey for the veteran player Dennis Hopson. Krause then signed an unrestricted free agent, Cliff Levingston, an older player who had previously played well for the Atlanta Hawks. Michael Jordan was persuaded to defer some of his earnings to a later season so that the team could stay under the league's salary cap. Management then rented a small jet aircraft to fly the team on road trips. While doubling travel costs, this reduced the fatigue on long trips away from home. Finally, a new, complicated half-court offense was installed in order to give more players scoring opportunities. The goal was to create an offense in which Michael Jordan would score a lower percentage of the Bulls' points, while simultaneously increasing the total points scored by the team. In sum, for management the time was at hand. The future would be sacrificed in order to win the championship in 1991.

The Bulls marched through the 1991 season with the best record in their conference. In the playoffs, they first destroyed the New York Knicks without losing a game in the series. Then they demolished their old nemesis, the Detroit Pistons, by winning the first four games of the best-of-seven series. Playing great defense, the Bulls controlled the tempo of the games. Perhaps most importantly, the reserves played well, giving the starters important breathers during the games.

Next, Chicago played the Los Angeles Lakers. Taking four of five games, the Bulls dominated the Lakers to win the championship. As usual, Michael Jordan played like a superhuman and won the Most-Valuable-Player award. However, the difference in 1991 was that he received support. Scottie Pippen played like an All-Star, and John Paxson knocked down long-range jumpshots that seemed to squelch every Laker rally. For the Bulls' management, the future was at hand. They took steps that potentially mortgaged the team's future, and the gamble brought a long-sought NBA championship to Chicago.

The present versus future judgment call was also made by commanders in the Persian Gulf war. I spoke to a thirty-year-old pilot shortly after he returned to the United States after flying thirty-two F-16 missions into Iraq. He told me that when the air war began in January 1991, the Air Force followed a clear, future-oriented philosophy. The pilots were told, "No target is worth dying for." The goal was to conserve planes and to avoid having U.S. personnel return in body bags. The strategy was implemented by flying the planes above 6,000 feet in order to avoid the majority of the antiaircraft fire. If pilots missed a target one day, they could always come back and get it the next.

However, when the ground war began, with American troops directly engaging the enemy, targets had to be hit the first time, which meant flying as low as possible. Going in low is extremely risky. Below 3,000 feet, small-arms fire can shoot down an F-16, and the change in tactics resulted in increased losses by the Air Force.

Early in the hundred-hour ground war, the pilot received a radio call directing him to an area just south of Baghdad. A Special Forces operation had been discovered by the Iraqis, and eight Americans were being attacked by forty to fifty enemy troops. There was no room for a mistake, and the pilot had to fly his plane lower than he had ever flown before. Screaming in less than 300 feet above ground, he unleashed bombs that drove off the Iraqis. AH-64 Apache helicopters then arrived to pluck the Special Forces team from the grasp of the enemy. In this instance, the future was at hand, and the F-16 pilot risked his life to save the Special Forces troops.

Making the Present versus Future Judgment Call

In "modern" societies, such as the United States and Japan, time is viewed as a road that emerges from the past, moves through the present, and extends into the future. People believe that what we do now will influence the road's course into the future. If we save in the present and use our time wisely, the road will lead to a better life. On the other hand, if we abuse our time now, the road will crumble and perhaps end prematurely. We have reified time. We have taken this abstract concept and made it into something concrete. Thus, we speak of "wasting," "saving," "buying," "borrowing," and even "killing" time.* With such a world view, people can make either of two errors: living in the present and failing to build the road into the future, or living in the future and failing adequately to tend to the present.

That most difficult financial investment decision of all—when to sell a stock—illustrates how present versus future judgment calls work. The belief among skilled professionals is that investors tend to err most frequently by selling their gains and holding their losses. For example, Gerald Loeb strongly recommended the guideline of letting your profits run and cutting your losses. Born in 1899, Loeb was a successful investor and stock market guru for much of the

---

* The Western view of time is not shared throughout the world. One study compared the accuracy of bank clocks, the speed people walked on Main Street, and the rapidity with which customers could buy stamps in post offices in several countries, including Japan, the United States, and Indonesia. The idea was that these were indicators of the importance of time in the society. The results revealed that in Japan, bank clocks were more accurate, people walked faster down the main street, and stamps could be bought most quickly. Not far behind was the United States. But Indonesia lagged strikingly. People in agrarian cultures, such as Indonesia's, have a very different view of time. For them, it moves in a circular manner with the seasons and generations. The goal is to maintain a way of life. The people know that next year they will be doing the same thing they are doing this year, just as their great-great-grandparents did and their children's children will do.

twentieth century. Referred to as the "Dean of Wall Street," he suggested that while it is good insurance to cash in on some of your profits once they become substantial, the gains from selling too early are usually counterbalanced by the huge losses you can take by holding your losers. Similarly, one of the "money masters" on Wall Street, Philip Fisher, said that perhaps the silliest thing an investor can do is "selling out just because a stock has gone up a lot."

Why do investors reveal a tendency to sell winners and keep losers? One answer lies in the present versus future dilemma. Because we tend to overemphasize the present, we want to avoid taking losses while simultaneously wishing to take our gains in the here and now. Thus, because selling a losing stock results in a loss in the present, we tend to hold onto it in the hope that a gain can be made later. Similarly, because selling a profitable stock leads to a gain in the present, we tend to make the sale too early.

When deciding whether to sell a stock, peerless decision makers ignore what the stock has done in the past. They will ask whether the money received from selling the stock now is equal to or greater than the likely benefits that would result from holding the stock and selling it in the future. They compare the future prospects of the company with those of other possible acquisitions. But peerless decision makers also understand that future outcomes should be discounted and that small rewards must be taken in the present in order to sustain an effort. Thus, when gains become substantial in a stock, they will sell a portion in order to reap some rewards in the present.

In the last chapter, it was argued that peerless decision makers should avoid looking back when making judgment calls. The primary message of this chapter is that when making a choice, they should also assess the benefits and liabilities that can occur in the future *as well as* in the present. When time traps evolve, and losses and gains occur at different points in time, peerless decision makers carefully weigh the outcomes in the present versus those that may occur in the future. They recognize that we tend to overweight outcomes that occur in the present. But they also understand that the future is inherently unpredictable. As a result, future gains and losses must be appropriately discounted.

Some additional suggestions for making the present versus future judgment call follow:

· Keep in mind that quitting too soon results from overweighting short-term costs and underweighting long-term gains of a course of action.

- Refrain from using a change of strategy as an excuse for quitting.

- Encourage endurance by rendering quitting extremely costly—by publicly committing to an action, and by making large financial or time investments in that action.

- If endurance is paramount, burn your bridges and entrap yourself into a course of action.

- Avoid misadventures by not allowing short-term rewards to cause you to act in ways that could lead to long-term ill effects.

- Remember that people take more risks when they feel pain in the present.

- Avoid time traps by creating side bets that encourage desired behaviors and punish unwanted actions at appropriate points.

- Keep in mind that when both gains and losses occur in the future, people will tend to reveal future optimism.

- Maintain a balance between the present and the future by enjoying a portion of the fruits of past labors in the present and by investing the remainder.

5.

RISK VERSUS SECURITY

In the aftermath of Saddam Hussein's invasion of Kuwait and the destruction of Iraq, a lingering question remained. Why would he take such a risk? Earlier, I suggested that he missed the weak signals emanating from the United States that it would protect its interests in the Gulf. But that doesn't explain why he failed to withdraw from Kuwait after President George Bush pieced together a coalition of 30-plus nations and a military machine of over 600,000 troops. By early January 1991, the signals that the United States would attack on a massive scale were unmistakable. In order to more fully understand the possible motivations of Saddam Hussein, one must analyze the complicated trade-off between risk and security.

Human beings have an approach-avoidance conflict with risk. In some cases, we actively seek and relish it; in others, we can become petrified upon sensing the most remote possibility of a negative outcome. On the one hand, consider the process of treating water with fluoride. The fear that fluoride might poison water supplies has resulted in three of the ten largest cities in the United States failing to adjust their drinking water. Yet, after a generation of use, fluoride has revealed no measurable ill effects while simultaneously preventing dental cavities in 50 percent of our youth under seventeen years old. On the other hand, we comfortably ride in automobiles even though car accidents kill nearly as many Americans *every year* as those who died in the entire Vietnam War. Similarly, we spend less than $100 million a year to combat radon gas that seeps into homes and causes twenty thousand lung cancer deaths a years. Yet we spend $6.1 billion annually to clean up hazardous waste dumps responsible for at most five hundred cancer deaths a year. We constantly choose between risk and security. When we choose security in our personal lives, we not only select safety, but also the status quo and monotony. When we seek risk, we increase the potential for harm, as well as the possibility of change, excitement, and innovation.

Corporations must also choose between risk and security. Boeing Inc. represents a company founded upon risk taking. During World War II, the company prospered, making the B-17 Flying Fortress and the huge B-29 Superfortress that dropped the atomic bombs on Japan. When demand for warplanes ended in 1952, Boeing's managers gambled most of the company's net worth on building a prototype passenger jet. Going up against industry giant Douglas Aircraft and its prop-driven planes, Boeing built the first 707. The gamble paid off, and Douglas Aircraft was driven into bankruptcy. Boeing still bets the company with each new generation of plane introduced. If a new line of passenger jets failed in the marketplace, the multibillion-dollar investment required to launch a new model would sink the company. But Boeing's CEO, Frank Shrontz, is keenly aware that Douglas Aircraft failed because it refused to take risks. Shrontz said, "You don't succeed in this business by being cautious. I don't want to lose that can-do attitude. The willingness to gamble, whether in product innovation or product introduction, is very important. The worst thing for us is to overreact and get so conservative that we try to live off our past accomplishments."

While risk taking is necessary for growth, scattered through history are the remains of armies, corporations, and individuals who risked all and lost. In military annals one finds the ill-fated invasions of Russia by Napoleon and Hitler. In business, the savings and loan debacle emerges as a current example of excessive risk taking. With the deregulation of the industry in 1982, S&Ls had no limits on the degree to which they could concentrate their loans in a single area. In addition, they were free to invest in joint ventures, large real estate deals, and junk bonds, which their managers were wholly unprepared to evaluate properly. The net result is a $200 billion bill for the American taxpayer due, in part, to hundreds of weak companies attempting to grow their way out of financial difficulties by taking large risks.

When a great risk is taken and the player loses, the game ends quickly in a humiliating disaster. When Nikita Khrushchev backed down in the Cuban missile crisis in 1962, the entire world knew nearly instantaneously that the Soviet Union had lost its dangerous gambit. In contrast, when the error is conservatism, the outcome is drawn out and less visible—opportunities are lost, growth stops, and a war of attrition eventually leads to defeat. In playing out a risky strategy, the decision maker hopes to reap large gains while recognizing that a probability exists that a large loss may also occur. In contrast, when a conservative strategy is set, the chances of taking a loss are minimized. Unfortunately, in most instances the gains experienced are also small. Thus, the choice between risk and security is based in part upon how highly decision makers value the gains versus the losses that may occur.

Gains, Losses, and Risk Taking

An important scientific goal is to identify "universal principles" that explain behavior across a wide variety of situations and in varied fields of study, be it economics, psychology, or biology. One such universal principle is the law of decreasing marginal effect. The law states that the reaction to each new unit of a stimulus declines as it is added to the previous amount. Thus, economists and psychologists have observed that each additional dollar obtained offers less value than the preceding one. (The principle is called "decreasing marginal utility.") If you are a homeless person, a hundred-dollar bill means a great deal because it is all the money you have. If you are in the middle class, the hundred dollars is nice, but no big thing, because you have a home, a car, and a bank account. If you are wealthy, you tip the bellboy with it.

The law of decreasing marginal effect explains not just how people feel about money but even how they respond to changes in levels of light or sound. For example, as the actual loudness of sound increases by one unit, we perceive it to increase by less than one unit. Our hearing apparatus is constructed in a manner that allows us to hear very loud as well as very soft sounds. If each additional increment in actual sound level caused a similar increase in perceived sound level, our ears would be "blown out" by extremely loud sounds. To combat such a problem, our hearing evolved so that with each additional increment in actual sound intensity, we perceive a lesser increase in sound level.

The law of decreasing marginal effect works for losses as well as gains. Thus, each additional loss means less than the first loss. Think of a basketball team playing a twenty-five-game season. Imagine that the team has played twenty games and won each of them. Consider how the players would feel if they lost their twenty-first game. After the long winning streak, that first loss would be taken hard. Now, compare this experience to how they would feel if they had lost their first twenty games and then lost the twenty-first game. One more loss would have little impact. Of course, the team members care about how many games they lose. The twenty-first loss is simply not as bad as the first loss.

The law of decreasing marginal effect explains both conservative and risky patterns of behavior. Continuing with the basketball analogy, imagine that you are a coach and your team has won twenty games in a row. Things are going well, and you perceive yourself to be in a gain position. Your next game is with an extremely tough opponent, however. Will you take an unusual risk in order to win, perhaps by inserting an unproven but highly skilled player into the starting line-up? Most coaches will not take such a risk when in a gain position. The reason is that the possibility of an increase in team capability would be matched by the possibility of a decrease in performance. The law of decreasing marginal effect says that each additional increment of performance is less valuable. It also says that in such circumstances, regressing from a high level of performance would have greater negative impact than increasing performance a similar amount would have a positive impact. As a result, people will want to avoid taking risks and tend to stay with the status quo when they believe that they are in a gain position.

While people tend to avoid risks in such a gain position, they will also take greater risks when in a loss position. Suppose that you have the unfortunate experience of coaching a poor basketball team. You are going through a miserable season, and your next opponent is particularly tough. In this case, how likely is it that you would take the risk of inserting an unproven but skilled player into the line-up? In the loss domain, each additional defeat means less than the preceding one. As a result, you are willing to risk another defeat in order to have a chance of a victory. Your risk preference changes when in the loss domain. So, people will take greater chances.

Just how one's gain or loss position affects risk taking has been demonstrated in numerous experiments. In one research study, a first group of managers was given the following information:

A large car manufacturer has recently been hit with a number of economic difficulties, and it appears as if three plants need to be closed and 6,000 employees laid off. The vice-president of production has been exploring alternative ways to avoid this crisis. She has developed two plans:

Plan A: This plan will save one of the three plants and 2,000 jobs.

Plan B: This plan has a ⅓ probability of saving all three plants and all 6,000 jobs, but has a ⅔ probability of saving no plants and no jobs.

Faced with this problem, most managers chose Plan A. They wanted to ensure that the 2,000 jobs would be saved. By phrasing the problem from the perspective of saving jobs, managers viewed the situation from a gain position. Because people tend to be risk-averse when operating from a gain position, the managers avoided the more risky choice of following a plan that could save all of the jobs, but risked saving none.

In the same study, a second group of managers was given another set of alternatives that was phrased differently. This time the plans were phrased in terms of losses rather than gains. Here are the options:

Plan C: This plan will result in the loss of two of the three plants and 4,000 jobs.

Plan D: This plan has a ⅔ probability of resulting in the loss of all three plants and all 6,000 jobs, but has a ⅓ probability of losing no plants and no jobs.

When choosing between Plans C and D, managers more frequently selected the second option. Note, however, that the choice between Plans A and B and between Plans C and D is equivalent. Losing two of three plants and 4,000 jobs is equivalent to saving one of three plants and 2,000 jobs. By framing the choice in terms of losses rather than gains, the researchers changed the risk/security trade-off for managers.

The tendency of individuals to take risks when in the loss domain may explain in part why Saddam Hussein invaded Kuwait and then failed to withdraw as overwhelming forces were arrayed against him. Several factors appear to have placed the dictator in a loss position. The fact that the country was bankrupt was one such factor. The war with Iran had cost Iraq $500 billion and incurred a debt of $80 billion to Western nations. Iraq needed cash, and as a result, Kuwait's over-production of oil was viewed as a direct attempt to undermine Iraq's economy because it kept prices low. In an interview in September 1990, Iraq's Ambassador to the United States said, "When a country is bent on destroying you economically and when mediation fails, you are left with no course but to take military action." A second factor creating feelings of loss were the Arab defeats at the hands of Israel and Western nations. The incursion of Israel into Iraq to destroy its nuclear facility in the early 1980s still haunted Hussein. In February 1990, he stated that "a real possibility" existed that in the next five years Israel would embark on "new stupidities" as a result of encouragement by the United States. Similarly, the presence of the U.S. naval fleet, which had operated in the region for forty years, also nagged at Hussein. It symbolized the Western military superiority that had humbled Arab nations in the past. As one Middle East expert put it, "Saddam sees himself as the avenger of the Arab nation, history's instrument to redress the slights visited on Arabs for millenniums." The position of Iraq in 1990 mimicked that of Egypt in the early 1970s. In 1967, Egypt was humiliated by Israeli forces in the Six Day War. In order to avenge the loss, Anwar Sadat risked almost certain military defeat when he ordered the attack on Israel in 1973. In sum, being placed in the loss domain creates a country, corporation, or person ready to take extreme risks.

Gamblers at race tracks exhibit this same tendency to take increased risks when losses mount. Go to a race track and observe the parimutuel odds as the day progresses. Early in the day, the odds fairly accurately reflect the likelihood that the various horses will win. As the day goes on, however, a peculiarity surfaces. Longshots begin to receive more attention. The crowd shows an increasing tendency to make risky bets at the end of the racing day because of the law of decreasing marginal effect. As the end of the racing day approaches, more and more gamblers find themselves in a loss position. In order to get even, they are willing to take greater risks and bet on longshots. For example, suppose that you had been making $10 wagers all day and found yourself $100 down going into the last race. The law of decreasing marginal effect says that the loss of the first $10 is worse than the loss of another $10 after having already lost $100. Within the context of a $100 loss, forfeiting another few dollars feels okay, particularly with the possibility of breaking even. Hoards of people begin to bet on the longshots.

The greater risk taking that results from being in a perceived loss position explains in part why small companies tend to be more innovative than large companies. A major difficulty for large companies is maintaining a dynamic, entrepreneurial approach to business. As a company succeeds, it grows larger. In order to protect its gains, it becomes more bureaucratic and risk-averse. In contrast, small start-up companies *start out* in the loss domain. They are in debt, hungry, and driven to develop new products. So, smaller companies grow more quickly. They also create more jobs in the U.S. economy than large companies. As reported by *The Wall Street Journal*, during the 1980s small businesses created nearly all of the 20 million net new jobs in the economy. The number of jobs in the top 500 industrial companies actually decreased by 400,000 positions a year during the 1980s. Small companies must innovate and grow or they will die. In contrast, many large firms develop a conservative culture that focuses on maintaining the status quo and not losing what has been obtained.

A good example of the entrepreneurial spirit of small firms is U.S. Gold Corporation. The company is attempting to use genetic-engineered bacteria to eat dissolved ore and release gold. If the experiment succeeds, the company will be worth millions. If it fails, however, it will vanish. Much like hunting for oil, gold-mining discoveries tend to be made by small companies. A professor at the Colorado School of Mines once said, "To be a miner, you have to be a gambler." Bill Reid, one of the owners of U.S. Gold, agrees. "If you're not worried, you're not risking enough. I believe life should be an adventure, and we're having a hell of an adventure right now." Bill Reid and his brother David have little to lose if their firm goes bankrupt. David Reid told *The Wall Street Journal* that "If the project fails, he'll just sell his house, load up his van and go back to prospecting."

In some cases, large companies recognize the greater entrepreneurial spirit of small companies, and invest in them for that reason. For example, Homestake Mining Company owns a controlling interest in U.S. Gold. In other cases, the larger company simply buys the smaller one. In 1986, General Motors purchased Lotus PLC—a small and innovative British firm known for making fast, stylish sports cars, but which according to its chairman, Michael Kimberly, "staggered from crisis to crisis." After the purchase, GM's European division head, Bob Eaton, worked to maintain Lotus's independence because the engineers in the firm had a spirit and commitment that GM lacked. Eaton explained the reason for the entrepreneurial spirit at Lotus: "Lotus was a company that's been on the brink of failure—bankruptcy—since it started. In 1982 or 1983, on Monday of a couple of different weeks, they didn't have any idea of how they were going to make the payroll on Friday. That mentality of just barely staying alive caused a tremendous commitment to make things work."

The engineers at Lotus were more productive than GM's because they were hungrier and closer to the market. According to one auto analyst, "They were the perfect example of how adversity could bring out the best in an organization." When people perceive that they have their backs to the wall, they become innovative and driven to avoid final disaster.

The perception of being in a loss position, however, can also lead to poor decision making. A college football story illustrates this idea. On January 1, 1984, Nebraska played Miami in the 50th Orange Bowl for the national championship. Nebraska came into the game with a better record than the University of Miami. As a result, Miami had to win the game in order to become national champion. Both teams played well, and at the end Nebraska went on a long drive and scored. They were one point behind. What should Tom Osborne, the Nebraska head coach, do? Should he kick the extra point and with virtual certainty tie Miami but still clinch the championship? Or, should he take the far riskier route, go for two points and win the game? The crowd chanted: "Go for it, go for it, go for it!" Millions watched the game on national television. What would Osborne do?

In coaching lore the "book" says always go for the win. Tying a game is tantamount to taking a loss. The Miami coaching staff was sure that Nebraska would go for two. Their coach, Howard Schnellenberger, said that he "never even thought about sending in the kicking team." The total force of the environment said, "Go for two." While all of this was occurring, Pat Jones sat back watching the game from his easy chair in Oklahoma. The coach of Oklahoma State's football team yelled at the screen: "Just kick it, just kick it, and you're the national champion."

So what did Coach Osborne, one of the savviest coaches in college football history, do? He did what was expected—he went for the two-point conversion. When it failed, Miami won the game and the national championship despite a poorer overall record. Asked after the game why they didn't just kick the extra point, Coach Osborne said: "We didn't want to back into anything."

Osborne and his coaching staff were unable to shake off the psychological forces that pushed them toward a decision that cost them the national championship. Tom Osborne simply could not avoid the tendency to take a high-stakes risk when he framed his situation from a loss perspective.

High-Stakes Illustrations of Excessive Conservatism

The error of being too conservative can be just as dangerous as taking too much risk. Again, "big-time" college athletics provides a vivid example of the potential negative effects of conservatism in decision making.

In 1988, the Oklahoma State University Cowboys had the best offensive college football team in the country. Blessed with Barry Sanders, the Heisman Trophy winning running back; a great receiver in Hart Lee Dykes; a highly underrated quarterback; and an excellent offensive line; the team was nearly unstoppable. Unfortunately, the defensive team was a sieve, and opponents scored nearly as frequently as OSU. The team's coach, Pat Jones, told me that he still rues a decision he made in a game against the Cowboys' bitter rival —the Oklahoma Sooners—that could have meant a trip to the Orange Bowl and hundreds of thousands of dollars to the university. Yet, few are even aware of the decision and its possibilities.

Here is what happened. In the first half, the Sooners played well and ran through, over, and around the Cowboys. As usual, the team's defense played poorly. To make matters worse, the offense was sputtering as the Sooners focused on containing Sanders and Dykes. In the second half, though, the game began to turn. Sanders rushed for over 200 yards, and in the middle of the fourth quarter the Cowboys scored the go-ahead touchdown and took a three-point lead.

At this point, Coach Jones faced a crucial decision. After scoring the go-ahead touchdown, what should his team do? The "book" said to play conservatively, kick long, and try to stop the opponents. Another alternative was to take a huge gamble and execute an on-side kick. As Pat Jones said, "It would have been an off-the-wall call, but I considered it." In hindsight, the risky call had much going for it. Jones pointed out, "It would have played to our team's strength." In practice sessions he had installed two trick on-side kick-offs for the game. If the play worked, the Cowboys could probably have run out the clock. If the play failed, the Sooners would have gotten the ball, but they would probably have scored faster, leaving the Cowboys more time to come back and win the game with their potent offense. It was the type of game in which the team that had the ball last would win.

What actually happened? Pat Jones went with his instincts and played conservatively. The Cowboys kicked long. The Sooners took the ball, went on a long time-eating drive, and scored. When the Cowboys got the ball back, less than two minutes remained. They quickly marched down the field. On the last play of the game, a long pass went through the arms of a receiver in the end zone, leaving the Sooners victorious—again!

After the game, no sportswriters or fans accused Pat Jones of calling a poor play. He had reacted in a manner completely consistent with expectations. How often do you see on-side kicks made by the team that is ahead and in a gain position? But, consider what would have happened if after the Cowboys scored the touchdown, they had been a point behind, rather than three points ahead. Pat Jones would certainly have ordered an on-side kick because the team would still have been in the loss domain.

No one criticized the coach, and few were even aware that an alternative course of action was available. In our interview, Coach Jones summed up his thoughts: "It would have taken a lot of guts to make the call, and to this day it's the one decision that in hindsight, I wish I could change."

All else being equal, conservatism tends to occur when a person, corporation, or country perceives itself to be in a gain position. As a result of the law of decreasing marginal effect, each additional gain feels less positive than preceding gains. And taking a loss from that gain position is viewed as highly negative. As a result, decision makers in a gain position tend to become overly conservative and to avoid taking the risks necessary for growth.

Such errors of conservatism can be found in the life cycle of nations. Paul Kennedy argues in his *Rise and Fall of the Great Powers* that a great nation must develop a flourishing economic base as well as a strong military defense. The dilemma faced by such a nation is how to allocate resources between these two goals. On the one hand, a growing economy and military security are mutually enhancing. A powerful military must be supported by a diversified, strong economic base, and in turn, the economic machinery is protected and even extended by the military. Kennedy's thesis, however, is that great powers decline because in attempting to gain military security in the short run, they overextend themselves geographically and strategically. Too many resources are allocated to a parasitic military and not enough to productive investments. Other competing nations, which may be protected by the security umbrella, funnel more resources into economic investments and over the long haul create flourishing economies. Their industrial base eventually grows to the point where they can support a huge military, supplanting in power the nation that heretofore had protected them. According to Kennedy, such a pattern has repeatedly occurred throughout history. Three hundred years ago, Spain was a great power. Then it overextended itself, and became a third-rate economic and military power. Great Britain followed the same pattern, and it struggles today to remain a second-tier economic power. Kennedy argues that the same pattern threatens the United States today.

During the Persian Gulf war, Kennedy was chided for his pessimistic view of the future of the United States. An editorial in *The Wall Street Journal* maintained that the United States was not suffering from "imperial overstretch," as Kennedy had claimed; instead, the wizardry of its high-tech weapons and the ease of victory would help the United States recover its reputation and break its mood of self-doubt and defeatism. In response, Kennedy observed that the last thing the United States needs is "to seek its self-esteem on the battlefield." Rather, he suggested, "If the U.S. wishes to recover its 'reputation,' it might begin by repairing its inner cities, public education, crumbling infrastructure and multiple social needs, at the same time resisting the temptation to follow the path of Spanish grandees." Indeed, our nation's failure to repair the inner cities was vividly depicted by the Los Angeles riots that occurred in 1992 after the failure of a jury to convict a white policeman for beating a black man named Rodney King.

Michael Porter, the Harvard management guru, agrees with Paul Kennedy's basic thesis. He suggests that countries move through three stages. In the first, they are driven by geography, resources, and people. Next, they become driven by technology. Finally, they are "driven by wealth . . . which creates a backward-looking, rear-guard action to protect what they've got."

The risk/security trade-off is at the heart of the debate about the role of the military in the United States. The judgment call of how much to invest in the military in order to protect the American standard of living is the ultimate high-stakes decision. The law of decreasing marginal effect suggests that as long as the majority of voting citizens perceives the United States to be in a gain position, the error of conservatism is most likely to occur, resulting in attempts to protect the status quo by maintaining an overwhelming, but economically draining, military force.

When Risk Is Security and Security Is Risk

The judgment call of how much to invest in the military illustrates the idea that sometimes the search for security can actually lead to major risks. In seeking to obtain current high levels of national security by maintaining a huge military machine, we create a large risk of future economic decline. On other occasions, taking risks can increase security. It is as though a principle of opposites applies to high-stakes decision making.

Nowhere is this principle of opposites better illustrated than in the balance of nuclear terror after 1945. With the development of the atomic bomb, and a few years later the H-bomb, the United States lived a Faustian existence of having more destructive power at its disposal than it could possibly imagine. With his thirty-plus years of experience in the politics of using "the bomb," McGeorge Bundy published a book on the topic called *Danger and Survival*, suggesting that the incredible risk posed by the bomb caused political decision makers to become highly conservative in their decision making. The principle of MAD (Mutually Assured Destruction) created a situation in which a war between the countries possessing "the bomb" was nearly unthinkable. As a result, Europe avoided conflict for nearly half a century. The nuclear risk *created* security, albeit in a highly psychologically uncomfortable form.

The principle of opposites also applies to attempts to protect ourselves against nuclear warfare. In the early 1960s, President Kennedy was attempting to hammer out a nuclear test ban treaty with the Soviet Union. In addition, he tried to implement a national program of civil defense. According to Bundy, who at the time was the special assistant for national security affairs at the White House, Kennedy believed that the danger of nuclear war was real and that "a national shelter program could save tens of millions of Americans. It seemed a prudent form of insurance."

Kennedy announced the program in a speech on the Berlin crisis, and the public reaction was overwhelming. Near panic resulted.

Some wanted to build bomb shelters immediately because of the impending doom and began digging in their basements. Others assumed that the administration was preparing for war and opposed the shelters. Kennedy and Bundy viewed civil defense as a cheap form of insurance that should be non-threatening to the enemy. In contrast, many saw the proposal as tantamount to declaring an intention to go to war and as a means of making such a war acceptable. By taking what on the surface appeared to be a prudent, cautious approach, Kennedy was perceived to be engaging in the highest form of risk-taking behavior—preparing the country for a nuclear war. The program was scrapped, and only later was a scaled-down version developed that utilized community shelters rather than one in every home.

In sports, the principle of opposites is found in the saying, "The best offense is a good defense." The idea appears to work in the curious world of nuclear deterrence as well. According to Bundy's account, it was recognized both in the United States and in the Soviet Union in the early 1970s that attempts to use anti-ballistic missiles (ABMs) would only lead to the development and deployment of ever more sophisticated and dangerous offensive missiles. As a result of the recognition, the Anti-Ballistic Missile Treaty of 1972 was signed, which all but barred defensive systems. Again, the world seemed turned on its head—the conservative strategy of creating a ballistic missile defense would have led to increased risk.

President Ronald Reagan's Strategic Defense Initiative (SDI) in March 1983 also exemplifies the principle of opposites. On the surface, SDI (or the so-called Star Wars) appeared a prudent course of action. As stated by President Reagan, its goal was "to give us the means of rendering nuclear weapons impotent and obsolete." Undoubtedly, President Reagan's motives were sound. Indeed, his reasoning made a good deal of sense. He said: "It is inconceivable to me that we can go on thinking down the future, not only for ourselves and our lifetime but for other generations, that the great nations of the world will sit here, like people facing themselves across a table, each with a cocked gun, and no one knowing whether someone might tighten their finger on the trigger." Our intuitive psychological reaction is that basing our defense on mutually assured destruction appears to be mad.

Not surprisingly, leaders in the Soviet Union opposed SDI. Supporters of the program in the United States viewed the Soviet stance as indicative of weakness and as evidence that we should move even more quickly. The Soviet position, however, was completely consis-

122 · JUDGMENT CALLS

tent with the 1972 ABM Treaty and the thinking behind it. Putting missile defense systems in place would only lead to a race to build more sophisticated offensive weapons. Indeed, if a country had an impenetrable shield, it would possess the ability to launch an attack first, and then fend off a counterattack. Place yourself in the shoes of the Soviet Union's leaders. Would you ever allow a country to put such a shield in place? The basic logic of the SDI was flawed, and the attempt to increase security would have magnified the risks many fold.

Going to extremes either to seek risk or to obtain security frequently results in the converse occurring. For example, an alternative program to Star Wars has been proposed that appears to balance the risk/security trade-off. The objective of the program would be to build a small land-based system that would do two things. First, it would have the capability to defend the United States against an accidental attack. Such attacks would be limited in scope, and the capability of the system required to defend against them would not be threatening. The second objective would be to protect the United States and/or its ground troops from attack by leaders of hostile Third World countries, such as Iraq and Libya. The CIA estimates that by the year 2000, fifteen to twenty developing nations will be able to launch ballistic missiles—many of which will also have nuclear or poison gas capabilities. A small program to counter these capabilities could allow the United States to avoid blackmail threats.

In sum, perfect security is never achieved. Indeed, the quest for perfect security inevitably leads to risk. When security is gained in the short term by creating overwhelming military forces, a nation can mortgage its future. Even for individuals, the goal of obtaining complete financial security necessarily requires some risk taking. For example, if people put all of their savings in ultra-safe Treasury bonds (or worse, in a bank's safe), inflation will rapidly reduce their value. Even individuals in their sixties must take some risk in order to have financial security in their seventies and eighties by placing their money in prudent investments that have a good chance of keeping up with inflation.

The Need for Arousal and Risk Taking

Risk taking may result because individuals perceive themselves to be in a loss position. In other instances, some individuals possess a chronic, high need for stimulation, which causes them to take actions that seem crazy to many of us, like parachuting for sport. They also react to risky situations in an unusual manner.

A scene from the movie *Romancing the Stone* nicely illustrates the role of individual differences in the need for stimulation and risk taking. Michael Douglas plays Jack Colter, an adventurer in South America who makes a living capturing rare birds; Kathleen Turner plays Joan Wilder, a sheltered writer of romance novels, who, re-acting to a plea for help from her sister, ends up in Colombia, South America, paired with Douglas. In one scene the two are fleeing a corrupt police officer. As they run through the jungle in the middle of a rainstorm, the ground beneath them gives way and they begin to slide, tumble, and bump down a steep hill. They barely miss trees as they flip head over heels in a gush of mud and water. Finally, Turner splashes down in a pool of water on her rear, legs splayed. Douglas plops face down in her crotch. You expect them to emerge bewil-dered, groggy, and scared, and Turner reacts just as expected. Doug-las, however, pulls his muddy head from between Turner's thighs, and yells jubilantly, "Woo-ye, what a ride!" His unexpected reaction turns the scene into comedy. It represents the impulsive behavior of a person with a chronic need for high stimulation.

According to the psychologist Marvin Zuckerman, our goal as functioning human beings is to maintain a level of overall physiologi-cal arousal that is comfortable. In order to maintain the proper level of arousal, we engage in activities that stimulate us to the appro-priate degree. If we are underaroused, we seek activities that pump us up. If we feel overaroused, we engage in actions that are calming. For example, in order to calm themselves, people may garden, read a book, or take various types of system-depressing drugs, such as alcohol. In contrast, people who want to heighten arousal may turn to stimulating drugs such as cocaine, watch violent television shows and movies, or seek physical risk. Engaging in any risky activity—from gambling to jumping out of airplanes—is a quick means of raising one's blood pressure.

Some people are chronic thrill-seekers. As one psychologist de-scribed it, "If you ask accident-prone skiers if they are scared when they are on a high-risk slope, they'll say they wouldn't bother to ski the slope if they weren't scared. They want a slope that terrifies them. Parachuters say the same thing. After you take the plunge there's an immense relief and sense of well-being in facing a fear that doesn't materialize." For those who have a chronic need to maintain a high level of stimulation, it is possible to become addicted to sensation-

124 · JUDGMENT CALLS

seeking activities. Zuckerman further argues that high sensation-seekers crave excitement from such questionable sources as taking drug trips, to jumping into sexual adventures, to engaging in criminal activities.

The rush, the jazz, the adrenaline flow all describe the same intense feeling one receives from achieving a victory by conquering the fear of uncertainty. The heavy hitters on Wall Street, some of whom ended up in jail, described the same feeling. In a story in *Fortune* magazine, Dennis Levine told what persuaded him to make the insider trades that induced investigators to uncover Levine himself, then led eventually to Ivan Boesky, Michael Milken, and to the fall of Drexel Burnham Lambert.

Levine started out in 1978 as a $19,000 a year trainee who discovered the art of insider trading before authorities began their prosecutorial binge. He spent some time working in Europe where insider trading is not a crime. He readily rationalized his behavior by looking at the frequent runups of the stock price of takeover firms prior to the announcements as evidence that others were doing it. Levine began his escapades in 1979, and that year his trading profits reached $39,750. By 1986, he had leveraged his gains to $11.5 million through insider trading. "Eventually insider trading became an addiction for me," he explained. "My account was growing at 125% a year, compounded. Believe me, I felt a *rush* when I would check the price of one of my stocks on the office Quottron and learn I'd just made several hundred thousand dollars. I was confident that the elaborate veils of secrecy I had created—plus overseas bank-privacy laws—would protect me."

In sum, one reason why people seek out and enjoy risk is to feel the rush from the excitement. But remember that sensation seeking can be a general trait. One would expect individuals who seek arousal in one area also to seek it in others. Thus, when making important hiring decisions, managers should ask whether the job requirements demand a sensation-seeker or sensation-avoider. For example, sensation-seekers can be attracted to the stock market. When the markets become dull and listless, one can bet that these individuals will devise other means to find some action in addition to trading stocks. Such was the case in the spring of 1989, during the "March Madness" of the NCAA basketball tournament. It seems that the traders created a market composed of the competing teams. In the over-the-counter market, "bid and ask" prices were developed, and one found brokers, traders, and arbitragers. At one point, prices for the Georgetown Hoyas were $5,200 bid and $6,400 asked. One group created a $460,000 pool with players chipping in from $5,000 to $10,000 each. High sensation-seekers act as though they are addicted to obtaining the excitement that comes from taking risks. If a job requires high levels of conservatism and prudence (an example would be banking), executives should think twice about hiring a sensation-seeker. In contrast, if the job requires considerable risk taking (an example might be managing a small, entrepreneurial company), the confirmed risk taker may make a perfect match.

On Managing Risk by Using Rules of Thumb

An approach to balancing risk and security involves developing rules of thumb for action. Rules of thumb—or heuristics, as they are termed—specify easily understood guidelines for decision making. Heuristic devices differ from computerized algorithms or decision calculus models, in which data are input into a mathematical formula and the correct answer is spewed out. Heuristics provide easily followed rules that result in satisfactory, but not perfect, decisions. They have several advantages. They are quick to implement, simple, and frequently based upon years of experience.

One heuristic frequently followed by successful corporations goes as follows: "Strive for incremental rather than quantum improvements." When an incremental strategy is used, small improvements are introduced in a continuous manner. As a result, small risks are taken repeatedly, but the company avoids taking the large risk that could sink it. As a result of incremental change, the organization is in a constant state of making minor changes that become part of its culture. In contrast, quantum change breaks the flow of work and sends shock waves through the organization.

Breaking the rule of incremental change can lead to dire consequences, as illustrated by the attempts of General Motors in the 1980s to halt the slide of its ever-shrinking market share. GM spent over $40 billion on modernization and new facilities during the 1980s. A significant proportion of this incredible sum went to purchase state-of-the art production equipment, such as robots. One industry analyst said that GM "ended up investing in million dollar solutions for ten-cent problems." The company attempted to make quantum, rather than incremental, jumps in the use of technology. The result was near chaos.

Another classic example of the failure to use incremental improvements was found in the experience of the Hamtramck plant, brought on line in the mid-1980s to build the Cadillacs of the future. The plant opened with 260 robots and 50 automated guided vehicles to ferry parts. It proved a nightmare, reminding some of the 1950s B-grade movie *Robots from Hell*. The robots sprayed each other instead of the cars, smashed windshields instead of installing them, and crashed into each other and the cars. In one instance, hundreds of damaged Cadillacs had to be shipped to an old-fashioned plant where they were painted with hand-held sprayguns. In another instance, a robot quit and shut down the entire assembly line. An electrician was summoned. He read through the manual and could not figure out the problem. A manufacturer's representative from out of town was flown to the scene. He stepped up to the robot, looked at it for a minute, pushed the reset button, and the robot sprang back to life. After a full year of operation, the plant was completing only half the planned number of cars.

In contrast, many Japanese companies work on the principle of incremental improvement. For example, when Toyota built a plant in Kentucky identical to one in Japan, visitors were amazed to find a traditional factory, lacking the scores of robots that they expected. The goal of the firm was to minimize risk in the United States by using existing technology. Because the equipment was identical to that used in Japan, if robotics or other problems occurred, the solution could be quickly found. Once the plant was running smoothly, new technology could be gradually introduced. Japanese companies are using the same incremental approach to enter the lucrative aerospace industry. Rather than attempt to make the quantum leap of building their own passenger or military jets, they chose to build under American licenses in order to begin the learning process. In addition, Japanese companies are winning contracts to supply critical components to plane manufacturers in the United States. A senior vice-president at Boeing said of these companies, "Today they're looked at by the world as subcontractors. Fifteen years from now they'll be major players however you define it."

Perhaps the most basic risk-reducing heuristic is the principle of diversification. Various familiar maxims express the concept of "diversification," such as "Don't put all your eggs in one basket." While the axiom is basic, even professional managers and investors frequently ignore it and suffer the consequences. Indeed, the failure to follow the principle of diversification is one of the fundamental reasons for the current problems in the U.S. financial system. The first bailout of a billion-dollar bank, the Bank of the Commonwealth, happened in Detroit in 1972. The Federal Reserve gave a variety of reasons for saving the bank, but the basic fear was that if it closed, a domino effect would occur and banks would start failing throughout the system.

What interests us here, however, is the cause of the Bank of the Commonwealth's problems. It seems that beginning in the late 1960s, when long-term interest rates began to go up because of the cost of the Vietnam War, the bank's managers gambled that they were seeing a short-term rise in interest rates. As a result, they began investing greater and greater percentages of the bank's capital in long-term, low-grade municipal bonds. When the rise in interest rates proved to be a long-term phenomenon, the bank failed. As one analyst stated, the bank's principals "ignored the time-honored banking policies of diversification of risk, laddering of maturities for a continual turnover of securities, and picking quality issues. They steadily bled away the bank's liquidity." The bailout cost the FDIC $35.5 million. Similarly, the second billion-dollar bank bailed out by the Federal Reserve, First Pennsylvania of Philadelphia, also suffered from a lack of diversification. In First Pennsylvania's case, however, the bank loaded up on long-term U.S. Treasury securities and used short-term borrowings to pay for the bonds. When short-term rates went above long-term rates in the early 1980s, the bank collapsed. This bailout cost the FDIC $325 million.

In comparison to the problems of the savings and loans, however, the bailout of banks represented mere pocket change. Prior to 1981, when Congress changed the regulations, S&Ls lent money almost exclusively to homeowners. Of course, this policy created problems because it meant that the S&Ls were not diversified. When interest rates ballooned in the early 1980s, the S&Ls began to hemorrhage money. In 1981, Congress decided to solve the problem by rewriting the regulations so that S&Ls could diversify their investments, and in the mid-1980s some S&Ls jumped aboard Michael Milken's junk bond machine. Buying long-term junk bonds gave the S&Ls a means of locking in extremely high rates of return. They could borrow short term at lower rates to finance the purchase of the junk bonds. Further, because the government insured depositors to the tune of $100,000 each, the S&Ls could offer consumers high interest rates in order to attract their money while assuring them that their deposits were completely safe. Michael Milken's message was persuasive. In buying a portfolio of junk bonds, it would make no difference if any one bond issue went sour; the high rate of return and the diversification across the securities of different companies solved the problem.

As a result, many S&Ls purchased junk bonds, and the firms grew rapidly. (To give just one example, within five years, the capitalization of Columbia Savings and Loan grew from $360 million in assets to $10.4 billion—most of it junk.)

In 1988, Congress recognized that a $50 billion problem existed. The S&L industry was rapidly becoming insolvent, due in part to the excessive purchase of junk bonds. To solve the problem, Congress legislated that by 1995 S&Ls would have to junk their junk bonds. The trouble was, what would the S&Ls do with the billions of dollars of junk now in their portfolios? The answer was, sell the bonds. But who would buy them? As a result of the enforced sale, their value plummeted due to the basic laws of supply and demand. Everyone wanted to sell and no one wanted to buy. A $50 billion problem had suddenly become a $200 billion problem.

Again, the problem was one of diversification. Financial companies need to diversify across time, industries, and instruments. In the late 1970s, banks were closing because they failed to diversify across time by placing too great a percentage of their assets in long-term securities. In the early 1980s, banks in Oklahoma and Texas were killed because they sank too great a percentage of their assets in one industry—oil. In the late 1980s, many S&Ls crumbled because they failed to diversify across instruments by relying too much on junk bonds and risky real estate deals.

The principle of diversification works outside of business and finance as well. In the 1970s, decision makers at NASA made a near-fatal error when they placed all of the United States' spacecraft eggs in the basket of the shuttle. When tragedy struck and the Space Shuttle Challenger blew up in 1986, the U.S. space program stopped dead in its tracks. Recently, the pattern was again repeating itself in the space program. In the early 1990s, NASA and the Bush administration pushed a $50 billion program to launch a series of huge weather satellites to investigate the earth's climate in order to determine whether the earth is growing warmer. Many scientists argued that the satellites were "too big, too expensive, too complex and too late." Rather than building something so big and technologically risky, they felt that NASA should develop small satellites, which are cheaper and can be launched into orbit much more quickly.

In addition to diversification and incremental change, other risk-reducing heuristics have been proposed. During the Apollo moon program in the 1960s, a great deal of effort was expended developing rules of thumb at NASA. The managers recognized early that the

principle of "safety before everything" was simply impossible because a manned rocket would never get off the ground. The impetus
for the development of the rules came from Chris Kraft, the director
of Flight Operations, and the person who became known as "the
teacher." The heuristics were inserted into other mission rules to
handle two separate types of situations: When insufficient time existed to think through a problem, and when intuition might lead to
wrong answers.

Interestingly, the Apollo staff at first resisted the rules. They argued that the situations would never be exactly the same as those
practiced. But their attitudes changed as the program matured. The
associate director of Flight Operations explained it this way: "If
you'd worked your way through problems, then when you saw a
problem, whether you knew exactly what it was or not, you started
recognizing the characteristics of it—and understanding the system,
you could work your way out of it."

The mission controllers would have preferred rules such as "Protect the crew at all costs." But this type of rule would have led to
paralysis. Thus, more helpful heuristics were formulated. As we saw
earlier, one of the first was: "If you don't know what to do, don't
do anything." This rule was counterintuitive because the controllers
instinctively wanted to act when faced with a problem. Teaching
controllers to recognize their own ignorance became an important
goal. A great deal of their training time was spent demonstrating to
them how they could be fooled.

One of the most important judgment calls faced by the controllers
was when to abort a mission. In the case of Apollo XII, lightning
struck the spacecraft as it ascended through clouds. It temporarily
paralyzed the electrical systems in the ship, but somehow the spacecraft made it into orbit. Once in orbit, the question was whether or
not to attempt a trans-lunar injection. Would the electrical systems
hold up? In order to deal with the problem, another heuristic was
employed. It stated: "You will continue only if the next thing that
happens to you—and it's the worst thing you can think of to couple
with the problems you already have—is still survivable." After
checking the spacecraft's electrical systems in minute detail, the engineers could find no problems. The one system that could not be
checked was the pyrotechnics that released the parachutes for the
landing. But if that system failed, it would kill the crew whether or
not they went to the Moon. Craft argued that the greatest risk in the
mission was the launch. Once in orbit, you want to stay there and

complete the mission—as long as the next problem is survivable. As a result of this reasoning, the flight continued. Happily, it was completed successfully.

Many rules of thumb are industry-specific. In 1988, I interviewed a series of executives in small oil firms who had survived the bust of the 1980s. I asked them what kinds of rules of thumb they employed. Many involved controlling risk. Some examples included:

—Don't bet more than two times monthly income on any one oil well.
—Don't use your own capital on exploratory wells.
—Costs go up geometrically when you drill beyond 6,000 feet.

The men and women who followed such rules were able to weather the plunge in oil prices that forced many of their peers into bankruptcy.

A basic principle is that peerless decision makers identify and utilize the rules of thumb that apply to their specific line of work. But judgment calls do still exist in using such heuristic devices. For example, should one slavishly follow the diversification principle? One of the most successful investors of this generation, Warren Buffet, built his company, Berkshire Hathaway, Inc., by following the rule of never committing more than one fourth of the partnership's capital in a single investment. Yet the investment that caused his company to take off violated that rule. In 1963, American Express became involved in a scandal, and its stock price fell by almost 50 percent. Recognizing a once-in-a-lifetime opportunity, Buffet poured 40 percent of Berkshire Hathaway's capital into American Express. Two years later, he sold out for a $20 million profit.

Warren Buffet violated the principle of diversification because he believed that the potential rewards compensated for the added risk. When he made his fateful judgment call to violate the rule, he understood the potential consequences, both good and bad, of his decision. Peerless decision makers *consciously* apply rules of thumb when making high-stakes decisions. Problems can develop, however, when risk-reducing heuristics creep in surreptitiously.

An important judgment call for manufacturers developing new products concerns when to move from the R&D stage to pilot production. In an interview with a research chemist for a *Fortune* 500 firm, I discovered the implicit use of a risk-reducing heuristic. He was describing how his group approached the problem of developing a new process for extracting pure methane from natural gas. As expressed by the Ph.D. chemist, the rule states: "Lower the risk of failure by delaying for as long as possible the start-up of the new process, while simultaneously working on the production facility and on basic research and development." Basically, the research scientists and engineers wanted to lower the risk of failure by delaying commercial start-up for as long as possible while learning everything they could through additional testing. The scientists recognized that their goals differed from management's. The managers wanted to get the product out quickly in order to obtain a return on their investment; the scientists, in contrast, wanted to avoid any chance of failure. The scientists' heuristic was developed in order to maximize the impression that they made on managers. By delaying production, they increased the likelihood of success. If they worked on the development of production facilities without management's knowledge, when the order finally came "to produce or else," they could start up very rapidly. The problem with the rule of thumb was that it delayed development of the project. In this era of global competition, the ability to innovate quickly is paramount. In sum, it is important to identify non-verbalized rules of thumb that may be detrimental to the firm.

On Computerized Decision Making

In addition to using rules of thumb to manage risk, decision makers can also employ computers to assist them. A number of computer-aided approaches exist. In one, the decisions of experts are carefully examined, and a computer program is developed that models the experts' approach to the problem. The computer software then asks the novice decision maker a series of questions on issues that the expert would consider. The novice feeds in the information, and the computer cranks out a recommendation. (Note that experienced, as well as novice, decision makers frequently find expert systems useful.) Another approach is to empirically derive a predictive equation that best fits the data from hundreds of similar decisions. When a new problem of the same type is encountered, the decision maker feeds in the appropriate data, and the computer cranks out a recommendation. Such computer systems are highly useful when the decision is one that occurs frequently. In such circumstances, experts really exist and/or equations can be developed and tested. An example would be a bank determining whether or not to give someone a credit card.

The problem is that computerized decision making is largely inappropriate when one must make a high-stakes judgment call. By their very nature, judgment calls occur infrequently. Equations cannot be developed and tested from prior experience, and experts will disagree. Indeed, no evidence exists that complex models do better than heuristics, even for quite simple problems. In one well-researched book on forecasting, Stephen Schnaars argues that "There is absolutely no evidence that complicated mathematical models provide more accurate forecasts than much simpler models that incorporate intuitively pleasing rules-of-thumb." No matter how sophisticated the model, it rests on basic assumptions. If the assumptions are wrong, the model will not predict accurately. Similarly, if decision makers are predisposed to one conclusion, they can "cook" the numbers that go into the mathematical model in order to get the desired outcome. In sum, the rule "Garbage in equals garbage out" still holds. Computerized models, however, have a seductive quality, because the garbage going in is concealed in the gilt-edged wrapping of mathematics.

Suppose that a financial model is being used to decide whether to invest in a new system to rust-proof the frames of automobiles. It is quite easy to develop a mathematical model that includes parameters for the costs and benefits of the process. The model will also include discount factors that account for the time value of money. The up-front costs of purchasing and installing the equipment are easily calculated, and because they occur early in time, their full value is included in the calculations. In contrast, the benefits of having rust-free cars are difficult to quantify and must be developed on the basis of human judgment. Further, cars take time to rust, and the negative effects on customer satisfaction and future sales only occur far into the future. As a result, the discounting formula that calculates the "net present value" of the benefits will dramatically reduce them. If a decision maker is opposed to installing the process, all that he or she has to do is feed into the model pessimistic estimates of the positive outcomes of using the process or discount them excessively. The computer will then spew out the desired answer justifying the decision.

Of course, this example is based upon the now infamous Ford E-coat affair discussed earlier in the book. As we saw, it took Ford over twenty years to install the corrosion protection process in all of its plants. The finance and accounting people who controlled the firm ensured that the numbers fed into their models would result in a conclusion that the process could not be justified.

Another classic example of "cooking the numbers" occurred in Vietnam. The Pentagon brass desired an optimistic attitude in the reporting of the war. Secretary of Defense Robert McNamara wanted the entire war effort quantified so that decisions would have the benefit of numbers. (By the way, McNamara had also installed the rigid cost analysis systems at Ford.) In order to present the war's status optimistically, statistical data—such as body counts and the number of Viet Cong—were systematically fabricated. The numbers were created simply in order to justify the actions and decisions of the White House and the Pentagon.

The General Electric Compressor Debacle

In 1988, General Electric had to take a $450 million pretax charge against earnings because its revolutionary refrigerator compressor proved a failure. The company voluntarily replaced 1.1 million defective compressors in refrigerators scattered around the world. When asked to describe the extent of the problem, one GE executive exclaimed, "How do you think the engineers at Thiokol felt when the [Space Shuttle] Challenger blew up?" The fiasco illustrates many of the risk versus security issues discussed in this chapter, particularly the need to follow the heuristics of incrementalism and diversification.

GE's problems began in 1981, when the appliance division's market share began to plummet. As a result of an outdated design from the 1950s, manufacturing costs were extremely high. While it took GE sixty-five minutes to build a compressor, rivals in Japan and Italy could make one in just twenty-one minutes. The net result was a huge price disadvantage. A consultant brought in to evaluate the situation told management that they would either have to buy foreign compressors or develop their own.

Management debated the issue and, to its credit, decided to build its own compressors. The company committed $120 million to build a brand new plant in Tennessee that would produce a revolutionary rotary compressor using one third the number of parts in conventional compressors. If it worked, it would leapfrog the foreign competition and help GE regain technological leadership in the competitive industry. Management bet its entire $2 billion refrigerator product line on successfully developing a largely untried technology.

This strategy, however, violated the principles of incremental change and diversification. Not only did the company bet its fortunes on a new technology (i.e., it used a revolutionary rather than an incremental approach), but it also placed the rotary compressor in all of its refrigerators (thereby violating the principle of diversification). Rather than move slowly and introduce the compressor in a single new refrigerator model, so that the risk would be limited, the company decided to install it in all of its refrigerators. Finally, rather than thoroughly testing the compressor under realistic conditions, managers hurried the process.

Why did the GE managers take such a huge risk? One explanation is that they perceived themselves to be in a loss position. With profits and market share declining rapidly in the highly profitable refrigerator market, something had to be done quickly. Because they framed the situation from a loss perspective, the management leaders were unconsciously willing to accept the huge risk. They even engaged in self-deception by refusing to acknowledge that such a risk existed. The division's chief said, "We told them it wasn't a moonshot. We knew how to make rotaries. We'd made 12 million of them in air conditioners." What the manager failed to realize was that making compressors for air conditioners was entirely different from making them for refrigerators. Refrigerator compressors must work harder, longer, and under more intense heat conditions than those of the small air conditioners in which the rotary compressors had previously been successfully used.

This frame of mind also caused managers to push the introduction of the new technology too fast. The company took shortcuts in the field testing of the new product. They ignored warnings by technicians that the motors showed signs of excessive heat. Curiously, the test reports coming back indicated that no documented failures had occurred. As one finance individual observed, this fact should have set off alarm bells—"It looked too good to be true." Another GE manager said that, in retrospect, "I'd have gone and found the lowest damn level people we had . . . and just sat down in their little cubbyholes and asked them, 'How are things today?' "

To its credit, General Electric did respond rapidly to the crisis once managers realized that their refrigerators were failing by the minute because of the bad compressors. When companies face product problems, all too frequently they will attempt to avoid taking a major short-term loss by ignoring the problem. In contrast to such shortsighted behavior, GE launched a total recall. Repair persons were sent to every purchaser that could be identified to replace the rotary compressor with a standard motor purchased from one of six foreign suppliers. As a result, no lawsuits have been filed, and the company's market share has held.

A number of factors to consider when making the risk/security judgment call include:

- When in a gain position, decision makers will tend to act in a risk-averse manner.

- When in a loss position, decision makers will tend to take greater than normal risks.

- Perfect security is never achieved and attempts to obtain it will increase, rather than decrease, risk because of the threat posed to others.

- People take excessive risks, such as gambling, in part to create thrills, increase arousal, and maintain an optimum level of stimulation.

- Risk is best managed by developing rules of thumb, such as:
  - If you don't know what to do, don't do anything.
  - Strive for incremental rather than quantum improvements.
  - Diversify, diversify, diversify.

But remember, situations vary. Warren Buffet built Berkshire Hathaway in part because he ignored the diversification rule and took a calculated risk. Similarly, the rule at NASA, "If you don't know what to do, don't do anything," cannot be followed in all circumstances. If your present path is leading irrevocably to a collision, any action is better than no action. Rules of thumb will differ according to the profession and the circumstances. They cannot be followed slavishly. Indeed, perhaps the best rule of all is just to use "good common sense."

6.

FINDING THE CAUSE

The young Navy test pilot had just taken off when the red warning light lit up like a flare: His jet had a hydraulic leak that would quickly make the controls useless. Immediately, he contacted the control tower, and it was decided that he should take the jet to 8,100 feet, aim it at the Chesapeake Bay, jettison the aircraft, and parachute down to land in the middle of the airfield. The pilot followed his instructions precisely. He took the plane to the correct altitude, pointed it in the right direction, held the appropriate air speed, and ejected. Then another major problem occurred. The parachute failed to open. As planned, he landed in the middle of the airfield. Unplanned was his 120 mile per hour airspeed. When medics picked up his body, it felt like a bag of fertilizer.

What caused the pilot's death? The other test pilots reasoned along the following lines: A chain of faults occurred. Someone screwed up and caused the hydraulic leak in the plane. Then, another guy failed to rig the parachute correctly. Next, the pilot failed to check the parachute. Finally, while plummeting toward the earth, the pilot had fifteen to twenty seconds to open the chute manually, which any guy with the "right stuff" could do. "Why just stare at the scenery coming up to smack you in the face?" they asked themselves. In the end, they decided that his death was his own fault.

In his classic book *The Right Stuff*, Tom Wolfe captured the mental gymnastics of fighter pilots who attempted to maintain their sanity as they watched classmate after classmate crash and burn. According to Navy statistics, in the 1950s and 1960s a one in four chance existed that an average pilot would crash and die in an aircraft during his expected twenty-year tour of duty. (These data exclude deaths during warfare, which are not considered accidental by the Air Force.) For test pilots, the risk was far greater. To handle the frequent funerals, the pilots had to deny the existence of chance as a killing factor. As Wolfe described the attitude, "There are no *accidents* and no fatal flaws in the machines; there are only pilots with the wrong stuff." The pilots must believe that blind Fate cannot kill them. Those pilots who survived blamed the victim in order to protect their own sanity.

People have an inborn need to understand why things happen. Knowing "why" helps us to solve problems and to anticipate, and perhaps influence, the future. Fortunately, the fundamental reasons for why things happen to us are limited to just a few sources. First, we can attribute our outcomes to ourselves; that is, because of our abilities and efforts, or lack thereof, good and bad things happen to us. Second, we can attribute what happens to factors external to ourselves, to chance/luck, to other people, perhaps to supernatural beings, or to the difficulty of the problem on which we are working. People also attempt to determine the cause of what happens to others. Again, the same internal versus external dichotomy is used. The cause of other people's good or bad fortune may come from inside them (i.e., from their ability and effort) or from external factors (i.e., luck or the nature of the task). To which of these sources we attribute an outcome will strongly influence our psychological well-being and even our subsequent actions. When an Air Force test pilot crashed and burned, his ex-colleagues attributed the cause to his lack of ability rather than to bad luck. An accident could happen to anyone. Thus, in order to handle the situation psychologically, the surviving pilots blamed the incident on the inferior skills of the dead aviator. Since they had the "right stuff," they could avoid similar disasters.

The attribution of "what caused what" is an important judgment call. Consider the story about the bartender from Pittsburgh. It seems that in addition to pushing drinks, he had a second job on the side collecting gambling debts. On one occasion a gambler from Nevada lost a great deal of money in the back room of the bar and left IOUs. Later he reneged on paying his debt, and the bartender was sent to Reno to collect it—at gunpoint if necessary. After a long search, he tracked the gambler down at his apartment. When the man answered the door, the bartender drew a gun and demanded the money. Shocked at the intrusion, the gambler said that he had to make arrangements to get the money and promised to pay that afternoon. The bartender believed him and left. Later that day, he returned, and when the door opened, he shoved a gun in the gambler's chest and pushed him back into the apartment. There, to his dismay, he found "cops behind every chair in the apartment."

The bartender told his story to Robyn Dawes while staying in a halfway house for first-time offenders. Dawes, a psychologist who specializes in the study of decision making, probed to find out to what the man attributed his incarceration. The man's reaction to the affair was moral outrage. How could that lowlife slimeball renege on his debt and then con the police into helping him? Then, unexpectedly, the bartender turned to Dawes and in a serious voice told him that he had learned his lesson. Surprised, Dawes listened eagerly for signs that the man had learned something positive from the experience. The bartender said that he would never go to jail a second time, "because I'll never go to Nevada again." As far as the bartender was concerned, it wasn't his fault. His incarceration did not result from bad luck or the intervention of a supernatural being out to get him. It was those people in Nevada. If he simply avoided Nevada, he was home free. By attributing his incarceration externally to those scoundrels in Nevada, and not to his own actions, he set himself up for continual run-ins with the law.

People tend to avoid attributing bad outcomes to their own actions. They rarely shoulder the blame for a failure. Indeed, when an individual owns up to a mistake, we are shocked. After the abortive Bay of Pigs invasion of Cuba, President Kennedy took public responsibility for the defeat. As a result, his popularity increased. Called the "pratfall effect," the same dramatic increase in popularity occurred with Attorney General Janet Reno after she took responsibility for the horrible death of more than seventy people in the Branch Davidian compound in Waco, Texas.

The tendency to attribute causality in order to put the best face on our actions results in "defensive attributions." These are exhibited in a wide range of settings, from the boardroom to the sports pages of newspapers. For example, a study was done in which researchers analyzed attributions for causality among athletes as recorded in eight newspapers for thirty-three major sporting events. Included in the analysis was the 1977 World Series and a variety of college and professional football games. Reactions as to why their team won or lost were analyzed in order to determine whether the players and coaches attributed the outcome to factors internal or external to their teams. A statement of internal cause for a win was represented by Billy Martin (the manager of the Yankees at the time), who said, "Piniella has done it all." Lou Piniella was the star of the 1977 World Series, and Martin felt that Piniella's performance was the reason for the win. An example of an external attribution after a loss was Ron Cey (the Dodgers third baseman) saying, "I think we've hit the ball all right. But I think we're unlucky." The results of the study showed that winning teams tended to ascribe the victory internally to themselves. In contrast, losing teams attributed their loss far more frequently to factors external to the team.

The determination of the underlying cause for events is vital for outstanding decision making. In one interview, I talked to the manager responsible for producing the LT-5 engine that powers the Corvette ZR-1. The prestige of Chevrolet and General Motors rested on successfully bringing to market this piece of engineering art—the largest, most complicated production automobile engine produced in the United States. As in all new projects, the launch of the LT-5 had its share of problems. The manager said that a vital component of successfully handling the difficulties was doing "root cause analysis." The goal of the procedure was to find the underlying cause, not the symptom, of the problem. He noted that too often the troubleshooting process stops at the symptom and never gets to the underlying reason for the difficulty. In order to combat the tendency to look only for superficial causes, he said, "You can never stop asking 'why?'"

In order to fix problems in the present and attempt to forecast the future in an uncertain environment, people attempt to identify the causes of outcomes. The attribution of cause forms one basis for making judgment calls. For example, President Bush and his advisers had to make a determination of the reason for the Iraqis' invasion of Kuwait. If the cause was an attempt by a country to retrieve land that was rightfully theirs, a low-key, measured response might have been appropriate. On the other hand, if the cause was the quest by a megalomanic tyrant (i.e., another Hitler) for supremacy of the entire Middle East, a much harsher response was required. The judgment call of using massive military force against Iraq was based in part upon the determination of the cause of Saddam Hussein's behavior.

On Illusory Correlation

In order to determine what causes what, people attempt to identify occasions when two events correlate with each other. In some instances, however, the association can be imaginary. "Illusory correlation" takes place when people erroneously believe that two events are strongly associated with each other. A classic illustration occurs when the predictions of stock market gurus incorrectly become associated with successful investing—an event that caused me much anguish a number of years ago.

The story of my tangle with a stock market guru began in late 1979, when my wife and I decided that we should start a family. It was a scary decision, and we knew that our lives would change in countless unpredictable ways. As a part of the planning process, it seemed prudent to begin an investment program in order to save for those extra expenses, such as college for the kids. No different from other decision makers discussed in this book, I suffered from overconfidence. I figured that if I spent some time on the topic, I could select stocks myself and do better than the average mutual fund. I assumed that my analytical abilities and hard work would enable me to succeed. I spent three months devouring everything that I could on the stock market. The net result was the development of a set of rules culled from the writings of the great investors, such as Benjamin Graham and Warren Buffet.

The stock market was hovering just below 1000. I just knew that it was about to break out to set new all-time highs. After opening an account with a discount brokerage firm in early 1980, I bought 100 shares of Consolidated Foods—now Sara Lee. The next day Joseph Granville, the famous financial guru, trumpeted to the world his great sell order. Obediently, the market fell like a rock. Only once before had the market fallen further: Black Tuesday in October 1929. At the time, Joseph Granville could move the market with a forecast. Using technical analysis, in which future prices are estimated based upon the past movements of the stock, Granville collected a large following of worshippers. Of course, the value of Consolidated Foods plunged. My reaction was horror. How could a guy who dressed in robes and tried to predict earthquakes have such a massive impact on the market?

I continued to follow my investing rules and persisted in buying stock for the next two years. Meanwhile, the market continued to go down. Then, some time in 1982, Joseph Granville again lifted his

voice to proclaim that a Great Depression was imminent and investors should sell all their stocks. By this time, however, he had lost his
following. Shortly after his second great sell signal, the market took
off on the huge rally of the 1980s, in which the Dow Jones Industrial
Average would move from below the 800 level to nearly 3000. So
much for market gurus like Granville. What happened to the investments that we made? By 1984, our investments had doubled in value,
and my wife and I decided to build a house, so we took our profits
and put them into bricks and mortar. Unfortunately, we built at the
peak of the oil boom in the Southwest, and within a couple of years
our housing investment was worth one-third less than what we paid
for it. Investing is indeed a humbling experience.

Despite great failures, such as Granville's second sell recommendation, why are so many otherwise bright people attracted to technical analysis and the various gurus who espouse it as an approach
to investing? One part of the answer lies in the illusory correlation
phenomenon. In the folklore of technical analysis, an explanation can
be given for every pattern of stock prices. The problem is that the
explanations are given after the fact. In statistics, this is called "over-
fitting." An equation can be developed after the fact to account for
any series of numbers—even if they are randomly generated. The
problem is that the same equation will be useless in predicting the
next series of numbers, if they are driven by chance.

In order to persuade us of their perspicacity, technical analysts
provide a number of historical examples in which this or that pattern
is followed by a certain change in stock prices. What they are doing
is giving examples of cases in which they achieved a "hit" with a
particular market indicator. That is, they made a prediction, and "lo
and behold," the market acted as expected. This pattern gives the
illusion that a strong correlation exists between the indicator and the
outcome. What the technical analysts forget to do is include the
"false alarms." That is, how often was the prediction made without
the expected change in stock price following it? Similarly, they avoid
giving us information on their "misses," or the times when the market changed when they made *no* forecast. In order to calculate a
correlation, you must look at the overall pattern of hits, false alarms,
and misses. The problem is that most people, even the highly educated, use only the frequency of hits to mentally determine the relationship between events. Thus, we are "set up" to believe the
prognostications of stock market gurus like Joseph Granville.

Illusory correlation can even exacerbate the boom and bust cycles
of the stock market. Watch the morning business show on CNN or

read the "Heard on the Street" column in *The Wall Street Journal*. Almost invariably, you will find the commentators going to great lengths to explain the cause for what is happening to the stock market as a whole or to an individual stock. These explanations can in fact influence the future action of a stock. A few years ago the person who wrote "Heard on the Street" used this phenomenon to his advantage. Before a column appeared, he would give tips to a friend, who would buy and sell stock in order to profit from the forthcoming change in prices. It didn't matter that his comments could have been (and probably were) worthless over the long term. If the accomplice knew what was said in the column before others did, money could be made, because in the short term people acted on its content.

A psychologist at Harvard, investigating the effects of providing explanations for stock prices, created an experimental market in which mock investors bought and sold stocks with play money. One group of investors actually received excerpts from the "Heard on the Street" column that purported to explain the movements in stocks. Another group received no such information. What he found was that the news stories influenced the investors, so that they became less cautious and created boom and bust cycles. In contrast, when only information on price was given, the novice investors would follow the old axiom of "buy low and sell high."

The boom and bust pattern was caused by investors heeding the analyst's explanations for the cause that fit the outcome after the fact. Because the environment is dynamic, in most instances both good and bad things are happening simultaneously to an individual company and to the economy as a whole. If a stock price moves up, the analyst identifies the good events as the cause. When the price goes down, the bad events must have caused the outcome. For any price movement a cause is found, when in fact the fluctuation is largely random. As a result, speculative bubbles can be created, which will eventually burst when another random fluctuation leads to a downturn and a cascade of newly pessimistic investors selling out. The outcome is a tendency to have boom and bust cycles in markets that result in part from people identifying illusory causes for price movements, which accentuate random fluctuations. Researchers have extensively investigated markets in experimental settings. Invariably, one finds boom and bust cycles occurring. In fact, when experienced business people are involved, the effects are often increased.

Illusory correlation is an insidious decision demon. The process begins when people believe that they have found the cause for something. In order to demonstrate the correctness of their judgment, they seek examples of cases in which the cause and effect occur together. For example, many argue that lie detector tests are valid devices for detecting deceitfulness. The explanation is that when people lie, they give off telltale physiological signs. Proponents will then cite examples of people who had failed polygraph tests and were afterward shown to have lied. What is forgotten is that they also need to look at the instances in which people were accused of lying when in fact they told the truth. Unfortunately, people rarely look for cases in which someone has been falsely accused. The evidence shows that polygraphs are no better than chance at detecting lying. The myth of the efficacy of lie detector tests belongs in the same category as technical analysis and astrology.

Historians, scientists, and journalists also succumb to illusory causation. A strong tendency exists for people to look for single causes to explain events. Similarly, we assume that big events must have had big causes. That is, the cause must somehow match the outcome. For example, today scientists are attempting to explain the demise of the dinosaurs. One theory holds that a gigantic meteor or comet hit the earth, changing the climate sufficiently to doom the species. The end of the dinosaur era was a big event—so the cause must have been a big event. Such a theory smacks of illusory causation. Indeed, the theory's opponents point out that the dinosaurs died out over a period that lasted millions of years—not quickly as implied by the meteor proponents.

Historians have a strong tendency to find single causes for major historical events. In looking for explanations for the rise of Nazism and the Third Reich, for example, historians have traced the origins back to the writings of various authors who enunciated the myth of Aryan supremacy. The process works well if one moves backward in time. But if one begins with the writings and attempts to extrapolate their impact forward, the projection of Nazism is only one of many outcomes that could have occurred. As noted by one critic, "Historians give an appearance of inevitability to an existing order by dragging into prominence the forces which have triumphed and thrusting into the background those which have been swallowed up."

An example of the "historical causation myth" influencing journalists occurred during the 1990–91 football season. In the fall of 1990, sportswriters wrote with awe of Joe Montana, the quarterback of the San Francisco 49ers. From 1981 to 1990, he led his team to four Super Bowl titles and eight out of ten Western Division, National Conference championships. Bob Oates, a sportswriter for the *Los*

Angeles Times, suggested that the cause for the 49ers' dominance was Joe Montana. Agreeing with one of Montana's teammates who had played in both leagues, Oates even suggested that the sole reason the National Conference won more Super Bowls during the 1980s than the American Conference was Joe Montana. The attribution of super-human capabilities to Joe Montana could affect a number of high-stakes decisions, from the betting patterns of high-rolling gamblers to the trading of players by management.

But consider the issue carefully. How likely is it that one player could account for the fact that the National Conference won eight out of ten Super Bowls from 1981 to 1990? Montana's team was involved in only four of the wins. Montana is a great quarterback. He is a likable celebrity. But he is not endowed with superhuman qualities. His teammate and the sportswriter were merely succumbing to the "historical causation myth." These individuals were looking for a singular reason for the 49ers' success, and Joe Montana was seen to be that cause. (By the way, the 49ers lost in the NFC Championship in 1991 to the New York Giants, in a game in which Montana was harassed continually and effectively by the Giants' defensive team.)

"Let's Sue the Bastards!"

The culture of the United States subscribes to the illusion that all events have causes that can be controlled. Because of the belief that unhappy events simply do not occur as a result of bad luck or chance, a cause must be found. Such thinking helps to create the highly liti-gious atmosphere that exists in America. The societal cost of exces-sive litigation is massive. Indeed, when the number of attorneys per capita in the United States is compared to that in Japan, we have a partial explanation for that society's high economic productivity. The United States has 279 attorneys per 100,000 people, in compari-son to only 11 in Japan. Americans want to find someone to blame even under the most peculiar circumstances—such as when giant mudslides race down mountainsides to inundate entire neighbor-hoods.

Towering above Los Angeles are the San Gabriel Mountains. Geo-logically in their youth, the mountains are still growing. Because they persist in growing taller, these mountains continually shed ma-terial as their sides disintegrate. As the city sprawls up the side of the range, homes are built on precipitous and crumbling slopes. Therein lies the rub—when the conditions are right, entire sides of mountains can begin to move, fast.

One California family, the Genofiles, lived in Shields Canyon, high above Los Angeles. On one fateful rainy night, they were awakened by a crash of thunder. Looking outside, they could see in the lightning flashes a "big black thing coming at us, rolling, rolling with a lot of water in front of it, pushing the water, this big black thing. It was just one big black hill coming toward us." The family was witnessing a calamitous freak of nature: a debris flow. Resembling fresh concrete, debris flows consist of water and solid material, laced with car-sized boulders. They periodically hurtle down the sides of the San Gabriels. A general contractor, Bob Genofile was aware of the potential problem and had built his house out of steel-reinforced concrete block to resemble a dam. The debris flow hit the house and entered like "the Blob" through the doors and windows, rapidly filling the interior. The family members huddled together on a bed, which began to rise toward the ceiling as the mass seeped in and lifted it. Within six minutes the house was filled. The muck stopped at the chins of the children, who had been caught between the bed and the wall.

Neighbors and rescuers assumed the worst when they saw the house seemingly filled to the ceilings with muck. The family, however, survived. They cleaned out the house, built a second story (which became their new home), and sued the city—claiming that the debris basins above them had not been cleaned and were poorly designed. The city settled for $337,500. As far as the Genofiles were concerned, it wasn't their fault that the house was ruined. It was the city's.

The debris flows occur irregularly—roughly once every ten years or so, and then from different parts of the mountain range. Why they occur is a scientific curiosity. Growing on the steeply angled ridges is chaparral, a dense, oily bush that nearly explodes when exposed to fire. Indeed, its life cycle depends upon fire, because its seeds will not germinate unless exposed to extreme heat. When the dry Santa Ana winds come in the fall, the chaparral is on the brink. A spark will set it off, and wildfires are indigenous to the landscape of the San Gabriels. After a fire has consumed the chaparral, a thin layer of ash covers the soil and nothing exists to bind it together. The fine soil tumbles down the slopes and begins to collect. Rains may come and add more material, called ravel. In addition, the ash from the chaparral reacts with the soil to create a kind of waterproof coating. Rain doesn't soak through; rather, it is repelled. As a result, when it rains, the water begins to run extremely fast over the ash.

While Los Angeles is arid and averages only 15 inches of rain a year, the San Gabriels can receive incredible torrents in short time periods. For example, in 1969, 39 inches of rain fell in less than nine days. Aperiodically, conditions coalesce to create catastrophe. First, fires occur and burn the chaparral. Next, a series of storms descends from the Pacific and dumps massive quantities of water into the mountains. The water sweeps over the ash. It forms streams, which are funneled toward canyons where their volume is multiplied. The stampeding water then picks up the ravel collected over the decades. The huge mass shoots out of the canyons to engulf everything in its path—housing developments included.

What we have here is a natural phenomenon of massive proportions that has been occurring for eons. Representing a recent addition to the geological landscape, human beings have come along and decided that they can control the problem with assorted barriers and catch-basins. Occasionally, however, events coalesce to such a point that the remedies pall in comparison to the natural forces. Such a situation occurred in 1968. Twenty thousand acres of chaparral burned above the town of Glendora. The city manager knew what would happen and went to every federal agency he could think of to get assistance to prevent a disaster. The reaction of the feds was that they could help only *after* the disaster occurred. He then went to the townspeople. He held town meetings and tried to persuade them to take action to avoid the inevitable. He was called an alarmist. The following January the rains came, and a gigantic debris flow hit the town. The townspeople then sued the city government for not doing enough—and won! What was the cause of the devastation? As far as the townspeople of Glendora were concerned, they were certainly not the cause. When the gigantic losses occurred, a great need existed to place blame, and the city government was a handy choice.

The ability to successfully sue others for accidental outcomes is a fact of life in the United States. Here are just a few examples. A seventeen-year-old college student sued a food company for allowing a beetle to get into a jar of yogurt. In her lawsuit, she claimed that when she pulled the dead beetle from her mouth, she became hysterical and went into shock. Later, her hair began falling out. She then became partially bald, resulting in extreme self-consciousness. This caused her to drop out of school and become a recluse. For her psychic injury, the jury awarded her $425,000. Now, I remember once opening a hamburger purchased from a regional burger chain and finding a large fly lovingly cooked into the beef patty. You know, my hair is thinning; I wonder. . . .

Then there was the case of the commercial jet that suddenly rolled over and plunged six miles toward earth before the pilot gained control. Three passengers sued for emotional distress and averaged over $40,000 in compensation each. Even more lucrative was the incident in which a construction worker was hit on the head by a one-pound piece of metal accidentally dropped by a co-worker. He had on his helmet and suffered no actual injury. He complained, though, of headaches, dizziness, and tightness of the forehead. A psychiatrist diagnosed the problem as unconscious fear and apprehension of going back to work. The company settled for $87,000, back pay, and medical expenses.

In another case, a seven-year-old boy named Ryan darted into the street on a bicycle. He collided with a city truck. As a result of the accident, the driver claimed that he injured his back when attempting to avoid the child. The city then sued the boy's family in order to cover its costs for workman's compensation and medical expenses. In writing about the incident, a professor at Berkeley noted that one day he was thinking about the lawsuit while shaving. He was pondering the question, "Don't accidents sometimes just happen and no one is at fault?" when he nicked himself. Upon seeing his own blood, he became dizzy. Lying down would require him to miss an hour of work, and he'd have to postpone some income-producing activities. Clearly, this was Ryan's fault. Certainly, he was due compensation. On the other hand, perhaps it was the actions of the plaintiff that caused the loss of income. From another viewpoint, however, if he hadn't been reading the newspaper, he would never have nicked himself. The manufacturer of the razor also had a hand in the problem. Warnings should be on the label to avoid daydreaming while shaving. As he reached for the phone to call his attorney, yet another thought hit him. Perhaps my lawsuit causes someone else pain, and they launch a countersuit. Finally, he simply got up to go to class. As he said, "Luck was with me, though. Through nobody's fault but my own, I was teaching *Alice in Wonderland* that day."

Even though the curious world of lawsuits may sometimes have the appearance of a legal *Wonderland*, high-stakes decisions are made by plaintiffs, judges, and juries. By ignoring the effects of chance and by finding blame for accidents when none exists, our legal system threatens the vitality of commerce in the United States.

Availability and Causation

When searching for a cause, we sometimes encounter another villain —the availability bias. This commonly used rule of thumb explains some misconceptions about a current high-stakes decision faced in the United States. What should we do about homelessness? In order to answer the question, one must begin by asking why we have so many homeless. In 1990, estimates of the number of homeless ranged from 1 to 4 million. One frequently given explanation for the explosion in the number of homeless people in the 1980s was the deinstitutionalization of the mentally ill. In 1986, *Newsweek* magazine in a headline story argued that the homeless are "America's castoffs— turned away from mental institutions and into the streets." In reality, however, the mentally ill appear to make up at maximum one third of the homeless.

Why do so many people attribute the cause of homelessness to mental illness, or that other affliction, drug addiction? The answer probably lies in what has been termed the "availability heuristic." When we attempt to determine the cause for an event, we will tend to search our memory for possible answers. Those thoughts most easily recalled from memory will be the ones selected for examination as causes. The problem is that what is available in memory is highly biased; in particular, information that is highly vivid and salient is most easily remembered. Think about the times you have encountered homeless people. Are there not instances in which you observe someone acting in a bizarre and unusual manner? Those who are mentally ill and homeless frequently act weirdly. They stand out and are remembered. When a person attempts to analyze the causes of homelessness, the memory of the strange street person comes to mind. The cause is then erroneously deduced—i.e., homelessness results from the deinstitutionalization of the mentally ill.

The availability bias can strongly influence judgments. Which factor causes more deaths in the United States—stomach cancer or motor vehicle accidents? In one study, the authors found that 86 percent of the respondents judged motor vehicle accidents to be the more frequent cause. In reality, more than twice as many deaths per thousand result from stomach cancer than from motor vehicle accidents. Why does such an enormous misperception occur? The answer probably lies in the frequency with which such deaths are reported in newspapers. For each occasion when stomach cancer is reported as the cause of death, auto accidents are identified in 137 cases. Instances in which auto accidents led to death are far more available in memory because of their greater publicity. As a result, we more frequently ascribe them as the cause of death than the unpublicized malady of stomach cancer.

In addition to publicity variables leading to availability biases, it has been found that more recent information tends to be remembered better than older information. Decisions within the corporate environment have been found to be influenced by such recent events. For example, one chemical company found that when its engineers looked for the cause of problems, they tended to discover them in the most recently encountered difficulties. After a series of misdiagnoses had cost the company a great deal of money, managers began to analyze carefully how the engineers were reaching their decisions. They found a 15 to 50 percent greater tendency to attribute the cause to problems that had occurred in the recent past, leading to losses averaging about $2.5 million a year.

The Internal Revenue Service slyly uses the recency effect in its efforts to discourage tax fraud. The agency shows a pattern of indicting several highly visible tax cheaters each March. The goal is to make strongly available in memory the potential consequences of cheating on tax returns just prior to the due date for tax filing. Similarly, companies have found that sales personnel attempt to persuade customers to buy the products on which they had most recently received training.

In sum, using one's memory to identify a cause is a chancy proposition. The key to avoiding availability bias is to recognize its existence. In addition, decision makers need to engage in a sufficient search for information to ensure that they have the correct facts on paper as well as in their heads.

The Resemblance Criterion and Causality

In 1843, John Stuart Mill observed that people are prejudiced by the belief that "the conditions of a phenomenon must *resemble* the phenomenon." As a result of the use of this "resemblance criterion," people assume that complex events must have complex causes. Similarly, emotional outcomes must have emotional causes. The magical thinking of "prescientific" societies illustrates the resemblance fallacy. For example, in the Azande culture, ringworm was cured by the use of fowl excrement. At first glimpse, one might assume that the Azande developed the procedure over thousands of years of trial and error learning. Hardly. The answer is that bird crap looks just like a ringworm infection. Therefore, for a civilization working via the resemblance fallacy, the foul material must cure the disease. Similarly, the cure for epilepsy was the burnt skull of the red bush monkey. It seems that the bush monkey moves in a spastic manner similar to those having convulsions.

Even in nineteenth-century Western medicine, the resemblance criterion continued in the guise of what was called "the doctrine of signatures." The essence of the doctrine was the idea that natural substances possessing medicinal value would have some external identification with the diseases they would remedy. As a result, the lungs of a fox were fed to those with asthma. Similarly, jaundice was treated by turmeric, whose yellow color matches that of the diseased victim. Early in the twentieth century, Walter Reed was lambasted by newspapers for his ridiculous idea that yellow fever could be caused by mosquitoes. How could something so small cause such a terrible disease?

The Fundamental Attribution Error

Test pilots, race car drivers, and others who hold the firm belief that accidents "don't just happen" but that the victim must have badly screwed up, act as though they believe in a "just world." Indeed, much of the population at large assumes that others get what they deserve in order to support a belief in an orderly and predictable environment. Such a belief allows us to make plans and to invest in ourselves in order to achieve long-range goals. In a purely whimsical world, it would not make much sense to commit oneself to long-term projects. As a result, we choose to act as though we live in a world in which people don't die needlessly and do reap the rewards of all their efforts. While the belief in a just world gives us psychological comfort and makes it possible to develop long-range plans, it also can lead to highly dysfunctional actions. The tendency to blame the victim is one outgrowth of such thinking.

The twenty-two-year-old woman was standing in the parking lot of a Fort Lauderdale restaurant when she was approached by a drifter from Georgia. She claimed that he kidnapped her at knife-point and raped her twice. The defense argued that she provoked the attack by wearing a white lace mini-skirt, a green tank top, and no underwear. The Florida jury agreed with the accused and found him innocent, based upon the reasoning that she had solicited sex. Said the male jury foreman, "We all feel she asked for it for the way she was dressed." Certainly, the young woman could have been more prudent in her choice of attire. She did not, however, go to the restaurant with the intention of having a guy threaten to kill her with a knife and rape her. But, didn't she contribute to the crime by dressing scantily? Aren't women socialized to wear panties and keep their knees together? One reason why such precautions are necessary is to have a defense should they become a victim.

Victim-bashing extends throughout the legal system and society. Consider the case of the beautiful model Marla Hanson. After she resisted her landlord's advances, he sent two goons out to slash her face with a razor. At his trial the defense attorney claimed, based upon no evidence whatsoever, that Hanson "preyed on men." The judge went along with a defense line of questioning in which she was made to define an anatomical obscenity that her landlord used to describe her. Occurring in New York City, the degrading trial prompted Mayor Koch to ask publicly: "How many times must a victim be victimized?"

Some authors have argued that this phenomenon extends to how society deals with a variety of its problems. The bias can be subtle, as when well-meaning liberal-minded people argue that poverty occurs because some people are different and can't help being poor. Or, that racial inequality occurs because black families are abandoned by their male members. Just as the test pilots blamed their fellow pilot for his own death, juries blame women for rape, and society blames victims for their problems.

The "blaming-the-victim" phenomenon represents but one manifestation of a larger tendency called the "fundamental attribution error." When observing and evaluating others (particularly those we don't know), we tend to attribute the cause of their misfortunes to the people themselves. Thus, women are raped because they asked for it. A group is discriminated against because it lacks the ability or motivation to succeed. A coach is fired after a losing season because he failed properly to prepare and manage the team. In such cases, forces external to the person are ignored as causes. Less attention is placed on the fact that the rapist had a knife, that the minority group for centuries has received inferior education, or that the team had a series of injuries to key players during the season.

What happens when circumstances force people to engage in actions that others find abhorrent? Again, the fundamental attribution error tends to hold. Consider Peter Arnett's high-stakes decision to remain in Iraq in order to report for CNN on the Persian Gulf war. He was the only U.S. newsperson to stay on. While his newscasts on CNN were heavily censored, he attempted to describe whatever he was allowed to see. Arnett had previously reported with distinction on the Vietnam War: he covered some of the fiercest battles and obtained the unforgettable words of a U.S. Army officer, "It was necessary to destroy the village in order to save it." Risking his life again to report the news from Iraq, Arnett was pilloried for his actions. A congressman from Pennsylvania stated that Arnett was to Saddam what Goebbels was to Hitler. A Republican senator from Wyoming, Alan K. Simpson, called Arnett an Iraqi "sympathizer." CNN switchboards in Atlanta buzzed with callers asking why the network was broadcasting Iraqi propaganda.

After the war ended, Arnett appeared on the "Larry King Live" talk show. King asked Arnett how it felt to have people attacking you for doing your job. Arnett responded simply: "It comes with being a reporter. They want to kill the messenger." Those angry at Arnett were exhibiting the fundamental attribution error. They were ignoring the censorship shackles placed on Arnett, as well as his well-chosen barbs that slipped past Iraqi censors. In one case, he reported on a factory that had been bombed to smithereens. Iraq claimed that the factory had produced baby milk and that numerous civilian casualties resulted from the attack; the United States claimed that it was manufacturing poison gas. Reporting from the scene with an Iraqi censor at his elbow, Arnett was able to tell the world that the factory's "BABY MILK" signs were carefully printed in English. Unfortunately, most missed Arnett's subtle message. Just as we tend to blame victims for their misfortunes, we also blame messengers for the bad news that they bring.

What do we do about national problems, such as poverty in the United States? How should we respond to news reporters, whistleblowers, and others who bring us news that makes us uncomfortable about ourselves? Our understanding of such problems will influence how we respond to them, and how we react has high-stakes implications. To take just one example, billions of dollars are being spent to reduce poverty in the United States. If the fundamental causes are misunderstood, it is unlikely that the enormous spending programs will have any beneficial impact.

154 · JUDGMENT CALLS

Organizational Blame

When negative things happen to organizations, the people who run them attribute blame so as to minimize the organization's connection to the happening. Consider the annual report. This document presents the financial statements of a firm and includes the income statement, balance sheet, and funds flow statement. The Financial Accounting Standards Board (FASB), through its statements of "generally accepted accounting principles," specifies what information goes into the annual report. Ultimately, all of this is controlled by the Securities and Exchange Commission. With so many regulatory bodies involved, one might assume that questionable rationalizations would not find their way into these documents.

Two business professors did a study of annual reports in order to analyze the pattern of attributions made in the "Letters to Shareholders" portion of the reports. A total of 181 letters were analyzed. In these letters, management can describe verbally what happened in the previous year and give explanations for the company's performance. So, an example of a negative outcome attributed to external causes would read: "With the marked slowdown in building activity, there was a drastic decline in orders." An example of a positive outcome attributed to internal causes would read: "During the fourth quarter, the subsidiary's management lowered production costs substantially and recorded a strong operating profit."

As expected, the results of the study showed a pattern of defensive attributions. Favorable outcomes were attributed more frequently to internal causes (61 percent) than to external causes (39 percent). In contrast, unfavorable outcomes were attributed more frequently to external causes (59 percent) than to internal causes (41 percent). The idea that corporate management is hard-nosed and free of the human desire to protect its image is a myth. Corporations attempt to project and protect their institutional ego just as you and I seek to maintain our own self-image. In addition, it can be much less expensive to blame a person for a major accident. In the U.S.S. *Iowa* gun turret explosion, as we saw earlier, the Navy tried to pin the blame on a dead sailor. This way the Navy could potentially avoid launching a massive investigation of the gunpowder that fires the shells from the 16-inch guns. If the powder were found to be the cause, the costs of replacement would be extremely high.

Similarly, when an airplane accident occurs, strong pressures exist to place blame on human error rather than on design flaws.

Consider United Airlines Flight #811 flying from Honolulu to Auckland, New Zealand, in February 1989. The locks on the 747's cargo door failed, and the explosive depressurization sucked out ten passengers 23,000 feet above the Pacific Ocean. Management and the Federal Aviation Administration blamed the incident on the human error of maintenance workers when they closed the door. Yet the plucky detective work of one of the victim's parents revealed that management had ample warning of problems in the electrical system of the 747's cargo door. After a manned submersible vessel recovered the door from 14,200 feet of water, it was determined that the "probable cause" of the accident was "a faulty switch or wiring in the door control system. . . . " The premature attribution of cause to the maintenance workers represents a case in which it was cheaper and more face-saving to blame the incident on human error than on a design flaw in the door itself.

This pattern was seen earlier, in the spring of 1987, in the case of the Zeebrugge ferry that sank in the English Channel, killing scores of people. A wave of water passed through the open bow doors, causing the boat to be swamped. Again, human error was cited as the reason the bow doors were not closed. Yet the ferry between Zeebrugge, Belgium, and Dover, England, had left port for years with the doors open, and management knew of the procedure. Again, the tendency was to blame worker carelessness for an accident rather than look to management or equipment problems. Blaming accidents on worker error is frequently a means for managers to avoid looking at their own actions as the cause of a problem.

But the ability of organizations to reveal self-protective behavior is perhaps best seen in the plight of whistle-blowers. Just as messengers in ancient Greece were beheaded for bringing back bad news, so too are whistle-blowers blamed for bringing the attention of outside observers to problems within an organization. David Burns was a senior staff member at the Department of Housing and Urban Development's (HUD) New York office. Part of Burns's job involved approving housing projects. In one case he turned down a project for the elderly because he believed that it would create an undue concentration of subsidized housing in one area. As Burns tells the story, afterward, his boss pressured him to reverse his decision, which he finally did.

A couple of years later, after the Bush administration had come into power and his boss had left, Burns asked permission from his superiors to go public and report the pressure. It was 1989, and the HUD scandals were headline news. As a result of his actions, a neighborhood group successfully sued to block the construction. Burns's views were supported by the courts. The problem was that he quickly went into limbo in his own agency. The week after going public, Burns suddenly began to be excluded from senior staff meetings he had recently attended. He became an outcast at HUD. As he said, "For speaking out, I am looked at as an unstable oddball by the HUD leadership in New York." In sum, the need to avoid self-blame is ubiquitous, and it infects decisions made in organizations as well as those made by individuals.

Outcome Severity and Blame

When people assign blame, they tend to attribute greater responsibility as the severity of an outcome increases. Consider the Audi "sudden acceleration syndrome" scare. Early in 1986, reports began to filter in of possible problems with Audis, as well as with other cars having automatic transmissions. It was charged that they would accelerate suddenly and uncontrollably, causing accidents and deaths. The charges achieved national prominence in November 1986, when CBS's "60 Minutes" did a feature on the Audi and the sudden acceleration syndrome (SAS). The heart-rending story was told of a six-year-old boy who got out of an Audi 5000S to open the garage door. As his mother described it, she put her foot on the brake, shifted into "drive," and the Audi suddenly surged forward. Joshua was in front of the car and was fatally crushed when it crashed into the back wall of the garage.

After the CBS documentary, reports of SAS flooded the National Highway Safety Administration, and Audi's sales plummeted. In 1985, the German company had sold over 74,000 cars in the United States; by 1988, sales had plunged to less than 23,000. My wife and I happened to own an Audi 5000S at the time, and we were concerned. So I talked to some friends who are mechanical engineers. Their reaction was that there was nothing wrong with the car. It was a question of driver's error. The victims were simply putting their foot on the accelerator without realizing it. The same phenomenon even occurs to inexperienced racing car drivers. We were told to go out and buy used Audis if we wanted a great car for a low price. The clamor finally subsided in 1989 when the National Highway Safety Administration released a report finding that SAS was caused by driver error and not by any mechanical problem.

What was happening here? Were the victims lying? In some cases they may have been. In most instances, though, they were engaging in a defensive attribution process. It is difficult to admit that you wrecked a $20,000 + car because you mistook the accelerator for the brake. Or for a mother to allow herself to believe that she was responsible for killing her own son. People will naturally act defensively to avoid the blame. Particularly when combined with the publicity about SAS, it was easy to fall into the trap of attributing blame elsewhere. There was just enough ambiguity in the situation to allow SAS victims to charge that the car, not themselves, had caused the accident.

The same pattern of defensive attribution is frequently found in the memoirs of famous individuals. Richard Nixon in his memoirs blamed the U.S. Congress for losing the Vietnam War. Just enough ambiguity resided in the cause of South Vietnam's downfall to allow him to react defensively. Nixon was elected president because he promised to end the war. By attributing responsibility to Congress for the loss, he avoided blame to himself and his administration for allowing the war to continue for over four years after his election.

The Zone of Ambiguity and Causality

In order to anticipate the future and to believe in a just world, people attempt to identify the causes for outcomes. While searching for the answer to why something happened, most of us attempt to avoid blaming ourselves. In the final analysis, however, the reality principle must hold. If our attributions become too unrealistic, we are subject to ridicule. In addition, our future actions will become increasingly dysfunctional because they are based on false assumptions. Motivated distortions occur within that zone of ambiguity where judgment calls take place.

But blame has to be apportioned cautiously. Consider the case of the spotted owl. In 1990, the U.S. Fish and Wildlife Service placed the bird on the list of threatened species. As a result, it would have to be protected: over 8 million acres of forests would be set aside, resulting in the loss of over thirty thousand jobs in the Pacific Northwest by 1995. As one would expect, those whose livelihoods depend upon collecting timber from the forests were angry and frightened. How could a small, nocturnal bird, which few people ever even see, cost them their jobs?

Men and women in the timber industry wondered whom or what they should blame if their jobs vanished. A union leader pondered the question. Is it the owl? Is it the environmentalists, who want to see thousands of acres of forest protected? Is it the timber industry itself? Earlier on in the same region, furriers killed off their own livelihood by overhunting the fur-bearing animals living there. Then, in the gold rush days, prospectors did the same by depleting the gold. The pattern seems to be repeating itself today. A union leader agonized over the dilemma:

> What do I tell them, "It's going to be O.K."? I can't. Who do I blame? Do I blame the industry for raping the lands in the East and raping the lands in the West 50 years ago and not replanting? Do I blame my father? Do I blame my grandfather? Do I blame myself for not reading the paper every single night and being critically involved in these issues? How do I answer these people?"

Finding the cause, placing blame, and determining responsibility are all part of the same process. Because we are human, we attempt to identify the cause for outcomes. Most of the time we accomplish the task with accuracy. But in that zone of ambiguity where judgment calls take place, we have problems. Do we attribute the cause to ourselves, to others, or to luck and chance? Some principles to consider when searching for the correct cause include:

- Identify the *underlying* cause, not just the obvious symptom, in order to solve problems and to anticipate and influence the future.

- Avoid the tendency to attribute the cause for bad outcomes to situational factors and the cause for good outcomes to yourself.

- Do not assume that big events (e.g., the start of a war) result from single, big causes.

- Recognize that the cause for an outcome is not necessarily the factor most available in memory.

- The cause for an event is often erroneously perceived to be that thing most resembling the event.

- Placing too much reliance on the belief that the world is just and victims get what they deserve can result in errors of judgment.

- When people assign blame, they often erroneously attribute greater responsibility as the severity of the outcome increases.

- Distortions of causality occur more frequently when the stakes are high and outcomes lie in that zone of ambiguity where judgment calls occur.

7.
CHANCE VERSUS CONTROL

In *One Day in the Life of Ivan Denisovich,* Alexander Solzhenitsyn described the marginal existence of those living in the Stalin work camps. Through the eyes of prisoner #S-854, in gang #104, Solzhenitsyn vividly depicted the horrible conditions of the Siberian camps. The prisoner, nicknamed Shukhov, was about forty years old, balding, and missing half his teeth. He was convicted under Article 58, the dreaded Stalinist law that sentenced people to prison camps based upon the mere suspicion of disloyalty or disaffection. It seems that during a battle in World War II, Shukhov's military unit had been lost behind German lines. With nearly everyone dead, he had managed to escape and return to the Russian line, only to be picked up as a traitor.

Inside the camp, life was regimented but unpredictable. The daily routines could be broken at any time by the mercurial guards—who undoubtedly hated being there as much as the prisoners. A mason, Shukhov spent his days building walls in −20 degree Fahrenheit temperatures. In order to survive, the prisoners collected anything not tied down. On the day described, Shukhov found a piece of scrap steel, which at great risk he hid in his clothing. If the guards found it, he would surely be placed in the cooler. The food in camp was terrible, but the mess hall was wonderfully steamy and warm. Danger lurked even there, though, because a prisoner had to guard his bowl of gruel. The few hundred putrid calories were needed for the marches. Indeed, one of Shukhov's prized possessions was his spoon, which he carried at all times carefully hidden in his boot. The story concludes as the day ends with Shukhov about to fall asleep in his bunk bed. On the last page of the book, Solzhenitsyn describes in a most unexpected way the prisoner's feelings as he drifted off to sleep:

> Shukhov went to sleep, and he was very happy. He'd had a lot of luck today. They hadn't put him in the cooler. The gang hadn't been chased out to work in the Socialist Development Project. He'd finagled an extra bowl of mush at noon. The boss had gotten them good rates for their work. He'd felt good making the wall. They hadn't found that piece of steel in the frisk. Caesar had paid him off in the evening. He'd bought some tobacco. And he'd gotten over that sickness.

> Nothing had spoiled the day and it had been almost happy.

> There were three thousand six hundred and fifty-three days like this in his sentence, from reveille to lights out.

> The three extra ones were because of the leap years . . .

The publication of *One Day in the Life of Ivan Denisovich* created international outrage against the Soviet work camps during the Stalin years. Yet the book ends with the main character, Shukhov, going to bed happy because he had good luck that day. In his capricious and uncertain environment, Shukhov knew that he had little control and attributed his good day to luck.

Chance is a harsh taskmaster. Consider Harvey Oxenhorn. His major goal in life was to publish his book, *Tuning the Rig*. The story of his trip on an early twentieth-century sailing vessel to chart the migratory patterns of whales around Greenland, the book took years to write and longer to publish. He wrote at night and on weekends while working a demanding job. After signing a contract with one publisher, Oxenhorn encountered bad luck when his editor suddenly quit, the publishing firm was taken over, and the new management demanded that he return his advance. His agent recommended that he drop the project after other publishers turned the book down. But Oxenhorn contacted new agents, who refused even to read the manuscript. Finally, he found one sympathetic agent who fell in love with the book. Its publication by Harper & Row was a joyous occasion and ample reward for a writer who had persevered.

The day after publication, the new author drove off to visit his mother, carrying Mother's Day presents, including copies of his book. On the road to her house, an oncoming car crossed into his lane, slammed into his vehicle, and killed him. I read about Harvey Oxenhorn in a *New York Times* book essay. As a writer, I felt a strong kinship with him. Reading the essay, I increasingly identified with his aspirations and motivations. Then I reached the description of his untimely death, and I was devastated. How could "chance" rob us of this person at such a time? As John Kennedy once said, "Life is not fair."

On the other hand, Fate equally often brings good fortune. For example, why did the Apollo spacecraft that successfully landed men on the Moon have a three-person crew? One astronaut had to remain in the command capsule that circled the Moon. It then took two men to fly the lunar module to the Moon, land it, and blast it back to the command capsule. The decision to use three people apparently was carefully planned based upon the needs of the mission—or was it?

In reality, the decision was based upon completely different reasoning. The plan was developed in 1960: NASA anticipated flying a spacecraft directly from the earth to the Moon, landing it, and then flying the same ship back to the earth. At that point, computers were still highly primitive. In order to monitor the systems on the spacecraft, someone would have to be awake at all times. Thus, a decision was made to use Navy shifts of four hours on and eight hours off, which required a three-man crew. As a result, decisions were made to design the command module for three people. A whole series of other decisions then followed, based upon this requirement. It was not until several years later that scientists realized that going directly to the Moon and back in the same rocketship was impossible. It was totally fortuitous that the early intention to employ three people worked perfectly for the new plan of first going into a lunar orbit, then sending down a separate spacecraft to the Moon, and finally flying back to the command module in another rocket.

The brief stories of Shukhov, Harvey Oxenhorn, and the Apollo moon rocket all deal with the impact of good and bad luck in high-stakes contexts. Coming to terms with "chance," however, is something that human beings have great difficulty doing. Because of our discomfort with happenstance, we try to deny it, avoid it, and control it. So strong is our antipathy to the idea that outcomes can result in part from good or bad luck that we develop elaborate explanations for purely chance events. For example, during World War II, the people in London created theories to explain the pattern of German bombing during the Blitz. By deducing the German strike targets from the patterns, they attempted to predict where the next bomb would land. In reality, aside from such targets as the Docks, the Germans were merely aiming at London. It was purely chance where the bombs fell within the city.

People have a strong need to feel as though they control the events that happen to them. This need for control is violated, however, if too large a role is left for chance to determine what happens to us. As we saw in the last chapter, test pilots gain control by denying the existence of bad luck. In their minds, past crashes resulted from human error that they would be able to avoid. Londoners gained control by developing theories to explain the pattern of Nazi bombing. Once the pattern was discerned, they could act appropriately. People act as though they live in a deterministic world in which they gain control by identifying the underlying causes of outcomes—even if the outcomes themselves are totally unpredictable. The net result of this "creeping determinism" is a set of actions that give psychological comfort to people, but that can have quite detrimental effects on our decisions.

In most instances, the denial of chance is innocuous. In general, our good luck rituals and charms create few problems. But creeping determinism and the need for control can also lead people to make poor decisions. For example, people waste money when they hire astrologers, Tarot card readers, and other soothsayers. At a more sinister level, the desire for control, and the laying of blame, can lead to such evils as pogroms, when Jews were blamed for the Black Death during the Middle Ages.

Another manifestation of creeping determinism is the "illusion of control." Let's examine this peculiar phenomenon in more detail.

The Illusion of Control

The Las Vegas gambler took a deep breath and blew against the dice before he rolled them each time. A man standing next to him at the craps table asked, "Do you think that brings you luck?" The gambler replied, "I know it does. Las Vegas has a very dry climate, right?" "Right," the observer said, nodding. "So, the dice are usually very dry. I have a very damp breath, and I always exhale against a six and an ace. That not only gives the six and ace a little extra weight but makes them adhere to the table when they roll across it. The opposite sides come up—and the opposite side of a six and ace are an ace and a six."

"Does it really work?" the observer asked.

The gambler turned to him, and in all sincerity said, "Well, not all the time. The load of condensation isn't quite heavy enough. But I've been on a hot liquid diet all day, and tonight ought to be the time I break the bank."

The craps player was attempting to control a purely chance event by creating an elaborate strategy that had absolutely no chance of success. What resulted was an illusion of control, in which his expectation of success was inappropriately higher than objective probability warranted. This is a type of overconfidence that strikes most of us at one time or another. Illustrations are frequently found in the gambling world. In the realm of dice, slot machines, and roulette wheels, many people attempt to control events that are completely governed by pure chance. In fact, researchers have done experiments on how the illusion of control influences gamblers.

Suppose that you were given a chance to enter a lottery for the next Super Bowl. It costs $1 and gives you a chance to win $50. After you agree to enter the contest and pay your money, one of two things happens: (a) you are allowed to reach into a bowl to pick out your ticket, or (b) you are just handed a ticket. The next day someone comes up to you and asks how much you would charge to sell him your lottery ticket. Would you charge a different price if you had chosen your ticket than if it had been handed to you? Objectively, you should charge the same price to give up your chance to win. Whether you personally selected the ticket or the ticket was handed to you has no relevance to whether or not you will win. When this experiment was performed, the results revealed that those handed the ticket charged on average $1.96 for the stub. In contrast, those who chose the ticket themselves charged $8.67. The only explanation for this finding is that when the gamblers had a choice, an illusion of control was created. Because they chose the ticket, they acted as though they had a greater chance of winning.

Similar results were found in a study involving the throwing of dice. The level of betting was compared for two groups of people. One group would make a bet and then throw the dice. The other group would throw the dice (but not see the outcome), and then they would bet. The people who bet before they threw the dice made higher wagers than those betting after tossing the dice.

In another study, one group of people played the card game, "War," against a stooge, who acted as though he was really confident that he would win. Another group played the game against a "schnook," who acted unconfident and wimpish. A game of chance, War involves turning over cards from a well-shuffled deck; the person getting the higher card wins. The results showed that when people were playing the schnook, they bet significantly more each round than when they bet against the confident stooge. They seemed to reason that the confident person would have greater control and a higher likelihood of winning.

On Pilot Instructors and Regressing-to-the-Mean

The illusion of control extends beyond gambling behavior to influence a broad spectrum of decisions. In the mid-1960s, a psychologist was working with Israeli air force flight instructors to improve their pilot-training methods. During his discussions, he argued that it is better to reward good flying with verbal praise than to yell at those who just screwed up. The instructors reacted emphatically—he was wrong. One said:

> With all due respect, Sir, what you are saying is literally for the birds. I've often praised people warmly for beautifully executed maneuvers, and the next time they almost always do worse. And I've screamed at pupils for badly executed maneuvers, and by and large, the next time they improve. Don't tell me that reward works and punishment doesn't. My experience contradicts it.

The principle that reward is more effective than punishment in motivating people is one of the most well-established findings in psychology. In the face of this evidence, could the flight instructors have been correct? They were correct when they concluded that after performing a difficult maneuver well, a pilot would do less well the next time. Similarly, they were right when they recognized that after really blowing it, on the next try the pilot would improve. The change in performance, however, had nothing to do with whether the flight instructor rewarded or punished the student pilots. The change was caused by a chance-based phenomenon called "regression-to-the-mean."

Almost by definition, a new pilot has little mastery over the art of flying a performance jet. While he or she is generally able to keep the plane in the air, the outcome of any single maneuver is influenced not only by the mediocre skill level of the pilot, but also by factors beyond his control. As a result, when a really good maneuver is accomplished, it results as much from chance as from skill. Similarly, when the pilot blows it, the poor performance is unrepresentative of his general skill level. On the next maneuver, performance will regress to the mean or average outcome that one would expect from a new pilot. Thus, if a maneuver is executed well, on the next try it is likely to be less great. Similarly, if the maneuver is done poorly, the next attempt is likely to be much better.

The concept of regression-to-the-mean is perhaps most readily seen if the size of parents and their offspring are analyzed. If you compare the height of extremely tall parents to that of their children, you will find that almost invariably the children are shorter. Similarly, the children of very short parents are almost always taller than the mother and father. One factor determining the height of one's offspring is chance. As a result, the size of the offspring regresses toward the population average when the parents are either very tall or very short. Because chance has some impact on almost all outcomes, if an event diverges substantially from baseline levels, one can expect that on the next occasion the outcome will move back toward the baseline level because of the regression-to-the-mean phenomenon.

Just like the Israeli flight instructors, all of us have difficulty recognizing the existence of the regression-to-the-mean. The reason is that we allow little or no room for the effects of chance to influence outcome. We implicitly assume that outcomes are totally determined by people's ability and motivation (as with the instructor pilots), or by some hidden process, such as genetics influencing one's height. Genetics is a probabilistic, rather than a deterministic, science. Creeping determinism intrudes to blind us from recognizing that to varying degrees chance has an impact on what happens to us all.

When people fail to recognize the effects of the regression-to-the-mean phenomenon, they frequently assume that something internal to the person has occurred to cause the change in performance level. One of the major problems for rookie phenoms in the major leagues is the sophomore jinx. According to baseball lore, a great rookie season is frequently followed by a poor sophomore year. The press likes to intimate that the cause for the jinx is that success has gone to the player's head; as a result, he is less motivated and performs worse. But the more likely reason for the sophomore jinx is regression-to-the-mean. The high level of performance in the first year resulted in part from chance factors. Because those chance factors are unlikely to repeat themselves, next year's performance falls off.

Financial Investing and Regression-to-the-Mean

Next to gambling—and perhaps romance—the area in which more bright people do more dumb things is financial investing. One of the major causes of the great debacles in the financial world is a lack of respect for chance. The scenario goes as follows: Otherwise bright people have the misfortune to have a run of good luck. They interpret the series of good outcomes and the resulting financial success as occurring because of their own outstanding abilities and efforts. As a result, they lose their respect for chance and succumb to the illusion of control. They begin to take larger and larger risks, only to find (to paraphrase Ecclesiastes) that "in the end time and chance happeneth to us all."

In the high-stakes arena of stocks and bonds, chance plays a large role in determining outcomes of financial investments. The evidence reveals that future changes in the price of stocks cannot be predicted from past price changes. What changes the price of stocks is new information. These ideas are explained by the most important financial theory of the last half century—the "efficient market hypothesis." A great deal of misunderstanding exists about what an efficient market is. Said in the simplest of terms, an efficient market is one in which all of the information known about a stock is captured in its price at any particular moment in time. With thousands of extremely smart people attempting to predict future price movements, the market as a whole becomes efficient. Nothing in this simple definition implies that markets have to be orderly or that big changes in valuation cannot occur quickly. It says nothing about how individual investors or funds should perform. It says nothing about whether emotion and crowd behavior operate in the marketplace. What the efficient market says is that future changes in the price of stocks *cannot be predicted from past changes.*

Because predicting the future is extremely hard, people find it difficult to beat the market averages on a consistent basis. For example, studies of the performance of mutual funds show that on average the total return of the funds is less than that of the stock market. Indeed, an analysis by *Consumer Reports* revealed that in 1989, fewer than one in four mutual funds returned as much as the *Standard and*

Poor's 500. Over the previous five-year period less than one in seven beat the *S&P* 500. As a result, funds that buy a sample of stocks representative of the general stock market averages are difficult to beat. While in any given period some mutual funds or individual investors will do better than others, when the costs of commissions and overhead are added, on average the funds return less than the market as a whole. Indeed, the evidence strongly suggests that above-average performance during one time period is not predictive of above-average performance in the next time period. In the *Consumer Reports* study, the top ten performing mutual funds, as rated in 1987, were merely average performers between 1987 and 1990. In other words, they regressed to the mean.

The efficient market hypothesis also says nothing about the role of skill in the selection of stocks. If an analyst has an above-average ability to forecast the future earnings of firms, that person can beat the market averages. Of course, this is the basis for fundamental analysis, which is the only proven method for long-term success in the stock market. (In fundamental analysis, investors analyze the quality of the underlying basics of a company, such as products, management, and market, in order to forecast long-term growth prospects.)

A second method of predicting future stock prices is technical analysis. Technical analysts argue that the historical patterns of the movement of stock prices tell it all. To predict future price patterns, technical analysts employ a wide variety of tools to analyze past price data, such as new highs and lows, volume, odd-lot data, short interest ratios, and trend lines. The problem is that absolutely no evidence exists to support the efficacy of technical analysis. Indeed, when the trends of the price of stocks or stock markets are analyzed, one finds that they act and look as though they are caused by chance.

Fortunately, the odds are weighted in the investor's favor. Over long periods of time, the American stock market has always moved up. Investing in the stock market is like throwing a die where you win if the number 3, 4, 5, or 6 appears, and you lose only if a 1 or a 2 appears. While the patterns of the stock market are not predictable in advance, the dice are loaded to the investors' advantage. As long as they avoid foolish actions, such as allowing brokers to churn accounts, in the long run they will come out ahead.

What does all of this have to say about financial analysis? An option is to make use of the regression-to-the-mean phenomenon when investing in the stock market. Assuming that the movement of stock prices is determined in part by chance factors, which is an absolutely safe bet, at any particular point in time the prices of some stocks (or the stock market in general) will diverge from a baseline range. Thus, because of chance factors, in wholly unpredictable ways stocks can become overvalued or undervalued. Just as a rookie phenom regresses to the mean after a lucky first year, so too will overvalued stocks regress to lower prices. Similarly, by chance stocks can become *undervalued*. They, too, should then regress to the mean. But this time the direction of their stock price is up. Indeed, evidence exists that such "dogs" actually outperform high-priced "stars" in the long run.

The idea that the regression-to-the-mean phenomenon operates in the stock market is the basis for what has been called a "contrarian investment strategy." The strategy is straightforward. First, the investor finds a group of solid companies whose fundamentals (earnings history, debt load, and future prospects) look good. The investor then identifies those in the group which are selling cheaply in comparison to the rest and in comparison to historic market valuations. You buy these and wait. Over a time span, they will regress to the mean, which happily is up, and you will outperform the market. The case for contrarian or value investing is absolutely compelling. Peter Lynch, who successfully ran the largest, and arguably the most successful, mutual fund in the United States, Fidelity's Magellan Fund, said: "It takes remarkable patience to hold on to a stock in a company that excites you, but which everybody else seems to ignore. You begin to think everybody else is right and you are wrong. But where the fundamentals are promising, patience is often rewarded." Lynch described his experience with the drug company Merck. From 1972 to 1981, its stock price barely changed, yet its earnings were increasing by 14 percent a year. Then over a five-year period, its price increased fourfold. The wait was amply rewarded.

Chance and the Gambler's Fallacy

Like the regression-to-the-mean, the gambler's fallacy results from a lack of understanding of how chance influences the patterns of outcomes. The fallacy frequently occurs when a person is engaged in a task generally recognized to have a strong chance component, such as gambling on the flip of a coin. Suppose that a run occurs, and heads appear five times in a row. Naive gamblers often reason (wrongly) that since heads have happened five times in a row, tails are due; thus, instead of a 50 percent likelihood of a tail appearing, more like a 70 or 80 percent chance exists. Of course, such thinking is incorrect. Simply by chance, runs will appear on occasion. If the coin is "fair" (i.e., it has not been "loaded"), the likelihood of a tail appearing is 50-50, no matter how many times in a row heads have previously appeared.

The gambler's fallacy is the converse of the regression-to-the-mean. When people ignore the regression-to-the-mean, they deny chance as a factor causing the extreme performance. In the case of the gambler's fallacy, however, people are aware that chance is operating. For example, they know that a low likelihood exists that heads will come up five times in a row when a fair coin is flipped. But they also believe that somehow the process is self-correcting in order for the number of heads and tails to be equal. As a result, they overcompensate and assume that if a run occurs, the next event must break the run. Of course, they have just fallen into a trap. If the coin is "fair," the chances of a sixth head appearing after a run of five heads is still 50 percent.

The effects of the gambler's fallacy can be seen in a number of silly beliefs about stocks identified by Peter Lynch. One such belief was that "if it's gone down this much already, it can't go much lower." He cited the example of Polaroid in the 1970s, whose price peaked at $143.50 and then started to fall when earnings collapsed. As the price sank to $100 and then $80, many investors hung on, believing that it couldn't possibly go down much further. It finally bottomed at $14⅛. The investors acted as though a run was occurring and that soon it would correct itself.

How can an investor tell if an extreme event, such as Polaroid going down to $80 a share, represents a case in which it will regress back to a higher baseline level or go down even further? The answer is to carefully analyze the fundamentals of the stock when using a contrarian investment strategy. If the earnings are there, management looks sound, and the industry is solid, the low stock price is probably a chance blip. At some point the fundamentals will exert themselves, and the stock will recover (i.e., regress to the mean). On the other hand, if the stock goes down and the fundamentals are missing, no mysterious force will move it back up. In the marketplace, as long as a stock has a price, it can always go lower.

The gambler's fallacy causes people to act as though chance corrects itself through some mysterious guiding hand. A letter to Abby from the mother of eight daughters illustrates this effect. The woman wrote that she and her husband recently had their eighth child, and it was "another girl." The mother continued:

> I suppose I should thank God she was healthy, but, Abby, this one was supposed to have been a boy. Even the doctor told me that the law of averages were [sic] in our favor 100 to 1.

The doctor was right—the likelihood of having eight girls in a row is very low (actually 1 in 256). *However,* the chances of having a boy after having seven straight girls is still only 1 in 2. Although sperm cells are amazing little creatures (as are ova, I hasten to add), they have no way of determining the sex of their previous siblings and behaving accordingly to even things out. In fact, consider this question. What is the probability of having children born in the exact sequence: G-B-B-G-G-B-G-B? The answer is 1 in 256, the same as having eight girls in a row. Because each event is independent, the likelihood of having any specific sequence of girls and boys is 1 in 256.

Like the failure to understand the regression-to-the-mean, the gambler's fallacy is a frequent delusion. The familiar and erroneous adage that lightning never strikes twice in the same place illustrates the gambler's fallacy. The idea is that since the probability of lightning striking any one object is rare, the odds of its ever striking the same thing twice are infinitesimal. Such reasoning is clearly fallacious. Indeed, if lightning strikes an object once, it demonstrates that it is prone to being hit. Similarly, the Associated Press reported the following incident in a story headlined CELTICS TRY "STRUGGLING MAN" TO BEAT LAKERS 104–102.

> Boston—Kevin McHale [the Celtics' highest percentage shooter] was having a terrible game. But, with fourteen seconds left and the score tied, Boston coach K. C. Jones called a play for him to shoot.
> "I think K.C. figured I might be due," McHale said after the game.

McHale had just illustrated the gambler's fallacy. But K. C. Jones had gone to him because he was the team's best shooter, not because he was due. Missing a bunch of shots did not increase the likelihood that he would make the next one.

Unfortunately, even individuals in responsible positions can fall prey to the gambler's fallacy. *BusinessWeek* magazine did an article on the problems of rebuilding after Hurricane Hugo devastated South Carolina. In the aftermath of the destruction, administrators in many states began to rethink building policies along shorelines. Hugo cost taxpayers $1.5 billion, and many believed that the general population should not have to subsidize those who want to live on the beach. As one Florida planner said, "I'm dreading what's going to happen when something like Hugo hits Key West or Tampa." The president of Banker's Insurance Company, however, did not share the planner's concerns. His company anticipated writing $28 million in federal flood insurance policies in Florida and South Carolina in 1990. Justifying his exposure to the potential loss, he intimated that such a calamity could not possibly strike for many, many years: "Charleston just had their 100-year hurricane. What are the chances of that happening again?" Of course only two years later Hurricane Andrew devastated southern Florida. It is truly scary to realize that the president of a major insurance company fell prey to the gambler's fallacy. In matters of pure chance, what has happened in the past has no relationship to what will happen in the future. The same creeping determinism responsible for people ignoring the regression-to-the-mean effect causes the gambler's fallacy.

The Superstitious Decision Maker

In 1967, Ronald Reagan chose 12:10 AM as the precise time for his inauguration as governor of California. In 1984, President Reagan's departure to Europe was mysteriously delayed for several hours, creating havoc in the elaborate presidential logistical system. It seems that important events such as these in the Reagan White House were scheduled at least in part after consultations with astrologers. Scientists went into paroxysms at the news. As one astronomer said, "How can you control a science budget of billions of dollars when you believe in nonsense of this magnitude?" Equally angered were religious fundamentalists. A past vice-president of the Moral Majority said, "This is the last straw for a lot of religious people who treated Reagan as their political savior. He used to say, 'The answer to all life's problems can be found in the Bible.' I guess he put God on hold and consulted Jeane Dixon." Of course, astrologers were delighted with the news.

Superstition is a big business in the United States. Every metropolitan daily newspaper in the United States except for *The New York Times* carries a horoscope. Roughly five thousand people are employed as full-time astrologers. The results of a Chamber of Commerce survey indicate that Americans spend $35 million a year on astrology readings. Purportedly, the most money to be made is in financial astrology. One specialist said that successful astrologers can earn $100,000 a year predicting which stocks or commodities are best to invest in. (It seems that a company's astrological sign is determined by its date of incorporation.)

Astrology is but one of many approaches used by people to forecast the future and thereby gain control over their lives. For example, the ancient Oriental practice of *"feng shui"* appears to be catching on in the corporate community. Described as "like an engineering survey," *feng shui* has long been used by businesses in the Far East to plan buildings. The idea is that by changing your environment you can influence your luck. Thus, a New York graphic artist installed an aquarium containing six black fish to ward off evil in his apartment; in addition, he installed some red drawers and hung a little clock on his front wall. It seems that he had experienced six burglaries and had consulted a *feng shui* master who suggested the changes.

Of course, superstitions are found in all cultures. The Trobriand Islanders in the South Seas obtain much of their sustenance from the ocean. Among those who fished in the lagoon, where little danger existed and fish were plentiful, few superstitions were apparent. Those who fished beyond the reef, in the open seas, however, used numerous rituals and charms to help them. For the men who took the greatest risks, luck and chance were crucial, not only for bringing in fish but also for coming home alive. In order to gain control over unpredictable events, the Trobrianders developed elaborate ceremonies to placate the gods who controlled both the sea and the fish. Similarly, the Greeks and Romans prayed to their own goddess of chance. In Greece, her name was Tyche; the Romans called her Fortuna. She brought good or bad luck to people whether or not they deserved it. Temples were built to her. In drawings she is shown with a rudder to reveal her power to guide lives; she also carries a horn of plenty to show that she can do good as well as evil.

Why the Universal Belief in Superstition? In August 1990, the world lost one of its most important theorists on human behavior, B. F. Skinner. Skinner's arguments and experiments done over half a century showed that much of human and animal action can be accounted for by the reward and punishment that occur after an action. It is all quite logical. If an action leads to pleasure, we are more likely to do it again. In contrast, if an action leads to harm, we are less likely to try it a second time. Our behaviors are molded and shaped by their results—by the rewards and punishments that occur after our actions. Note the relationship between this idea and the illusion of control. We believe that our actions cause things to happen, even if the outcomes occur merely because of chance.

These simple ideas nicely explain superstitious behavior. Indeed, Skinner was able to quite easily induce pigeons or rats to act superstitiously. All you have to do is set up the circumstances. First, you need to find a reward for which the organism will work—say, a food pellet. Next, you make obtaining the food pellet contingent on some action—say, pressing a lever. Third, you allow the creature to learn to get the food by pressing the lever. Then, you apply the coup de grâce: You only give the animal the food pellet after a light comes on at random time intervals.

Here is what happens. The bird, which had previously learned to press the bar for food, presses the lever and nothing happens. This occurs several times, when suddenly the light comes on and the food pellet is delivered. Soon, the bird learns the relationship between the light, its pressing of the bar, and food. As a result, it badly wants that light to come on. So, it starts doing things to cause this to happen. It may scratch the corner of the container, turn in circles, or raise and lower its body in a bowing motion. Whatever happens right before the light flashes on is reinforced. The bird starts repeating the behavior, and accidentally it again occurs just before the light flashes. Relatively quickly, you find the bird engaging in weird and bizarre actions in order to make the light turn on. The behavior is superstitious, because it has absolutely no effect on the light. It is merely an illusion of control.

In the same manner, human superstitions evolve. A good or bad outcome occurs immediately after an action of some type. We have an implicit belief that our actions cause outcomes to occur. The coincidental pairing of action and outcome leads to the repetition of the behavior.

A slight elaboration on the behavioristic view of superstition is required to explain why the Greeks and Romans developed gods of chance. Again, such beliefs are based upon the need for control and the desire to avoid believing that events occur simply by chance. Some outcomes, such as causing rain to fall or earthquakes to occur, are simply too big for humans to believe that they can influence. After all, big events must have big causes. (Actually, researchers have shown that people act as though this is the case.) Thus, in order to account for such momentous happenings, big versions of people are imagined (i.e., gods). These gods, who have supernatural powers, control the wind, the rain, fertility—and our fortunes. Such gods oversee us and allow us to communicate with them. As a result, we can still gain some degree of control over rain, wind, and seasons by placating the gods, offering the appropriate prayers and sacrifices.

In the modern world, we still keep a variety of gods to whom we offer prayers and sacrifices in order to receive their wisdom. Although we know that these supernatural beings cannot directly control the weather or the economy, many place their economic well-being in their god's ability to forecast the future. Economists represent one breed of "supernatural" beings in whose hands governments and multinational corporations place their fate. With their jargon, abstruse mathematics, and impenetrable econometric models, they give the appearance of having a divining rod for the future. Indeed, as long as future events act like past events, economists are quite good at the forecasting game. However, when unexpected events occur, their forecasts do no better than chance. As the Nobel laureate Paul A. Samuelson pointed out, "I don't believe we're converging on ever-improving forecast accuracy. It's almost as if there's a Heisenberg indeterminacy principle and God Almighty himself doesn't know what investment will be 18 months ahead."*

The reason for the difficulty in making economic forecasts is that the future is inherently unpredictable. As one critic put it, "It's easy to forecast when times are stable. It's just this year, plus 5%, plus a small error factor. No big deal." What economists cannot do is predict the dramatic changes in the economy that lead to great dislocations, because the factors that cause these catastrophes, such as the development of an oil cartel or a war, are inherently unpredictable. For example, in the late spring of 1990, the price of oil had fallen to $16 a barrel. Economic forecasters saw no hint of a recession in sight. Then, in August, Iraq invaded Kuwait, the price of oil doubled, and the U.S. economy headed into a recession. Again, consider the price of leather between 1977 and 1988. While the price of most other commodities changed little, the cost of leather tripled. The change was not predicted, although in hindsight the reasons are obvious. First, demand for beef decreased, causing the supply of hides to fall.

*The Heisenberg indeterminacy principle says that the position and velocity of an electron cannot be measured simultaneously. The act of measurement influences the electron, making the analysis impossible. As applied to economics, the principle would suggest that the act of measuring and forecasting the economy will change its future course.

Second, yuppies went on a leather-buying binge. It became the "in" thing to purchase bomber jackets and BMWs with leather seats. Even senior citizens wanted Chryslers with interiors of rich Corinthian leather. The combination of falling supply and rising demand caused an upsurge in leather prices that was not forecast.

In sum, decision makers seek to gain control by hiring forecasters. But to paraphrase an old saying, "Forecasters are like lampposts. They're used more for support than for illumination." Economic forecasters, astrologers, and soothsayers have their place, but it is not alongside deities.

Monday Morning Quarterbacks and Creeping Determinism

In October 1983, Rangers, Navy SEALs, Delta Forces, and other troops invaded and captured the little island nation of Grenada. The Reagan administration hailed a great U.S. victory. Coming after the marine massacre in Lebanon and with the Iranian rescue mission debacle still fresh in the collective memory, the United States needed a military victory to bolster morale. The commanding officer of the force said, "We blew them away." President Reagan boasted that we "are standing tall again." As a result of the successful invasion, the Army handed out 9,802 decorations, including 812 Bronze Stars.

Some years after the invasion, doubts began to arise about just how successful it had been. Documents acquired through the Freedom of Information Act by *The Wall Street Journal* showed a far different picture. Instead of a precision military operation, one finds a series of snafus and bungled actions. Some quick examples illustrate the near disaster:

—*Example 1*. The Navy SEAL unit sent in ahead to install navigation beacons failed in its mission. While the reasons for the failure are classified, it is known that four of the SEALs drowned.

—*Example 2*. A-7 attack jets bombed the island's insane asylum, killing seventeen patients.

—*Example 3*. Thinking that Cubans were holed up at a base camp, Rangers were sent in to mop them up. During the attack, two

Black Hawk helicopters collided, killing three men. The frustrated Rangers who reached the camp found it deserted.

—*Example 4*. President Reagan argued that the attack was staged in order to protect 600 American students attending the island's medical school. The troops thought that the American students were housed at the school's Grand Anse campus. Only after the attack began was it discovered that most were at another campus. A phone call to any one of the students' parents could have verified their location. The list of errors goes on and on: maps arrived a week after the invasion. The troops didn't have enough batteries for their radios, etc., etc.

Meanwhile, the Cuban construction workers who were the island's major defense force put up a heroic fight. The U.S. commander credited them with making "an amazing turnaround of basic defenses." They were simply defeated by an overwhelming-sized force, using the most modern weapons and composed of the best fighting troops that the United States could muster. Given the heroism of his troops, what happened to Colonel Tortolo, the Cuban military officer in charge of the island's forces? He was sent back to Havana, court-martialed, broken to private, and ordered to Angola, where he was killed in an ambush.

Outcomes, rather than the quality of the decision process, dominate the evaluations of decision makers. When outcomes are bad, heads roll. The Greeks beheaded messengers who brought bad news. U.S. voters turned away Jimmy Carter, who had the twin misfortunes during his presidency of having to give Americans the bad news about conserving energy and about the Iranian hostage crisis. The Cuban military stuck it to Colonel Tortolo, who was unlucky enough to be in charge of the Cuban defense forces in Grenada. In contrast, when outcomes are good, even the most severe transgressions can be ignored. Thus, U.S. commanders in Grenada received commendations even though the operation approached a farce.

The effect of the outcome bias on evaluations is readily seen in the aftermath of severe flooding in Tulsa, Oklahoma, in 1986. In early October, massive rains struck north-central Oklahoma, and water began to back up behind Keystone Dam. Run by the Corps of Engineers, the dam serves multiple functions: it acts to control flooding, to provide recreation, and to provide the correct amount of water for the Kerr-McClellan inland waterway. As the rains continued, the managers faced the dilemma of whether to begin releasing extra water because of the possibility that, if the rain continued, they would have to let loose massive amounts later in order to save the dam. This was a classic judgment call: Should they choose to release extra water and cause certain minor flooding, or hold the excess water and risk major flooding if the rains continued? If they released water, and the rain stopped, they would look like idiots for causing unnecessary flooding. If they held water, and the rains continued, they would be criticized for causing massive flooding. The managers decided to delay the release of the water. Unexpectedly, the rains not only continued, but worsened. When huge quantities of water were released, a major flood resulted.

The people of Tulsa, newspapers, and congressmen were incensed. Investigations followed. The dam managers were put through the wringer. After months and months of total strangers questioning their judgment, competency, and general worth as human beings, the engineers were vindicated. The investigation revealed that based upon the information collected, they had made a reasonable decision.

Monday morning quarterbacking is easy because you know the outcomes of the decisions. In the 1600s a wise scientist named Arnauld, said:

A fault condemned but seldom avoided is the evaluation of the intention of an act in terms of the act's outcome. An agent who acted as wisely as the foreseeable circumstances permitted is censured for the ill-effects which came to pass through chance or through malicious opposition or through unforeseeable circumstances.

Once an outcome has occurred, people believe that it was inevitable. People exaggerate in hindsight what in reality they could anticipate in foresight. They even misremember their own predictions. Researchers have found that if predictions are compared before and after outcomes are known, you find that people change their prediction to coincide with the outcome. Even worse, they misremember their own estimate and change it in the appropriate direction.

Both hindsight and the outcome biases illustrate our tendency to ignore chance as a factor that causes outcomes to occur. Bad luck can turn good decisions into bad outcomes. Good luck can transform bad decisions into good outcomes. Because of the chance component, evaluations should be based upon the process used to make a judgment—not the outcome. If the decision maker collected the appropriate information, analyzed it properly, and reached a logical conclusion from the analysis, he or she made a good decision—regardless of the outcome.

When can outcome information be used for evaluation purposes? The answer is when tactical decisions are made in which judgments occur repeatedly under similar circumstances, such as making bank loans or weather forecasts. In these instances a performance record is developed. When decisions are implemented multiple times, chance effects cancel themselves out, and evaluations can be made based upon the overall outcome of the series of judgments.

On the Importance of Process

To what extent are businesspeople aware of others falling prey to the outcome bias? Based upon the risk-taking tendencies of managers, it appears that they are quite cognizant that their performance will be based upon the outcomes of their decisions. Particularly in large firms, where all decision makers (including the CEO) have someone evaluating their actions, managers become reluctant to take risks. If something goes wrong, they recognize that heads will roll. Thus, decisions are made to avoid failure, rather than to achieve success. As a result, it is important to train managers and boards of directors to focus on the process of decision making.

A golf metaphor helps to explain why a focus on process is so important. The swings of professional golfers share many commonalities. The motion is effortless, the head is still, the body remains behind the ball, wrists are uncocked late in the swing, and so forth. In one hundred swings, a novice golfer with some athletic ability will hit two or three drives as well as the professional; the rest are terrible because the swing is bad. The amateur uses the wrong process. In a similar manner, if decision makers use the wrong process in making a decision, occasional good results will occur. In more cases, however, the results will be bad. When evaluating the quality of strategic decision making—in making acquisitions, deciding whether to use liquid-fueled or solid-fueled boosters in the Space Shuttle, or whether to wage war—the decision process is the key.

One important element of the decision-making process concerns ethics. In one of my interviews, I spoke with Bob McCormick, the CEO of a mid-sized bank in Oklahoma. Once featured in *Inc.* magazine, Bob has managerial talent that could have taken him to the top of any financial firm. He represents that reserve of talented people stored in the small cities of America. We talked about the issue of means and ends in decision making. "Means are crucial," he said, "because they affect how people feel. The appropriate process allows you to sustain effort. The reason why you see burnout at *forty* in high finance is not the pace. Rather, it's the problem of compromising the means."

A recent study supports Bob McCormick's analysis. One hundred and eleven managers were given a battery of tests that assessed their ethical behavior as well as their stress levels. The results revealed that those executives scoring highest on the ethics portion revealed the least stress by showing lower amounts of hostility, anger, and fear. A great psychological toll is extracted when decision makers consistently take ethical shortcuts, place themselves in the gray area between lawful and lawless action, and compromise their personal principles.

The Judgment Call: Control versus Chance

Soon after H. Ross Perot joined GM's board of directors, he began to create waves. One GM norm that he broke involved talking to employees. Once he phoned a union representative to set up a meeting with workers at a plant. The union man was incredulous— Ross Perot actually wanted to talk to workers? In describing the situation, Perot quoted a talk that he had given to GM executives:

> You've got to remember there are guys on the factory floors as smart as we are. We got the breaks. We got to go to college. We had the parental support. We had a lot of things they didn't have, but these guys aren't dummies. They are not, quote, *those people*. They are not, quote, *labor*. They are just like us, except that the ball bounced a different way.

Few people recognize that chance plays such a significant role in their lives. Rather, they attribute their success to their own abilities, efforts, and skills developed through their own hard work. Ross Perot's beliefs are anomalous.

The recognition of the importance of chance is a modern phenomenon. For eons, human beings believed that events were largely controlled by divinities. They had no room for chance in the universe. It was thought that by throwing astragali (small ankle bones of sheep, goat, or deer), the forces of divine intervention would arrange the bones in a manner that would foretell the future. The practice seems to have been universal. In ancient times—from Greece to Korea to Egypt to the Americas—games of chance were used for religious purposes. The games of chance that we know today evolved from such divinatory rites.

As one would expect, not everyone believed that gambling outcomes were dictated by the gods. Cicero talked very sensibly about throwing dice: "Now and then indeed [a man] will make it twice and even thrice in succession. Are we going to be so feeble-minded then as to aver that such a thing happened by the personal intervention of Venus rather than by pure luck?" Indeed, some historians argue that one of the reasons why the Roman Catholic Church outlawed gambling in the Middle Ages was to eliminate the last vestiges of the pagan practice of casting lots.

It was not until the sixteenth century that mathematicians first developed the basics of probability theory and the recognition that events can be construed as only probabilistic in nature. Even into the early twentieth century, the universe was understood mechanistically. As suggested by Newtonian physics, every event has a cause. If you were smart enough and knew the causal relations, you could predict the future. It was not until the ideas of relativity, the Heisenberg uncertainty principle, and Chaos theory were developed that the world view really began to change.

The vestiges of the belief in a mechanistic universe still remain, however. Like that strange organ the appendix, which remains in our bodies long after it has ceased to be useful, the belief in a mechanistic world is still retained. As with the appendix, most of the time this vestige belief remains innocuous and benign. But occasionally it flares up to infect our judgments.

Uncertainty and chance, though, are required in our world. As the psychologist Robyn Dawes notes, without uncertainty we would know the future. The world would be dull, boring, and uneventful. We would have no hope. We would have no freedom of choice because only by *not* knowing with certainty the outcomes of our choices can we be truly free. Without uncertainty, we would not have ethics. Because the consequences of actions are uncertain, most ethical systems require that a decision must be made freely before it can be unethical. If no real freedom of choice exists, the system of ethics disappears.

Thus, we have a fundamental dilemma. We dislike uncertainty and do everything that we can to reduce it. On the other hand, uncertainty is a requirement for our world. Further, the degree to which chance influences outcomes varies across time and changes as situations vary. The judgment call that decision makers must make is to what extent an event was controlled by skill, effort, and understandable forces, as opposed to chance. Was the increase in earnings caused by outstanding management or simply good fortune? Did the employee's performance result from her outstanding abilities or from good luck?

One way to approach the control versus chance judgment call is to borrow an idea from Blaise Pascal, the seventeenth-century French scientist and philosopher. He suggested that a belief in God is a good wager. If you are wrong, you lose nothing. If you are right, you have saved yourself from Hell. Similarly, it is a good bet to err on the side of believing that events are controlled. If you are wrong, in most cases the worst that can happen is that you expend a lot of energy for little benefit. If you are right, you may find a solution.

The error of ignoring the effects of chance leads to inappropriate beliefs in superstitions, to following the recommendations of fraudulent seers, and to the evaluation of decision makers based upon outcomes rather than upon process. On the other hand, the price of *not* finding the cause of outcomes can be extremely high. While at times our perceived ability to control events becomes illusory, we gain much more than we lose from this powerful drive.

Some principles that may help you in the control versus chance trade-off are:

- The illusion of control is the erroneous belief that your actions can influence purely chance events.

- When an outcome diverges dramatically from a baseline, in the next instance it will tend to regress toward its average level.

- Elude the gambler's fallacy by keeping in mind that when a run of good or bad luck occurs, no mysterious force will change the probability of the next event occurring.

- Superstitions result from the chance association of a human action with a positive outcome, and lead to a repetition of the action in an attempt to gain control.

- People tend to exaggerate in hindsight what they could actually anticipate in foresight.

- Evaluate others' decisions on the quality of the process as well as on the outcome.

- Remember that chance is ubiquitous, and that without uncertainty we would have no hope, no freedom of choice, and a meaningless existence.

- All else equal, it is better to believe that an event was determined by a hidden cause than merely by chance.

8.

CHOOSING A FRAME
OF REFERENCE

How big is Cuba? Most people think of it as a small island below
Florida. The question of Cuba's size was a key issue in the debate over
whether to invade that island in the early days of John Kennedy's
presidency. When Kennedy's advisers sweated over the decision of
whether or not to press forward with the plan, the Commandant of
the Marine Corps, General David M. Shoup, lectured them on the
difficulties involved. To illustrate the magnitude of the problem, he
needed to change their perception of the island's size. Shoup first
placed an overlay of Cuba upon the map of the United States. To
everybody's surprise, Cuba was not a small island along the lines of,
say, Long Island. Rather, it was about 800 miles long and seemed to
stretch from New York to Chicago. Then he took another overlay,
with a tiny red dot on it, and placed it over the map of the United
States. The red dot was roughly the size of the city of Chicago.
"What's that?" someone asked him. "That, gentlemen, represents the
size of the island of Tarawa," said Shoup, who had won a Medal of
Honor there, "and it took us three days and eighteen thousand Marines to take it." While such pithy analyses would cause the marine
commandant to become John Kennedy's favorite general, his obser-
vations failed to hold back the forward momentum of the plan that
would lead to the Bay of Pigs disaster.

General Shoup used a map to frame the size of a military encounter. Frames of reference influence the perception of a decision problem just as an optical lens can clarify or distort information received through the eyes. They affect judgment calls by acting as filters that influence our expectations and our interpretation of events. As a result, they affect which factors decision makers consider in their analysis of a problem and the relative importance of these factors. By using a map of the United States, General Shoup forced decision makers to consider the size of Cuba as a factor in invading the island; his goal was to influence their estimate of the probability that the mission would be successful. A variety of decision frames exist, but one particularly important basis is the decision maker's area of professional specialization.

Professional Specialization Frames

A surgeon described the one sign that really sets off bells—"Patients take their fist and put it against their chest." In doing so, they portray the classic reaction to angina: the pain caused when clogged arteries impede blood flow to the heart. My father once described the pain to me as being "like a cement truck parked on your chest."

What should be done to treat angina? As one cardiologist said of the decision, "At the extremes, it's very easy. A severely diseased left main artery goes right to bypass. Mild angina can be treated with medicine." Few cases, however, fit the extremes. Just as the captain of the U.S.S. *Vincennes* had to decide whether to shoot or not, cardiologists must decide whether "to cut or not." In the zone of ambiguity, matters become complicated because the stakes are so high. A bypass costs an average of over $23,000, requires a minimum of about three months of recuperation, and kills about 2 percent of the patients. On the other hand, angioplasty (inflating a small balloon in the artery to compress the blockage) costs less than $10,000, patients can return to work in five days, and the procedure has only a 1 percent death rate. But angioplasty has drawbacks, chiefly the fact that it is more temporary than bypass surgery.

One factor that influences the choice between bypass surgery and other less invasive approaches is the specialty of the physician. As a Fort Lauderdale cardiologist put it, "When you show a surgeon a case of significant coronary disease, there's only one cure for it: surgery. When you show it to a cardiologist, there's only one cure for it: angioplasty." Professional training can form a frame or lens through which people view the world. The frame distorts some information, lets in other information, and completely shuts out other data from consideration. Heart surgeons are trained to cut and will look for reasons to practice their trade. Similarly, cardiologists are trained to use drugs, angioplasty, lasers, and other means to assist patients. Each specialist views the patient's symptoms through the lens of his or her training.

Within organizations, differences in the professional frames of reference of key executives can create major conflicts. For example, at Ford Motor Company in the 1960s, one could find three distinct frames operating. Historically, Ford had been a company dominated by a manufacturing lens. The focus on production was illustrated by the classic Henry Ford line: "We'll give the consumer whatever color he wants, as long as it's black." Those with a manufacturing orientation want to have long product runs, few models, and maximum efficiency. By the 1960s, however, the manufacturing frame had been replaced by the ongoing battle between those with a marketing frame, those with a finance frame, and those with an engineering/technical frame.

In organizations, the technical frame is at its best when it causes executives to focus on producing innovative, high-quality products in an efficient and timely manner. At its worst, the technical frame results in look-alike, cost-ineffective products designed for the engineer rather than the customer. A marketing frame at its best causes managers to focus on developing products that fulfill the needs and wants of consumers. At its worst, the marketing viewpoint results in a P. T. Barnum focus on hype and product misrepresentation, in which gimmicks are used to foist inferior products onto consumers. The finance frame, when appropriately used, keeps costs under control and the company on firm financial footing. Improperly utilized, the finance lens focuses attention on achieving short-term profits and stifles innovation.

The battle over whether or not to produce the Mustang depicts the collision of frameworks at Ford. The idea for the Mustang came from Don Frey. One year Iaccoca's junior, Frey was an engineer—a product man who loved cars. For Frey, a car was an end in itself. When he looked at a car, he wondered what it felt like, how it handled, how much power it had. But around Ford, Frey was viewed as a disrespectful egghead. Henry Ford II once said, "The trouble with Frey is that he's too goddam smart for his own good. Maybe, he's a genius. Maybe not. But he's certainly a pain in the ass."

While Frey represented the technical product man, Lee Iacocca symbolized the marketing man. When Iacocca looked at a car, his reaction was, would the public buy it, how many options could be added to it, and could he sell it to finance? In addition, Iacocca was the consummate politician within the firm who knew that to get your way, you have to know how to use power.

Frey originated the idea of the Mustang as an inexpensive, two-seat, sporty car to go up against GM's Corvette. The goal was to build a vehicle that would appeal to the expanding youth market. The market researchers, however, reported back that only about fifty thousand units of such a vehicle would sell. Finance took these numbers and nixed the project. They argued that it would diminish standard volume. "Standard volume" meant simply last year's sales, which the finance people naively assumed could be sold the next year without anything being changed. Maintaining standard volume guaranteed profit without risk in the minds of the finance group. Unless a new product could surpass standard volume, it should not be produced because it was too risky. A new product that added to the budget without guaranteeing sales was described as "decremental." The Mustang was deemed decremental. Even after Iacocca came up with the terrific idea of putting jump seats in the back and marketing research increased sales estimates to between 100,000 and 125,000, finance still attempted to nix the project.

The Mustang case also illustrates the use of a political perspective in which players use power, persuasion, compromise, and cunning to implement their ideas. The problem faced by Iaccoca in launching the Mustang was largely political in nature. His strategy for implementing his ideas involved bringing Henry Ford II along very slowly. He avoided going through channels to reach him because that would awaken the finance behemoth. Rather, he would show Henry his ideas in informal settings. His goal was to create a situation in which Mr. Ford would grow to believe that the car was his.

But the Mustang proved to be a tough sell. Finance continued to oppose it, based upon the ill-conceived standard volume heuristic. When Iacocca finally got Mr. Ford to the design center, the CEO said, "I don't even want to talk about it."

Iacocca then took a major risk. He began to talk up the car informally inside Ford corporate headquarters. Worse, he began to leak information about it to the automotive press. Reporters and other outsiders then began to pepper upper management with questions about this hot new car and when it would be introduced. Finally, Ford went back to the design shop and said, "I'm tired of hearing about this goddam car. Can you sell the goddam thing?" Iacocca responded, "Yes," and Ford shot back, "Well you damn well better."

Iacocca's risk taking didn't stop there. Right up to the Mustang's launch, market research still estimated that demand would exist for only 100,000 or so units. Early sales, however, were hot, and Iacocca persuaded top management to add a second plant. Eventually three plants built Mustangs with a capacity of over 400,000 units. The Mustang came out in 1964, and in the first year 418,812 units were sold. In the first two years the car made over $1.1 billion in net profits —in 1964 dollars. Iacocca's photo appeared on the cover of both *Newsweek* and *Time* in the same week. But Iacocca had overstepped the bounds of political power. He had become a public figure, which did not sit well with Henry Ford II. Over the next ten years their relationship would deteriorate.

In the mid-seventies, Henry Ford was touring the design studios. He encountered a young designer who excitedly showed him a clay model of a new car. The effusive young man said, "Look Mr. Ford, we've got a hot new car here. Why, it could be another Mustang." Ford looked at him and said, "Who needs that?"

Political versus Technological Frames. Governmental organizations also suffer conflicts between individuals who approach problems with divergent professional frames of reference. One such instance occurred in the early days of NASA during the Kennedy administration.

April 1961 was a terrible month for the newly elected president and his administration. The first blow occurred on April 12, 1961, when the Soviet Union successfully launched *Vostok I*, which placed the first man into earth orbit. By blasting Yuri Gagarin into orbit, the Soviets frightened the American people. Congressmen called for wartime mobilization in response to the threat. Egyptian President Gamal Abdel Nasser said there was no doubt that "the launching of man into space will turn upside down not only many scientific views, but also many political military trends." A newspaper in the Philippines questioned whether the launch might show the superiority of the Communist system. The second blow to the Kennedy administration was the Bay of Pigs fiasco, which got under way just five days after the historic Gagarin flight. The ill-fated invasion by Cuban refugees trained by the United States would last only three days before being crushed.

The same day that the news of the Bay of Pigs fiasco was being communicated to the American public, John Kennedy met with Vice

President Lyndon Johnson on the space program. Johnson had long been enamored of space and would become one of the Apollo program's strongest advocates. At this meeting, Kennedy asked Johnson to get answers to a series of questions, the first of which was: "Do we have a chance of beating the Soviets by putting a laboratory in space, or by a trip around the moon, or by a rocket to land on the moon, or by a rocket to go to the moon and back with a man? Is there any other space program which promises dramatic results in which we could win?" The meeting represented a major shift in attitude because less than three weeks earlier, John Kennedy had been a reluctant participant in the space program. In fact, the day after Gagarin's successful orbital flight, Kennedy had stated in a press conference that the United States should not attempt to match the Soviets in space; rather, Americans should find "other areas where we can be first and which will bring more long-range benefits to mankind." The politics of the situation, however, changed Kennedy's mind.

A month after the Soviet Union's spectacular feat, the United States finally had a space triumph: Alan Shepard successfully flew a suborbital mission that lasted just over fifteen minutes. While the success of the mission was crucial, Kennedy had still not made up his mind whether or not to go to the moon. In order to help with the decision, the president frequently probed the feelings of others. Jerome Wiesner, a scientist from MIT who headed the Ad Hoc Committee for Space, talked about an incident in which Kennedy felt out Tunisia's president, Habib Bourguiba. Kennedy said: "You know, we're having a terrible argument in the White House about whether we should put a man on the moon. Jerry [Wiesner] here is against it. If I told you you'd get an extra billion dollars a year in foreign aid if I didn't do it, what would be your advice?" Bourguiba stood silent for a few moments, then replied: "I wish I could tell you to put in foreign aid, but I cannot."

As a scientist, Wiesner viewed the issue through a technological lens. While previously serving on the President's Science Advisory Committee, Wiesner and others had opposed manned exploration of space. The reasons for the opposition were logical: (1) you don't gain anything scientifically; (2) it is much too costly; (3) and when failures occur, people are killed. But as Wiesner listened to the feedback that Kennedy received from others, he realized the inevitable. As he said, the decision to go to the moon was "a political, not a technical issue." Technology was being used to serve political ends. In Wiesner's view, Kennedy had three choices: "Quit, stay second, or do something dramatic. He didn't think we could afford to quit, politically, and it was even worse to stay second. And so he decided to do something where we had a chance of really beating the Russians."

Three weeks after the successful Mercury flight, Kennedy asked Congress for funds to go to the moon. In the highly charged political atmosphere in which American prestige was on the line, Congress approved the project. A high-risk program such as going for the moon could only have been initiated within a setting in which the decision makers viewed themselves as being in a loss position. The Bay of Pigs debacle and the specter of Russians in orbit created a situation in which America was behind. They were losing, and as a result, they were willing to take a major monetary and prestige gamble to go to the moon. But the key point is that the decision was made for political, not technological, reasons.

In 1992, American policy makers were trying to decide whether to build a gigantic space station in preparation for sending a man to the planet Mars, and several parallels existed between the Apollo and the space station projects. The space station was being pushed by a vice president (Dan Quayle in this instance) who was enamored of space just as Lyndon Johnson had been. Again, many scientists viewed the project unfavorably. Dr. James A. Van Allen, who discovered the earth's radiation belts, said, "It's advertised as the world's greatest invention, but its scientific uses are pretty dubious." Further, the scientific goals could be accomplished much less expensively by using unmanned rockets.

Opponents of the space station used its high costs as a means of swaying opinion against it. One strategy was to discuss the project in terms of its overall costs. The General Accounting Office has estimated that over its thirty-year life span, the space station will cost $81 billion. Of course, such analyses strike a raw nerve at NASA. But one official felt that despite the cost overruns and the high total price, the project was worth it. "It's like building a house," he said. "If you start to calculate what it's going to cost over a lifetime to furnish it and heat it, and operate it, you'd never buy it. The lifetime cost is very high. But you say, 'I want a house.' We want a space station."

Using the metaphor of a house to describe the space station was a highly effective strategy on the part of the NASA official. Metaphors and analogies act as "mini-frames" to set up people's perspectives. Concrete and vivid, such metaphors effectively communicate nuances of meaning. The use of a housing metaphor for the space station creates images of home fires burning, of protection, of a friendly, safe haven.

What will happen to the space station and the Mars expedition?

With roughly $5 billion already spent, it has taken on a momentum of its own. As one scientist said, "It's going to get built. When you've got all those employees and contractors, and that big an operation at stake, a project has to be more obviously preposterous than the station in order not to happen." The scientist had recognized the sunk cost effect discussed earlier in this book. Once a project is "turned on" and significant sums have been spent, it is nearly impossible to "turn it off" because of the erroneous principle that money spent previously should impact upon future decisions. One thing we can be sure of is that political, not technological, factors will determine whether the space station is built, because Congress is inherently a political body.

Framing the Space Shuttle Program. Political considerations overruled scientific judgment to launch the Apollo moon program, and America did win the race to the moon. Americans take great pride in this technological success story. But an important factor in the success of the Apollo program was that, while politically inspired, the politicians stayed away from its actual operation. The scientists and engineers were given the autonomy necessary for them to work effectively. In the development of a highly technical enterprise, politics and engineering cannot be mixed.

The Apollo program's director, Jim Webb, was able to announce proudly that the program came in on time and on budget. The reason was that Webb went through a two-step process. First, he had NASA engineers and accountants carefully estimate how much it would cost to place a man on the moon. Second, he applied the heuristic that all research and development projects cost twice as much as estimated. He took the figures, doubled them, and gave these to the president.

An example of what happens when politics are allowed to intrude into the day-to-day running of scientific endeavors is found in the difficulties of the Space Shuttle program. Like the Apollo initiative, the Space Shuttle was born of a political process. Even after the program was initiated, however, political considerations constantly intruded, with disastrous results. All too frequently political judgments overrode technical considerations. The end result was the Challenger calamity and the continuing problems that plague the program in the 1990s.

In 1970, NASA managers projected that the Space Shuttle could be built for from $10 to $15 billion. At the time, the Nixon administration was heavily involved in the Vietnam War and was experiencing an extremely tight budget. As a result of a series of political compromises, a temporary and inexperienced head of NASA, George Low, agreed to an $8 billion budget. Tom Paine, the previous NASA head, was appalled by the decision. Paine argued later that the downfall of the shuttle program resulted from a series of small political compromises. As he says, "The road to hell is notoriously made small step by small step. The devil always has a very tiny bargain." The Nixon administration kept picking from the program a $100 million here and $100 million there, and finally it was whittled down to a cost of $5.1 billion. The initial allocations for the Space Shuttle were roughly one third of the original projected costs.

At the Nixon White House, a major focus existed on using cost-benefit analysis to save money. When applied to the shuttle project, the penny pinching created a series of trade-offs that resulted in catastrophe. First, the decision was made to use solid-fueled rockets to help boost the shuttle into space. Building a totally reusable system that employed liquid-fueled rockets was too expensive, according to the bean counters. Old-timers, such as Werner von Braun, viewed this decision as a highly dangerous one. Once started, solid-fueled engines cannot be turned off. If a malfunction occurs, it will progress until a catastrophic failure results. Later, the photos of the ever-enlarging flame of hot gases emerging from the side of the Challenger booster just before its explosion would vividly illustrate precisely such a problem.

The focus on reducing costs rather than emphasizing safety could also be seen in the decision not to develop an escape system. In von Braun's view, the combination of solid rockets and lack of escape system made the system too dangerous for manned flight. A military general, who acted as a liaison between NASA and the Department of Defense, described the trade-offs in the following words: "NASA didn't do it because it was stupid. They did it because they were forced to do so . . . we can never be perfectly safe and it's always a human decision as just how much is enough. But in this case how much was enough was not determined by the scientists and engineers but by the politicians. . . ."

Large-scale science projects are launched via a political process. After their initiation, however, political intrusions must be minimized. One factor that harmed the shuttle program was the appointment of key managers chosen for their ideological considerations rather than for their technical and managerial skills. Such problems became particularly acute in the Reagan administration, which zealously placed conservatives with little relevant experience in key administrative positions in the organization. Ultimately, the political intrusions into the program doomed it. The politicizing of NASA also resulted in a dismantling of the careful testing procedures developed during Apollo. The paper trails that could track mistakes to a single person went up in political smoke. An Air Force colonel assigned to assist Sally Ride in the investigation of the Challenger catastrophe described the feelings of the panel members: "It just unraveled like Watergate. We felt betrayed. It was one thing to understand the technical reasons for the solid rocket explosion. But NASA had always put its people above everything. To hear how they put off and covered up the needed repairs and to know it killed your friends is a little hard to take."

Did the Challenger disaster wake people up and get the shuttle program back on track? Evidence exists to suggest that a short-term, cost-reduction, financial frame of thinking continued to bedevil the program. In the summer of 1990, I talked to a mathematician who worked for Morton-Thiokol (the producer of the exploding booster rocket) after the Challenger explosion. His job was to conduct critical-items risk assessments: the goal was to identify the types of problems that could cause catastrophic failure of the shuttle. One hundred and fifty-three failure modes were identified. Examples included debris falling off at launch and damaging the ship, lightning striking the shuttle, joints failing, and propellant cracks causing explosions. At the top of the list of problems was one solid rocket booster igniting before the other. (This was also Werner von Braun's major fear over twenty years ago in the use of solid propellant boosters.)

The young mathematician came to believe that the O-rings, which caused the Challenger explosion, are now one of the most tested and safest parts of its design. However, as so often is the case in a complex system, changing one factor influences a series of others. At the joints the booster rockets are flexible. The metal where the joints come together is placed under pressure because of the buffeting of the spacecraft at launch and its "pressuring up" as the propellant ignites. A great deal of friction results, which heats the metal and causes "fretting of the joints." In effect, the metal is case-hardened from the heat, which makes it brittle. The problem is that engineers do not know how far through the metal the brittleness extends. If it goes all of the way through, the metal could shatter, leading to burnthrough and another explosion.

The mathematician wrote a memo explaining the problem and arguing that the situation should be classified as "Crit-1," or of highest priority. He told me that the response of his superiors was that

Morton-Thiokol could never admit to such a potential disaster. Nothing was done, and the young mathematician quit in disgust.

The combination of political and financial frameworks operating throughout much of the shuttle program had two major characteristics. First, the hiring of key administrators was based far too much upon ideological rather than technical expertise. Second, the financial frame tied the program to a "hold-down-the-costs" attitude. This penny-pinching approach resulted in an underfunded program that made a series of trade-offs, leading to an inherently risky design.

Military versus Political Frames. Another professional frame of reference is that of the military. At its best a military perspective emphasizes such values as discipline, security, efficiency, and a controlled aggressiveness. Problems occur, however, when aggressiveness becomes uncontrolled, when security turns into an overwhelming focus on secrecy, and when discipline develops into an intolerance for opposing views. Applied inappropriately within a political or business arena, the decision to view problems through a military lens can lead to catastrophe. Indeed, even when applied to wartime problems, the inflexibility that can result from a military viewpoint creates major problems. Such was the case in the 1973 Arab-Israeli War.

On October 6, 1973, in a surprise attack, Egypt and Syria quickly achieved a series of stunning victories over the unprepared Israelis. Only after a series of desperate battles was Israel able to stem the advance of the armies. Eventually it accepted a peace treaty in which much of the land that Egypt had lost in the 1967 war was returned. Why had Israel been caught so off guard?

In reality, Israeli leaders had ample warning of an impending attack. Twice, the CIA told Israeli intelligence of the existence of a plan to attack Israel, called "Operation Badr"—the first time, four months before the attack, and the second, just three days before. Unusual Egyptian military movements along the Suez Canal were also observed and reported. Even Prime Minister Golda Meir noted that the departure of Soviet advisers and families in early October was remarkably similar to the events prior to the 1967 war. The head of Israel's naval intelligence said that war was imminent. Reports analyzing the 1973 war concluded that all of the information was available for Israel to have recognized the impending attack.

What caused the near-fatal breakdown in decision making? The answer appears to lie in the military framework used by the Israeli leadership to analyze the situation. As some experts put it, Moishe Dayan and other leaders believed that it was simply implausible that the Egyptians would fight a war they could not win. The Israeli leaders had secret information that the previous Egyptian war minister had concluded that Egypt should never again fight a war with Israel if victory was not certain. Looking through their military lens, the Israeli leadership knew that Israel had overwhelming military superiority. Therefore, no attack could be forthcoming.

What the leadership failed to consider was that countries sometimes fight wars for political rather than military purposes. One historian quoted Anwar Sadat, the Egyptian president, as coming to the conclusion that "it would be better and more satisfactory for the Egyptian people to fight a war and lose, than not to fight at all because defeat was likely. . . ." Indeed, in 1972 Sadat had fired the war minister, who had argued against fighting an unwinnable war. As we saw earlier, individuals, companies, and even countries will take great risks when they perceive themselves to be in a "loss" position. After losing the 1967 war and the Sinai to Israel, Egypt was placed in just such a position.

The difference in the perspective of the military and political is also illustrated by the attitude of Admiral William J. Crowe over the *Vincennes* incident in the Persian Gulf in July 1988. As head of the Joint Chiefs of Staff at the time, Crowe focused on the military implications of the change in the rules of engagement. These changes occurred prior to the *Vincennes* incident and were implemented in order to allow American forces to shoot first. Crowe's goal was to save the lives of U.S. military personnel, avoid the loss of ships and planes, and maintain control over the area. From a military perspective, being able to shoot before being fired at makes perfect sense. Thus, when examined through a military lens, shooting down an Iranian passenger jet was unfortunate, but something that could happen in a war zone. Iran was in large part responsible for the tragedy. Its military leaders ordered boats to attack the *Vincennes* and then allowed a passenger jet to take off from a military airport. For Admiral Crowe, the events even had one positive outcome. He told me, "You know, Professor, after the passenger jet was shot down, we didn't have any more incidents in the Persian Gulf."

However, a political frame must have a wider field of view than the military perspective. Viewed through a political lens, one sees the potential connection between the loss of the Iranian passenger jet and the bombing of Pan Am Flight #103 over Lockerbie, Scotland. Ultimately, the political frame must take precedence over the military. At its best, a political frame encourages decision makers to compromise, to moderate their views, and to examine problems from multiple perspectives. At its worst, however, a political frame takes on heavy ideological overtones. Rather than using a wide field of view, it can become myopic and focus on achieving short-term gains at the polls.

The "New Coke" Debacle. Business executives may also employ a military frame to analyze problems. In 1985, Coca-Cola decided to change the taste of Coke. Responding to a long, slow decline in market share, and to the Pepsi Challenge, corporate officers announced with much fanfare that a different and better soft drink had been developed in a "new" Coke. Public response was swift. Within a few days a mass revolt was under way. Lawsuits were filed. Over forty thousand letters poured into corporate headquarters in Atlanta, Georgia. One said: "I don't think I would be more upset if you were to burn the flag in the front yard."

Eventually, Coca-Cola capitulated and brought back the old flavor in the form of Coke Classic while still leaving "New Coke" on the market. Three years after the introduction of New Coke, its sales represented only 2.3 percent of the market, despite the fact that the company spent twice as much on advertising for the new product as on the Classic. One Pepsi executive said, "Its market share has the half-life of uranium. Every time I look, it's gotten smaller." What happened to the marketing strategy of Coca-Cola? After all, taste tests had demonstrated that people liked the "new" Coke better than the old.

The decision by Coca-Cola to change the taste of Coke was made after long and careful study. But perhaps the single factor most responsible for the decision was the results of the Pepsi Challenge, in which person after person would be shown on television selecting Pepsi over Coke in taste tests. A rational group, the executives at Coke decided that if taste was the problem, a change in the taste of the beverage would solve the problem. They had to create a soft drink that would beat Pepsi in taste tests.

Coca-Cola executives viewed themselves as fighting a war against Pepsi Cola. Thus, a military perspective dominated management thinking. The mission assigned to Coca-Cola scientists was to develop a formulation that would surpass Pepsi in taste tests; in addition, the testing would have to be done in total secrecy in order not to alert the enemy of impending attack. To maintain that secrecy, the researchers kept the tasters in the dark as to which brands of soft drinks they were comparing. They would compare "brand A" to "brand B" without any idea that it was Pepsi and Coke they were tasting. But the researchers ignored one important psychological principle: Expectations strongly influence perception, which especially applies to taste. This principle was illustrated by an experiment sponsored by *The Wall Street Journal*. During the summer of 1987, when both Pepsi and Coca-Cola launched advertisements in which Pepsi challenged Coke Classic and New Coke challenged Pepsi, *The Wall Street Journal* commissioned a taste test to help clarify the muddled situation. When the identities of the brands were not revealed, the test showed that 70 percent of the one hundred tasters confused the three colas. When confronted with their confusion of brands, some consumers became defensive and accused the testers of shaking the bottles; others blamed the results on the use of plastic cups rather than glasses. Had the labels been placed on the colas, however, the results would have mirrored the tasters' prior expectations. Coke drinkers would prefer Coke and Pepsi drinkers would prefer Pepsi. Further, consider what would have happened had the Coca-Cola executives initially asked brand-loyal Coke drinkers to compare the new beverage to their old favorite, which was being discontinued. Of course, they would have immediately learned that a major problem was about to occur.

Perceiving themselves in a battle for survival with Pepsi, Coca-Cola executives viewed the world through a military lens. The military frame caused managers to focus on maintaining secrecy, thereby ignoring a scientific principle that expectations influence perception. By not labeling the colas being tested, the researchers obtained an inaccurate picture of what would occur. As a result, it was impossible to anticipate the staggeringly negative emotional response to the change.

Legal Frames. In the litigious society of the United States, a legal frame is taking on increased importance. Viewing the world through a legal lens can have its benefits. The law provides a formal set of rules that governs interrelations between parties. As a result, following the law can keep people and companies out of trouble. A partner in a prestigious Denver law firm described the role of corporate lawyers for me in the following way: "Most business people have a goal in mind. They focus on what can go right to reach the goal. As an attorney, I focus on what can go wrong. My goal is to help the entrepreneur identify alternatives with the least number of negatives."

On the other hand, a legalistic perspective can seriously impair progress. In order to avoid any possible legal problem, one solution is to do nothing. The result is a strong tendency to avoid risk taking. In addition, approaching problems from a legal frame can discourage open communications. I learned of the inconsistency between open communication and a legal perspective firsthand. In the early 1980s, I was actively researching how consumers react to product recalls. A friend asked if I was interested in testifying in a lawsuit filed by the parents of a young girl who had been seriously scalded by a hot-water vaporizer that overturned one night. After investigating the incident, it was clear that corporate managers had known for at least a couple of years that the product had serious problems, yet the managers decided to take no action to recall the product. In the trial, I described how product recalls are done, and gave my opinion that the company should have recalled this product. The jury awarded the plaintiff more than $3 million in punitive damages.

After the trial, the plaintiff's attorneys congratulated me for a job well done. My friend, who had dropped out of his academic career in engineering to make his fortune as a professional expert witness, was interested in recruiting me into his profession. He turned to me and said in all earnestness, "John, you are good at this. But, if you want to do more, you need to stop writing." I was incredulous. "Stop writing?" That was and is the single thing I like to do most in my profession. As I look back on the incident, though, I believe that he was right. In subsequent cases, opposing attorneys requested everything that I had written relevant to the topic. In trial, I found myself dealing with what I had written in the past rather than with the matters at hand. My research and writing made the process of testifying infinitely more difficult.

While a legal frame can pose problems, because of our litigious society, a corporation must be able to view the world from the lens of a legal frame. In *Talking Straight*, Lee Iacocca discussed his approach-avoidance conflict with lawyers: "Altogether, Chrysler has about a hundred lawyers on the payroll—more than the number of stylists or interior designers we employ—and that doesn't include the hundreds of outside lawyers we have to hire every year." The problem, however, is that the law is often ambiguous, ". . . and the easiest way to stay out of trouble is not to do anything. Of course, that's also a good way to go broke." To solve the problem, Iacocca hires lawyers who are also businessmen. As he said, "I want lawyers who tell me how to do something and stay within the law, but who still have enough moxie to stand their ground when they have to."

Just as I found that the legal frame seeks to discourage open communications, Iacocca observed the same pattern: "The sad fact is, being forthright and honest can set you up for those who aren't. Watergate gave stonewalling a bad name, but whether you're guilty or innocent, the first advice you often get from a lawyer is 'clam up.' " In business, however, not communicating with customers can lead to major problems. When things go wrong, consumers want to get accurate information quickly. The problems of Ford Motor Company with the Pinto illustrate the conflict between the legal frame, which focuses on limiting communications, and the marketing frame, which thrives on open communications. The troubles with the exploding Pinto gas tank occurred in the early 1970s, while Iacocca was still at Ford. He noted that the Pinto "was a legal problem and a public relations problem, and we chose to deal only with the legal problem." As a result, Ford was vilified by the press, which greatly increased public suspicions of the company. "Ever since then," Iacocca said, "whenever we've had a similar choice to make at Chrysler, we've done the exact opposite. We've chosen to look past the legal consequences and go public with the whole truth." Indeed, when one looks at the facility and openness with which Chrysler handled the speedometer tampering case in the early 1990s, one would have to agree that the company learned a lesson from Ford's mistakes.

In sum, while viewing problems from a legal frame is paramount today, one must recognize that a trade-off exists. A legal perspective can inhibit innovation and close communications. As a result, it is important to balance the legal perspective with a marketing orientation that encourages open communication and the free exchange of information.

Framing Risks

The way in which risks are framed can have a major impact on how people react to them. This issue was faced early in the development of the American space program. D. F. Hornig spent ten years on the President's Science Advisory Committee under Eisenhower, Kennedy, and Johnson. In this capacity he participated in a variety of high-stakes decisions. He was involved in the early stages of the Mercury space program, and one of his tasks was to put together a committee of scientists to estimate the probability of success for Alan Shepard's forthcoming suborbital flight. The task was daunting. For the sake of this discussion, let's assume that in the Mercury flight one hundred things could go wrong and that each was independent of the other. If each component had only a 1 in 1,000 chance of failure, there would still be a 10 percent chance that the flight would fail. Over the course of five flights, there would be a 41 percent chance of a catastrophe.

The question that Hornig faced was, how should you present such information to President Kennedy? How do you frame it? Do you tell him that over a sequence of five flights we have a 4 in 10 chance of killing the astronaut and seeing the space program go up in smoke? Hornig describes how he handled the dilemma:

> What we told him was roughly this. The space craft is about as complicated as a high performance jet fighter. It is made of similar materials, in the same factories, under the same management, with similar quality controls. It is built by the same group of workers. We have, therefore, looked into the first flights of new types of high performance fighters. We have listened to the transmissions from test pilots under crisis conditions—when you couldn't believe their blood pressures and heart rates. And from that comparison we believe the probability of catastrophic failure is about 5 percent.

Hornig went on to say that if a catastrophe occurred, the events could be explained to the American people in terms of the hazards of a test pilot. When framed from the perspective of a test pilot, the odds of dying in the Mercury capsule appeared to be acceptable. Americans were quite familiar with the short expected life span of test pilots. This perspective, however, was quite different from that of a systems engineer. Systems engineers are trained to *overdesign* for safety. When failures occur, those framing the problem from such a perspective have major psychological difficulties in handling the outcome.

Such was the case with the fire that killed three Apollo astronauts during ground tests in January 1967. The fire strongly affected Joe Shea, who was a key figure in moving the Apollo program from drawings to rockets. Indeed, it was purely by chance that he was not in the capsule with the astronauts when it was engulfed by flames. In analyzing the reasons why Shea took the accident so personally, one flight director suggested that it represented the difference between engineers who came out of the world of systems engineering and those coming out of the flight-test business. Systems engineers believed that if you were smart enough and good enough, you could figure a way to do the task without hurting anyone. In contrast, the flight-test people had a different view. Shea said, "You understand that the risk is there, and when it happens it's terrible, you wish it didn't happen, you wish you were smarter, but you know it's going to happen and so you learn to live with that. You worry about it a lot and you think about it a lot but when it does occur it doesn't kill you. You lose crew. Pilots die flying experimental aircraft."

Not only does framing influence how one approaches a risk, but it also influences how people respond to decision outcomes. Those who could frame the Apollo fire from the perspective of the test pilot handled their grief much more easily than those who viewed the situation through the lens of the systems engineer. Conversely, the horrible tragedy of the Challenger Space Shuttle explosion was made far worse because NASA framed the program as though it was a commercial airline. In their effort to garner public support, officials had moved it from the experimental to the routine. A congressman was flown into space. Even a schoolteacher was scheduled for launch. Unfortunately, she was one of those aboard the Challenger.

Because the public viewed the Space Shuttle from a commercial airline perspective, the visual scene of the Challenger explosion (with the solid fuel boosters spinning awkwardly away from the fireball) created massive dissonance for Americans. Commercial jets are not supposed to blow up in flight. An important lesson from the Challenger disaster is the importance of correctly framing the nature of programs to the outside public. Today, the Space Shuttle program is still experimental. Estimates are that a 50 percent chance exists that in the 1990s we will lose another shuttle. NASA officials would do well to make every effort to frame the program as experimental to the public in order to minimize the negative publicity that will inevitably result when another spacecraft is lost.

As the story of the Challenger explosion suggests, how the public frames risks can dramatically influence reactions to a disaster. Paul Slovic, an international authority on risk perception, wrote in the prestigious journal Science about one industrial accident that has produced more societal costs than any other. The incident produced no deaths and little if any future physical harm to people or animals. Yet it devastated the company to which it occurred, and stopped an entire industry dead in its tracks. After more than a decade college students considering a career in the industry continue to be scorned by their classmates. The disaster of which he wrote was the Three Mile Island nuclear reactor accident that occurred in Pennsylvania in 1979. His research revealed that the public fears nuclear accidents above all others, even though experts rate nuclear power as far less risky than many everyday activities in which we engage. Indeed, the top three risks—according to the experts—were driving motor vehicles, smoking, and drinking alcoholic beverages. Nuclear power was rated number 20 in risk, and as less dangerous than riding bicycles, owning handguns, or generating electric power via non-nuclear means. The studies also show that dangers perceived to be unfamiliar and out of personal control are perceived to be the most risky. For this reason, most people have much greater fear of riding in a passenger jet than driving a car, even though air travel is far safer. As Paul Slovic said, "An accident that takes many lives may produce relatively little social disturbance (beyond that experienced by the victims' families and friends) if it occurs as part of a familiar and well-understood system (such as a train wreck). However, a small accident in an unfamiliar system (or one perceived as poorly understood), such as a nuclear reactor or a recombinant DNA laboratory, may have immense social consequences if it is perceived as a harbinger of further and possible catastrophic mishaps."

The public has little understanding of, or control over, nuclear reactors. As a result, the industry is framed as being extremely risky, and even small accidents that harm few people create near-panic conditions. A similar problem is currently faced by oil companies. In March 1989, the huge oil supertanker *Exxon Valdez* ripped open on Bligh Reef in Prince William Sound, Alaska. While damage to the environment was certainly severe, not one human being was killed as a direct result of the gigantic oil spill. Yet it cost Exxon over $3 billion and immense negative publicity.

I spoke to Gene Smith, who acted as on-site financial controller for the entire operation launched by Exxon to clean up the gigantic oil spill. Exxon headquarters contacted him the week after the accident and asked if he wanted to go to Alaska to monitor the enormous financial transactions that would take place. He said yes, not realizing that he would have to leave his family behind for a year and a half and work fourteen-hour days, seven days a week. Gene appeared to be distressed by the public's reaction to Exxon's clean-up efforts. Exxon's mobilization was done under conditions that resembled wartime operations. Many individuals endured severe personal hardship to participate in the clean-up. From his perspective the firm made an all-out effort to solve the problem; yet it was assailed publicly for its actions.

To make matters worse, some of Exxon's massive effort was wasted. As the controller said, "the best clean-up was done by winter storms." A study performed by the National Oceanic and Atmospheric Administration supports his contention. It found that by 1991, Prince William Sound had nearly recovered, and that the re-

204 · JUDGMENT CALLS

covery would have been quicker had Exxon not been forced to blast beaches with jets of hot water to clean off the oil in response to the public outcry. It seems that more small organisms died from the hot water than from the oil. The chief scientist at the agency said: "Sometimes the best, and ironically the most difficult, thing to do in the face of an ecological disaster is to do nothing."

When people frame a technology as potentially uncontrollable and not understandable, great risks are perceived. If an accident occurs, demands for quick action follow, even if doing less is in fact wiser than doing more.

Historical Frameworks

When decision makers face a high-stakes judgment call, they frequently look to history to find similar events in the past that may help them in their present dilemma. In general, historians argue that the past can and should be used to enhance decision making. Harry Truman compared the North Korean crossing of the 38th parallel in their invasion of South Korea to events in World War II, such as Japan's seizure of Manchuria from China and Hitler's annexation of Austria in 1938. Using these incidents as frames, Truman had little option but to commit American troops, because the lesson from World War II was to resist aggression and avoid appeasement. Similarly, when Iraq invaded Kuwait in 1990, George Bush compared Saddam Hussein to Hitler. Framing the problem in such terms forced the United States to embark on a huge troop build-up in order to avoid appeasement.

Extreme care, however, should be employed in using historical analogies because, applied incorrectly, they can be used to justify *poor* judgments. For example, the misuse of historical frames is found in the justification for America's participation in the Vietnam War. Political and military analysts frequently referred to the Korean conflict as a historical parallel to Vietnam. Very early in the war, General Maxwell Taylor made such a mistake. In discussing the potential of sending troops to Vietnam, he characterized Korea as having terrain comparable to that in Vietnam. This description was inaccurate. In comparison to Vietnam, Korea has more open terrain, which is more suitable for conventional warfare employing tanks and airpower.

Lyndon Johnson also used Korea as an analogue to Vietnam. But he focused on the political implications. He knew that Korea had been a political trap, and he feared that if the war in Vietnam was not over quickly, he would be attacked for failing to win it. As a result, he wanted American troops to go into Vietnam and be aggressive, win, and get home. While Lyndon Johnson used a Korean frame to correctly deduce the problem that would prove his undoing, the generals were deceived by the terrain analogy. Their misassessment of the military situation would act to prolong the war and fulfill Johnson's worst fears. Of course, the correct historical frame in Vietnam was the defeat of the French in that country. But the arrogance of American decision makers created a situation in which the reasons for the failure of the French in Indochina were not applied to their own situation. Why wasn't the French failure in Vietnam considered relevant? One can only speculate; but a possible reason was that the French had been beaten by Nazi Germany, while the United States had been victorious. In addition, the French had failed in their quest to build the Panama Canal, while the United States had succeeded.

One of the most frequent uses of historical frames is to kill an idea by likening it to a previous debacle. At Ford Motor Company a sure way to cause managers to think twice about a new car idea is to raise the specter of the Edsel. Similarly, likening U.S. involvement in a military situation to "another Vietnam" throws cold water on the intervention. History was also used for such a purpose during the Cuban missile crisis by John Kennedy's advisers.

John F. Kennedy possessed a keen sense of history. He required each member of the National Security Council to read Barbara Tuchman's book, *The Guns of August*. His goal was to imprint in each person's brain the realization that otherwise intelligent leaders can blunder into world wars that no one wants. During the Cuban missile crisis, John Kennedy and his advisers frequently used historical analogies as a means of framing the problem at hand. On Tuesday, October 16, 1962, Kennedy was informed that a U-2 spy plane had taken pictures of missiles in Cuba. That day he assembled an advisory team, which immediately began to develop options. Gathering in the Cabinet Room of the White House, three options quickly emerged: (1) take out the missiles by bombing them; (2) take out the Cuban air force along with the missiles; or (3) invade Cuba. At this early point in the decision process, Kennedy felt that the minimum action would involve taking out the missiles. He said, "We're certainly going to do number one. We're going to take out these missiles."

The analysis went on for several days. The idea of bombing Cuba was distasteful to some of the advisers—particularly Robert

Kennedy and George Ball. On audio recordings of the meetings, listeners can hear Robert Kennedy say, "I would say that, uh, you're dropping bombs all over Cuba if you do the second. . . . You're going to kill an awful lot of people, and, uh, you're going to take an awful lot of heat on it." At this point George Ball invoked the historical analogy of Pearl Harbor, whereupon Robert Kennedy passed a note to his brother that said, "I know now how Tojo felt when he was planning Pearl Harbor." Later, Robert Kennedy would describe a surprise bombing of Cuba as "a Pearl Harbor in reverse, and it would blacken the name of the United States in the pages of history."

Fortunately for the world, John Kennedy and his advisers took six days to reach a decision. By not doing anything until they knew what to do, they avoided the precipitous action of bombing Cuba. While we can never be sure, it seems likely that by using Pearl Harbor as a historical analogy, George Ball and Robert Kennedy may have turned President John Kennedy away from what in retrospect would probably have been a terrible decision.

Selecting the Appropriate Frame

So far, we have discussed a number of sources of frames of reference, including historical and professional specializations. Because historical frameworks can have a positive or negative impact on decision making, the judgment call involves deciding which historical incident is relevant to the current situation. Some analysts have suggested that in order to analyze historical analogues, decision makers must first carefully define the current situation. Next, information should be sorted into what is *known*, what is *presumed*, and what is *unknown*. One can then compare the current situation to potential historical parallels for likenesses and differences. The process must be performed dispassionately, though, because choosing the wrong historical frame can lead to major policy errors.

Six professional frames have been identified in this chapter: technical, financial, marketing, political, military, and legal. Which of the six frames should one choose when faced with a judgment call? No cookbook recipe exists to answer this question, but the principle of multi-frame superiority is one of the fundamentals of high-stakes decision making. Faced with a judgment call, the decision maker should examine the situation from a variety of perspectives. Indeed, one of the worst offenses committed by decision makers is to view the world through a uni-dimensional lens. Even at the highest levels, managers can take a one-sided perspective. Robert McNamara in his book *Blundering into Disaster* described just such an occurrence in discussing three near misses of atomic annihilation. According to McNamara, one of the near misses occurred during the 1967 Arab-Israeli War when he was the Secretary of Defense. In early June, intelligence sources indicated that Egypt was about to launch a surprise attack on Israel. The reaction of the Israelis was to launch a preemptive attack; and, despite the efforts of President Johnson, they executed the plan swiftly and with deadly force. The Israeli forces threatened to totally eliminate the Egyptian army, which was supported by the Soviet Union. It was this situation that brought America and the Soviet Union to a point of nuclear confrontation.

On the day of the preemptive attack in June 1967, McNamara reached his office in the Pentagon at 7:00 A.M. Shortly after his arrival, the general on duty in the War Room called McNamara to report that Aleksei Kosygin, the prime minister of the Soviet Union, was on the Hot Line and wanted to talk to President Johnson. McNamara's first reaction was, "Why are you calling me?" The general responded that the Hot Line ended at the Pentagon. McNamara's incredulity at this state of affairs is best captured in his own words:

> It may sound absurd, but I had been Secretary for three years since the Hot Line had been installed, and because it had never been used, I was not aware that the teletype facility terminated below my office. In shock and surprise I told the general that we were spending some tens of billions of dollars a year on defense and, within the next fifteen minutes, he had better find a way to divert a few of those dollars to facilitate an extension of the teletype to the White House.

The installation of the Hot Line had been analyzed from a military perspective. The reasoning probably went something like this: "The Hot Line will only be used in time of war. Under such circumstances, all hell will break loose, and the President will most certainly be in the Pentagon. Further, in order to maintain complete control over the communications instrument, it should be in the most secure place possible—the War Room in the Pentagon." Those who installed the device appear to have lacked the breadth of vision to recognize that the Hot Line would most likely be used in order to *prevent* war. Thus, it should be as close as possible to the place where the President spends most of his time—the White House.

A problem in applying the multi-frame rule is that few people have the breadth of training to view the world accurately through divergent sets of lenses. In an article in *The Wall Street Journal*, Don Frey argued that one reason why Japan and Germany have a competitive advantage is that far more of their CEOs have a technical background. Perhaps reflecting his experiences at Ford Motor Company and Bell & Howell, where he was the CEO, he lambasted the trend for American companies to be headed by financially oriented types, the "beanies," as he calls them. As he accurately noted, universities in the United States turn out proportionately more MBAs than engineers as compared to either Japan or Germany. Because of his frame of reference, Don Frey has a visceral distrust of finance. While he admits that MBAs do have the best interests of the company in mind, their problem is that they are trained too narrowly. He pointed out that "financial control and measurement is all they know . . . too often the financial types do not realize that beans must be earned before they are counted." Given this "fact of life," how do you solve the problem? Again drawing on his own experiences, Frey suggested that non-technical CEOs should assemble a set of technically competent and trusted advisers.

Even in his own analysis, Frey too was looking through his own narrowly focused lens. His solution to "financial myopia" was to use a retinue of technical advisers. Such a policy may only result in replacing one filter with another. The goal of peerless decision makers should be to surround themselves with a variety of advisers, each of whom carries a divergent frame of reference. A place to start may be with individuals who can perceive problems through the various frames discussed in this chapter.

Some ideas to consider when making the judgment call of which frame of reference to choose are:

- Decision frames act as lenses that may clarify or distort information.

- It is best to analyze problems through various frames, using alternative professional perspectives and historical analogies.

- Six frequently used professional frames are: financial, technical, marketing, military, legal, and political.

- Employing metaphors and analogies as "mini-frames" helps to communicate vividly nuances of meaning.

- If risks are framed as uncontrollable and unfamiliar, people will experience anxiety and dread.

- Match the decision frame to the problem.

- When using historical frames, compare the present situation with the historical analogy based upon what is known, presumed, and unknown.

- Select high-level managers in part for their ability to examine problems through multiple frames of reference.

9.

REASON VERSUS EMOTION

"Amateur hour," "a game of chicken," "egos run amuck," "the Jonestown defense." These were analysts' metaphors for Bendix Corporation's attempted acquisition of Martin Marietta in 1982. This deplorable saga clearly reveals the interplay of reason and emotion in high-stakes decision making.

For several years prior to 1982, Bendix Corporation, headed by William Agee, had systematically divested itself of "lackluster" businesses in order to build an acquisition war chest of some $500 million. Meanwhile, corporate analysts assiduously searched for undervalued companies that would fit with Bendix. The one corporation that consistently appeared on their lists was Martin Marietta—an important defense contractor. Assisted in the development of the strategy by his wife, Mary Cunningham, Agee offered to purchase Martin Marietta stock for $43 a share ($12 over the market price).

The bid made by Bendix, however, was less than Martin Marietta had spent on modernization in the previous five years. Marietta's president, Thomas Pownall, and the board of directors immediately reacted negatively; they didn't like the offer, nor did they like Agee or Mary Cunningham. To develop a defense against a hostile takeover, Pownall contacted Martin Siegel at Kidder Peabody. Siegel suggested a novel approach: Have Marietta make a counteroffer for Bendix. The directors liked the idea, and the company offered to acquire 50.3 percent of Bendix's stock at $75 a share.

Some called the defensive reaction the "Pacman defense," because each company attempted to take over the other. The tactic also possessed elements of the game of chicken. Unless one of the companies turned away, both would be damaged. One analyst described the standoff as irrational, saying, "It is inconceivable that people would create a company like that. It would not be a merger but an implosion of two companies." Another analyst called the Martin Marietta approach "the Jonestown defense." As a metaphor for the clash, he was using the specter of the Reverend Jim Jones's followers escaping persecution by committing mass suicide. The acquisition war threatened to take two strong companies and turn them into a single weak firm burdened by excessive debt.

Bendix executives and Bill Agee hoped that once they started buying Martin Marietta's shares, its board of directors would capitulate. When asked about the reaction of his company's board, one insider at Martin Marietta said, "If Agee thought our guys were going to roll over and play dead, he's nuts." Another Marietta strategist said to *Wall Street Journal* reporters in the middle of the fray, "To us, Agee looks a little naive. I don't think he has plotted carefully enough the countermoves we might make."

After Martin Marietta responded by offering to acquire Bendix, Agee upped his offer to $48 a share. Making a classic mistake, he was merely bidding against himself. He then went to Martin Marietta to persuade its board that it was in their company's interest to go with the buyout offer. Here, Agee made another mistake by taking his wife with him. A vice-president at Joseph E. Seagram & Sons, Mary Cunningham was Agee's constant adviser. Bringing her to the bargaining table infuriated the Martin Marietta board. One member said that "Just the thought of losing their company to a guy who is being advised or guided by Mary Cunningham was more than they could stand." The action further stiffened the resolve of Marietta.

Finally, it dawned on Agee that Marietta's board was not playing chicken. At this point *Fortune* magazine described Agee as a "shaken man." Now, the tables were turned, and the hunter had become the prey. In order to defend his company, Agee brought out his "white knight"—Allied Corporation. In response, Martin Marietta brought out its bully—United Technologies, which also began buying shares of Bendix. Both Allied and United Technologies were larger companies; in addition, their CEOs hated one another. It seems that the CEO of United Technologies had once worked for his counterpart at

Allied and was anxious to get even for past wrongs. Suddenly, the fray had grown exceedingly complex.

The final deal was anticlimactic and one in which all companies lost. Allied bought out Bendix, but the merger resulted in a weaker company with a large debt load. Martin Marietta remained an independent, but substantially weaker, company because it, too, piled on debt. In all, over $4 billion was spent, and the only people to profit were stock arbitragers, buyout artists, and attorneys.

The acquisition of Martin Marietta began as a rational effort to acquire an undervalued company and, as a result, increase the market value of Bendix. But egos quickly became involved, and emotions dictated move and countermove. The consensus among Wall Street insiders was that the executives let personal ambition dominate sound business judgment. Rather than base their decisions on rational business and financial considerations, the players allowed anger and fear to dominate their decision making.

The Ubiquity of Emotion in Decision Making

Emotion: we expect it to influence decision making in high-contact sports, such as American football. But one would think that captains of industry, who control billions of dollars and the financial lives of thousands, should rise above human passion. The Bendix/Martin Marietta fiasco destroyed that myth.

When high-stakes decisions are involved, emotions inevitably intervene to influence judgment. For example, to the uninitiated, world championship chess appears to be a totally intellectual endeavor in which pure reason is applied to defeat an opponent. In reality, however, the pressure of the competition releases the full gamut of emotions—from fear to elation to hate. In 1981, Anatoly Karpov defended his crown as the world chess champion against the Soviet defector, Viktor Korchnoi. Shortly into the twelfth game of their match, Korchnoi suddenly became furious with Karpov and snapped, "Stop squirming in your chair, you sniveling little worm." The epithet, resounding in the staid realm of international chess, had enormous emotional impact, and it stunned the spectators. The two chess grandmasters, Karpov and Korchnoi, hated each other. Three years earlier in a championship match, both men had recruited accomplices to put hexes on one another. Korchnoi brought in two robed mystics, who meditated in the front row of spectators. Karpov used a more high-tech approach, importing a parapsychologist from the Soviet Union. Perhaps his clairvoyant was more effective because he won the match.

In late 1990, Karpov would play for the world title against Gary Kasparov for a total purse of $3 million, a sum sufficient to make most of us choke a little. Kasparov is to Karpov as a Porsche is to a Mercedes. Kasparov plays a fast, passionate, aggressive, open, risk-taking game. Karpov's style is plodding and conservative, but brilliant. When Karpov beat Korchnoi in 1981, Leonid Brezhnev cabled him: "Our whole country is proud that in a strenuous and persistent struggle you displayed consummate skill, inflexible will and courage —in a word, the qualities that make up our Soviet character." If Karpov represents the Soviet Union of Brezhnev, then Kasparov illustrates Russia under Boris Yeltsin. His goal is to take chess to the people. One reporter described Kasparov as wanting "the fan to understand his exhilaration, wonder, anger, or, if he should lose, his mortification." Kasparov was quoted as exclaiming, "Chess is a passionate game, but people don't know. The game can't exist in empty space—it needs a public."

Kasparov's passions extend from his love for the game to his hatred for Karpov. Brooding about his nemesis, he said, "He is a creature of darkness. He is not like a human being. He is angry and evil. He represents something alien to the crowd." Kasparov eventually won the long match, but at any moment onlookers expected sparks to fly. Aware of the potential, the organizers placed a special partition under the table to prevent the competitors from getting in their kicks under, as well as on top of, the board.

Emotions drive people to action. Tommy Lasorda, the manager of the Los Angeles Dodgers, told this story: When he was in the eighth grade, he volunteered to be a school-crossing guard because the teachers took all of the guards to see a professional baseball game at the end of the year. After he braved wind and cold that year, his wish was fulfilled. He put together an autograph book, and waited in a walkway at the park to get some signatures. Finally a player came through, and the young boy asked for his autograph. The player brushed him aside, saying, "Get the hell out of the way."

The incident angered Lasorda. He looked up the name and remembered it: Buster Maynard. Some years later he was pitching in the minor leagues, and who should come up to bat but Buster Maynard, "the same sonofabitch who wouldn't give me his autograph." The first two pitches that he threw knocked Maynard down. By this time the hapless old pro was beginning to realize that something was up. He said, "You throw at me again, and I'll come out to the mound." So, Lasorda threw at him again, and Maynard charged.

After the game, Maynard sought out Lasorda, who was still looking for a fight. Maynard said to him, "Before today, I didn't even know you existed. Why did you throw at me?" When Lasorda explained that it was because the player had refused to give him an autograph as a boy in the eighth grade, Maynard just walked away shaking his head.

Without emotion to serve as an impetus to action, little would happen in this world. When does the United States get into a war? Entry tends to occur only after an incident has created sufficient anger to goad the president, the lawmakers, and the public into action. Regulatory agencies tend to be created after a major event causes sufficient emotion within the Congress. For example, the Food and Drug Administration (FDA) was established in large part because of the emotions stirred by Upton Sinclair's book *The Jungle*. His description of the horrendous conditions in the meat-packing houses moved the Congress to action. Here is just one passage from the book:

> Some worked at the stamping machines, and it was very seldom that one could work long there at the pace that was set, and give out and forget himself, and have a part of his hand chopped off. . . . Worst of any, however, were the fertilizer men. . . . These people could not be shown to the visitor,—for the odor . . . would scare any ordinary visitor at a hundred yards, and as for the other men, who worked in tank-rooms full of steam, and in some of which there were open vats near the level of the floor, their peculiar trouble was that they fell into the vats; and when they were fished out, there was never enough of them left to be worth exhibiting—sometimes they would be overlooked for days till all but the bones of them had gone out to the world as Durham's Pure Leaf Lard.

Other books have stirred passions sufficiently to help get laws passed. In the 1960s, Rachel Carson's *Silent Spring* spurred congressional action on the environment. And Ralph Nader's book *Unsafe at Any Speed* led to the creation of the National Highway Traffic Safety Administration.

Rationality in Decision Making

If emotion has such a pervasive influence on decision making, what does it mean to make a reasoned and rational decision? Many different views of rationality exist. For Plato, "rationality" was the part of the soul that stood in opposition to animal desires. According to Aristotle, the "rational" level was the only immortal component of the soul. Decision theorists tend to view rationality as helping us to avoid contradictory trains of thought. Rationality does not necessarily lead us to any particular conclusion; rather, it is the key to avoiding logical errors of reasoning. As one authority on decision theory explained, rationality "dictates what *cannot* be concluded, *not* what can." The problem with an approach that defines rationality in terms of avoiding logical inconsistency is that madmen, such as Hitler, can be viewed as rational. By creating myths (e.g., Jews are dangerous and the purity of the Aryan blood must be maintained), it was possible to deduce quite logical justifications for the Holocaust.

Another approach to rationality is called subjective expected utility (SEU). When applied properly, it focuses on the starting points of the train of thought as well as the logic of the deductive process. The base ideas of SEU are old and go back at least to Benjamin Franklin, who recommended a version of it. In a letter to Joseph Priestley (the British chemist who discovered oxygen), Franklin described how to make complex choices. He suggested taking a sheet of paper and listing the pros and cons of engaging in an action. Next, the person places weights on the pros and cons in order to show the relative importance of each. Over a period of several days, he (or she) then crosses out the evenly weighted pros and cons and eventually selects the option having the greatest weight.

The SEU model merely extends Ben Franklin's intuitive approach. Based upon this model, a rational decision has the following five characteristics: (1) the decision maker identifies what options are available for action; (2) he identifies the possible outcomes of each option; (3) he estimates the likelihood of the various outcomes happening; (4) he calculates the value of the various outcomes; and finally (5), he combines the information according to appropriate rules of probability theory to estimate the subjective expected utility of each option. The option with the highest SEU is then chosen.

The table on pages 217–18 presents a simplified SEU analysis that I made of a decision faced by President George Bush in October 1990. After Iraq invaded Kuwait, the United States rapidly deployed troops and equipment to the Middle East and created an embargo against the country. By early October, roughly 200,000 American troops were in the vicinity. The problem faced by the president was whether or not he should order the invasion of Kuwait. In the analysis, two options were identified—either invade Kuwait immediately or leave the embargo in place indefinitely in hopes of starving Iraq into submission—as well as a number of possible outcomes for each course of action. In addition, values were assigned to represent the likelihood that each outcome could occur, and the positive or negative weight of each outcome should it occur. When I made the calculations in October 1990, the SEU of invading was 4.8 units and the SEU of maintaining the embargo was 6.0 units.

A simplified Subjective Expected Utility (SEU) analysis of a possible Kuwait invasion by U.S. forces in October 1990

Step 1. Identify alternative decisions: (a) invade immediately or (b) leave the embargo in place.

Step 2. Calculate SEU by identifying outcomes, their likelihood, their utility, and summing across options. (Utility estimates are on scale where 1 = bad outcome and 10 = great outcome)

OPTION A: INVADE KUWAIT

Outcome 1—The invasion is spectacularly successful. American forces suffer relatively minor casualties with only 500 soldiers killed in action. The price of oil then stabilizes at $22 a barrel. (Likelihood = .25; utility = 8.0)

Outcome 2—American forces are met with unexpectedly tough opposition and Iraq retaliates with poison gas. The invasion turns into a long bruising affair. The U.S. takes 30,000 casualties. After a year of massive attacks, Kuwait is recaptured, but the price of oil stabilizes at $45 a barrel. (Likelihood = .65; utility = 4.0)

Outcome 3—Iraq blunts the American attack, inflicting massive casualties. Iran, Syria, and Egypt then join together to form a united Islam nation. Israel is invaded, and the war expands dramatically. Quickly, 500,000 casualties occur. The

(continued)

price of oil skyrockets to $150 a barrel as all Middle East oil is cut off. (Likelihood = .10; utility = 2.0)

Option A's SEU = $(.25 \times 8) + (.65 \times 4) + (.10 \times 2) = 4.8$

OPTION B: MAINTAIN EMBARGO

Outcome 1—After six months of the embargo, Saddam Hussein is assassinated. Iraq gives up, abandons Kuwait, and agrees to pay war reparations of $20 billion. The cost of oil falls to $15 a barrel. (Likelihood = .25; utility = 10.0)

Outcome 2—Iraq suffers, but stubbornly holds on. Libya, China, and Iran increase their efforts to supply food and supplies to the beleaguered country. As the suffering mounts, Syria moves over to Iraq's side. Meanwhile, unrest stirs in the U.S. as the costs of the huge military presence in the region drain the economy. The cost of oil fluctuates between $25 and $45 a barrel as war fears come and go. (Likelihood = .50; utility = 4.0)

Outcome 3—After six months of the embargo, Iraq forms an alliance with Iran, Libya, and Egypt, which attacks Israel. The entire Middle East blows up, 500,000 casualties occur, and oil prices move to $150 a barrel. (Likelihood = .25; utility = 2.0)

Option B's SEU = $(.25 \times 10) + (.5 \times 4) + (.25 \times 2) = 5.0$

Step 3. Conclusion: *Delay invasion.* The embargo strategy SEU of 5.0 is higher than the invade strategy SEU of 4.8.

Thus, the SEU analysis—which admittedly used probabilities and outcomes as perceived by this author in October 1990—indicated that *not* invading Kuwait had the higher subjective expected utility. Of course, different answers could have resulted by simply changing the probabilities and the estimates of the negative or positive value of the outcomes that could occur as a result of each course of action. A common practice is to do what is called a "sensitivity analysis" and systematically change the estimates in order to see how the decision might be influenced.

As events would unfold, President Bush made the judgment call to invade Kuwait and Iraq. With the enormous military success of the operation, how does that make the SEU analysis look? The answer is that the succeeding events confirmed the analysis. Recognizing that the United States lacked sufficient military forces in the region, President Bush took steps to change the probabilities of the outcomes from those extant in October 1990 when the SEU analysis was performed. First, he nearly tripled the size and military potential of the American force. Second, he obtained United Nations support for the possible use of force after the deadline of January 15, 1991. Third, he put together a coalition of countries against Iraq in which each would have a great deal to lose if the attack failed. Thus, he increased the odds of a successful invasion and decreased the odds of having poor outcomes result. His actions dramatically changed the SEU analysis to the point that it favored taking action over leaving the embargo in place.

The SEU model requires decision makers to justify the estimates of likelihood and the positive/negative outcomes that could result from alternative courses of action. Wishful thinking must be eliminated from the analysis. The process is lengthy, and when done properly, is far more sophisticated than the brief example in the table indicates. The approach can be applied to mega-high-stakes decisions, such as whether or not to attack Iraq and Kuwait. It can also be applied to more mundane questions, such as do we open a new manufacturing plant, or do we recommend that our client settle a lawsuit for $200,000 or go to trial and hope for a much larger award from a jury?

In sum, rational decision makers reveal two major characteristics. First, their decisions follow the rules of SEU and probability theory. Second, their assumptions, which form the basis for the analysis, are thoroughly tested so that wishful thinking and factual errors are eliminated.

The Virtues of Irrationality

Using the SEU model to make rational decisions is appropriate as long as you have plenty of time and are not facing a competitor (or enemy) who has access to the same information as you. If your opponents know your assumptions and your strategy, they can blunt your efforts at every turn. In these circumstances, maintaining security becomes extremely important. In addition, in some situations appearing to have the capacity to act irrationally can give you a significant advantage in a conflict. Causing the other side to believe that you may act irrationally arouses both fear and hesitation.

In the movie *Lethal Weapon*, Mel Gibson plays a cop on the verge of losing it. In an early scene, Gibson is searching through a forest of Christmas trees for a drug dealer who has escaped. As Gibson moves from tree to tree, he is suddenly grabbed from behind and feels a gun barrel at his head. The drug dealer's eyes glisten confidence, because he just found his ticket out of the mess. Hearing the commotion, the police quickly encircle the pair. Gibson looks out and yells repeatedly to the police, "Shoot 'im, shoot 'im, shoot 'im!" The punk's confident look begins to vanish. Then Gibson puts his nose in the dealer's face and says over and over, "Shoot me, shoot me, shoot me." The irrational behavior causes fear, and when the punk loses concentration for a split second, Gibson grabs his gun, butts his head into the guy's face, and disarms him.

One of the attractions of *Lethal Weapon* and *Lethal Weapon II* was the sight of Gibson walking on the edge of insanity and using it to his advantage. Now, I know that you are thinking something like "In 'real life' people don't go around making other people believe that they may be crazy." This reminds me of a major I encountered in Vietnam. A Green Beret type, he wanted to make sure that everyone knew he was tough and could kill without mercy. His peculiar habit was finding puppies and biting off their heads. When people suggested that such actions might be cruel, he would laugh and remind them that the Vietnamese would just eat the puppies anyway. I have to admit that I never saw him in the act of decapitating a puppy. The legend simply followed him around. And I, like others, steered a wide berth around this guy.

Again, you are right, though. The puppy-gulping story is weak evidence for the thesis that creating the impression of irrationality can give you a power advantage. The gap between acting crazy for a purpose and actually being crazy is narrow. Perhaps the major simply played with only a partial deck of cards. Can an irrational person undertake the rational act of appearing irrational? Such a question might be worth scarcely five minutes of conversation at a cocktail party were it not for the realization that the strategy has been used by presidents. Presidents with their finger on *the* button have sought to make an enemy question their rationality.

One researcher conducted eighty-four interviews with defense policy makers on the use of nuclear weapons. Each of the respondents had a role in formulating, evaluating, or carrying out defense policies in the United States. The theme reiterated by a number of policy makers was the importance of appearing irrational. Dwight Eisenhower was given as an example of someone who used the "crazed-man" tactic effectively by invoking the specter of unleashing Curtis

LeMay—the general who headed the strategic air command and whose bombers carried the H-bomb. Calling Eisenhower a "shrewd president," the policy maker being interviewed remembered him in crucial situations as pointing to LeMay and saying:

Look, heh—listen—you know this is really a mad dog, but I keep him for those situations where I might be reluctantly compelled to unchain him. Now, you don't ever want to get me into a situation where I'm even thinking of unchaining him, but at the same time you understand that it might be necessary.

Richard Nixon also used the tactic. In his book *The Real War,* Nixon compared international relations to stud poker with a hole card. The players are dealt one card face down—the hole card. Then four cards are dealt one at a time—face up. After each card is dealt, bets are made. Nixon argued that because America is an open society, the other side can see each of our cards. In order to create some uncertainty, we must have a hole card that our enemies cannot see. This hidden card is the ability to act irrationally:

The United States is an open society. We have all but one of our cards face up, on the table. Our only covered card is the will, nerve, and unpredictability of the President. . . . If the adversary feels that you are unpredictable, even rash, he will be deterred from pressing you too far. The odds that he will fold increase greatly, and the unpredictable President will win another hand.

Apparently, Nixon viewed himself as playing out the "crazed-man" strategy in his dealings with North Vietnam. He reportedly wrote in his diary, "The North Vietnamese really thought that the President was off his rocker. . . . It was absolutely essential for them to think that." Nixon wanted the North Vietnamese to think that he might use nuclear weapons in Vietnam. The chief-of-staff in the Nixon White House, H. R. Haldeman, wrote:

We were walking along a foggy beach after a long day of speechwriting. He said, "I call it the Madman Theory, Bob. I want the North Vietnamese to believe I've reached the point where I might do *anything* to stop the war. We'll just slip the word to them that, 'for God's sake, you know Nixon is obsessed

about Communism. We can't restrain him when he's angry—
and he has his hand on the nuclear button.' "

During the Kuwait crisis, Saddam Hussein used the madman
strategy. Possessing the military capability to launch missiles
against Saudi Arabian oil fields and to unleash poison gas and biolog-
ical weapons, Hussein attempted to bluff and bluster his way
through the crisis. For the United States, the risk of moving in
quickly after the Kuwait invasion to bomb Iraq into the Stone Age
was too great. Hussein had the capability to inflict unacceptable
losses; he had previously shown himself willing to use poison gas.
Further, while launching a rocket attack against the oil fields of
Saudi Arabia would be tantamount to committing suicide, he seemed
just crazy enough to do it. As a result, the reaction of the United
States had to be measured and cautious until an overwhelming military force was put into place.

Of course, the "madman" strategy is also used in business. The
defense employed by Martin Marietta had such a quality. Its mastermind, Martin Siegel, called it "the deadman's trigger." As a major
weapons contractor, the firm used military jargon. Noting the strategy's similarity to the U.S. nuclear strategy, called MAD (Mutually
Assured Destruction), Martin Marietta called its plan against Bendix
ASSCAP, or "Assured Second Strike Capability." Whatever the name,
the policy was one based upon the threat of irrationality—if you
attack, then we'll bring us both down.

The tactic can be used effectively by individuals as well. In the
late 1970s, business colleges began to hire women on their faculties.
At many schools, reactions among the male faculty members varied
from enthusiasm to outright rudeness. Generally, the women encountered a low-key but relentless, joking type of male chauvinism. In
isolation, the jokes and small put-downs were trivial. The problem is
that the effect accumulates. Over the long run, after many incidents,
the impact is high. It is like a fifteen-round boxing match. The small
jabs at the beginning of the match have little impact. Over fifteen
rounds, however, you can go down for the count.

At one institution, after a year or so of taking the jabs of one
faculty member, two of the women professors finally had enough.
After he made one too many snide remarks to them in the hallway,
they jokingly took him into his office. They laughed with him about
various male problems, such as heart disease, prostate difficulties,
baldness, and so forth. Now this male professor prided himself on
always keeping a dozen or so perfectly sharpened pencils carefully

arrayed so that he could write his mathematical equations precisely and fluidly. The women proceeded to take each pencil, jab the point down on his desk, and break the lead into little pieces. Of course, no voices were raised or angry comments made; everyone laughed. Hey, this was just good fun.

The Freudian implications of the act, however, were intentional and comprehended. Indeed, the behavior of the women was irrational when seen within the staid confines of academia. They broke the norms of decorum. But their point was made. Male faculty members could no longer assume that the women would idly accept the low-key harassment. It would be returned in kind, the laws of decorum be damned. The frequency of the quips slowed dramatically, and ten years after the incident the male professor still talks about the crazy women who broke all of his pencils.

Emotion in Estimating Probabilities and Values of Outcomes

Two factors that rational decision makers have to consider are: (1) the likelihood of the various outcomes that could result from a decision; and (2) how good or bad those outcomes are. This analytical approach is generically termed an "expectancy-value model." That is, people develop an expectancy of the likelihood that various outcomes may occur from an action, and they place a value on the positive or negative aspects of the outcomes. The expectancy-value model has been found to be quite effective in predicting choices, even when they are made intuitively. (It is also the basis for the SEU model of rational behavior discussed earlier in this chapter.)

Expectancy-value models have been successfully applied to a number of different types of decisions. For example, when people determine the amount of risk in a course of action, they will consider likelihood and value. The greater the likelihood of bad outcomes occurring and the more negative their value, the greater the risk perceived. Deterrence models of crime use the same model. According to these models, the motivation to commit crime goes up as the likelihood of being caught decreases and as the severity of punishment decreases. Researchers have also used the expectancy-value model to explain worker motivation. That is, the greater the rewards from the work and the greater the likelihood that a given level of effort will bring a given reward, the higher the motivation level. Even models of attitude formation approach the problem similarly. People's attitude toward another person, a company, or whatever can be predicted by determining their perception of the likelihood that the object has certain characteristics and the value of those characteristics.

Because people intuitively consider the probabilities and the values of outcomes in making decisions, most of our decisions have at least some degree of rationality. In fact, people tend to call the decision of another person irrational when it is inconsistent with what they themselves would have done. The likely cause of two people reaching different decisions, when given the same information, is that they have developed different expectancies and applied divergent values in assessing the problem.

Peerless decision makers recognize, however, that we should *not* expect others to use the same values and likelihoods as we do. For example, in the 1973 Yom Kippur War between Israel and the Arab countries, policy makers in Israel assumed that Anwar Sadat valued losing a war as negatively as they did. For Israel, a defeat would be catastrophic because it would threaten the entire state. In contrast, a defeat for Egypt was less negative than continuing to experience the humiliation that the country was already suffering as a result of the last war. Thus, from the Israeli perspective, an Egyptian-led Arab attack was irrational. But from Anwar Sadat's perspective, it was eminently logical.

How we weight outcomes positively or negatively is based in large part upon our personal values. Americans place high value on the individual. As a nation, we feel strongly the death of each American soldier. For us, each life is precious. In contrast, in nations where the value system focuses more on supporting the group and furthering the interests of the whole, individual rights are given less weight. If large numbers of troops die for the state, they are mourned, but the outcome is acceptable. The image of the tens of thousands of Iranians dying in the mass attacks against the fortified Iraqi positions during the Iran-Iraq War illustrates this argument. For the American public, such carnage would be unacceptable, and it would lead to a change in leadership. Within Iran, the massacres were considered unfortunate, but tolerable.

Nevertheless, Americans also have a strong tendency to believe that others share their values. This phenomenon is part of a general egocentrism in which people believe that if they perceive the world in a certain way, others will too. But when trying to anticipate what others will do, we must view the world from their perspective and attempt to understand their value system. By seeing their world through their eyes, we may be able to assess the probabilities of their actions, and the values that they attach to alternative outcomes. In this way, we enhance our ability to anticipate how they are likely to act.

The failure to appreciate the divergent values of another culture could be seen in American reactions to the events surrounding the Iraqi invasion of Kuwait. Thomas Friedman in *The New York Times* described the response of American officials to a report in an underground Kuwait newspaper about a dream Saddam Hussein experienced during the fall of 1990. Hussein dreamed that the Prophet Mohammed appeared to him and said that "Iraq's missiles were pointed in the wrong direction." Some Arabs interpreted the dream as indicating that Iraq would soon pull its troops out of Kuwait. When queried about the dream, the White House spokesperson, Marlin Fitzwater, said: "No comment on dreams. I have enough problems dealing with reality."

Within the American culture, dreams are given little credence. According to our value system, knowing that Hussein had a dream would not influence our estimation of the probability that he would respond to sanctions and get out of Kuwait. In Arab value systems, however, dreams have greater reality. As noted by a former Assistant Secretary of State for Near Eastern Affairs, "Reading the Arab world is not one of our national skills." For those who understood Arab thinking, the dream report was an important sign. One expert said, "Saddam lets it be known that he had a dream, and we joke about it. But it sounds very different to Arab ears. He is speaking Arabic again and that worries me."

The Influence of Anger and Fear

More than other emotions, anger and fear can jump in to influence how we perceive and value outcomes. Consider Tony Cimo, who was haunted by the murder of his mother and father by Rudolph Tyner. A street kid from Harlem passing through South Carolina, Tyner had fired a shotgun into their chests during a hold-up of the Cimos' convenience store. Police nabbed Tyner soon after the shooting, and in a trial he received a life sentence. A year later, however, the South Carolina Supreme Court ordered a new trial on a technicality. Cimo went into shock at the thought that this murderer could go free. He began to have nightmares and his anger built. Finally, he decided to take matters into his own hands. He hired a convicted killer, who was incarcerated in the same prison as Tyner, to kill him. After various attempts at poisoning Tyner failed, his head was blown off when he turned on a walkie-talkie filled with C-4 plastique explosive. For his action, Cimo received an eight-year prison term, of which he served three years.

To many of the locals in South Carolina, Cimo was a hero—a Charles Bronson taking the law into his own hands. How did Cimo feel about it? He said of his crime, "I don't know if what I did was right, but it don't lay heavy on my conscience. I'd do it again for the peace of mind I got out of it. . . . I just did what I had to do."

When we are angry, we are driven to action. We overestimate the chances of success, and focus on the positive outcomes that will accrue from our actions. Thus, the anger felt by Tony Cimo was so great that it drove him to commit a heinous crime. An otherwise lawabiding citizen, who builds chimneys for expensive homes, Cimo obtained psychological relief by avenging his parents' deaths. His hatred and anger minimized the negative consequences of being caught. Indeed, for Cimo the net outcome was positive.

When afraid, our expectations of success are deflated. We focus on the possibility of taking a loss, thereby overweighting the negative consequences of a possible failure in the decision process. Fear is a physiological reaction burned into our nervous system by eons of evolutionary experience. While those who by their nature lack fear may have an edge (as in the "madman" phenomenon), they also tend to lead shorter lives and have spectacular failures. For example, a lack of fear was in part responsible for the nearly disastrous Yom Kippur War between Israel and its Arab neighbors in 1973. The top military men in the Israeli armed forces at the time were tough, aggressive combat soldiers. Highly confident in their own capabilities and those of the Israeli armed forces, they held the Arab military in low esteem. In particular, Eliyahu Zeira, the head of the intelligence branch (called AMAN), was known for his precise predictions and self-confidence. He had no room for ambiguity. A quote from his testimony to a fact-finding committee illustrates this tendency:

> The Chief of Staff has to make decisions, and his decisions
> must be clear. The best support that the head of AMAN can
> give the Chief of Staff is to give a clear and unambiguous
> estimate, provided that it is done in an objective fashion. To
> be sure, the clearer and sharper the estimate, the clearer and

sharper the mistake—but this is a professional hazard for the head of AMAN.

Zeira's reputation was well known within the Israeli military community. When he was appointed head of AMAN, one general said, "Now we are heading for a catastrophe: there are three men at the top [Dayan, Elazar, and Zeira] who do not know what it means to be afraid."

Fear causes people to hesitate, to consider the downside of an action. It induces them to place a higher probability on a negative outcome occurring. Zeira's fearlessness caused him to maintain that the likelihood of war was "low" until less than twenty-four hours before the attack. In addition, he had told the Israeli Defense Forces that they would receive several days' notice of a war. These failures resulted in losses far higher than the worst possible scenario conceived prior to the war. Golda Meir used the word *shoah* to describe the disaster; *shoah* is also used to describe the Holocaust.

The hesitation caused by the fear response creates major difficulties, however, for those who must make quick, decisive choices. This problem is perhaps best illustrated by those who must hit a five-inch horsehide-covered ball, which is traveling a non-linear course at 80 to 90 miles per hour, with a round stick of wood. If the batter hesitates, if a muscle flinches, he is dead meat. At best, he makes an out. At worst, the imprint of the ball's stitches is etched into his skull. Baseball is a reaction-time game, and fear slows reactions.

When a batter digs in and aggressively steps toward the plate, a pitcher must protect himself. Batters who hit without fear can cost a pitcher his job. Pitchers respond by throwing high, hard ones near the batter's chin. Such pitches used to be called "beanballs"; now they are euphemistically called "chin music," but the result is the same. The batter begins to stride confidently to meet the ball, spies it rocketing toward his head, and unceremoniously sprawls on his back in a desperate attempt to avoid having the ball buried in his eyesocket. The next time up, no matter what his mind tells his muscles to do, he becomes just a hair tentative. He flinches just a little, and the pitcher has gained the upper hand.

The Thinking Man's Guide to Baseball opens with a one-word paragraph: "Fear." The author, Leonard Koppett, calls fear "the fundamental factor in hitting." Tony Kubek, the Yankee shortstop who played with Mickey Mantle, said: "I remember years and years ago, when I was first breaking in, Mantle telling me that at least once a year and maybe more, 'I wake up screaming in the middle of the night, sweating a cold sweat, with the ball coming right at my head.' "

In his book *Men At Work*, George Will takes the reader through the baseball world as seen through the eyes of the coach, the pitcher, the batter, and the defense. The topic of fear crops up repeatedly. Throwing brush-back pitches, or on occasion firing at the batter's body, is simply part of a pitcher's arsenal. Chin music is frequently used as punishment, according to Will. For example, one naughty action of batters that must be stopped is peeking: Batters occasionally have the audacity to look back at the catcher just before a pitch to see the location of his mitt and thus figure out where the ball will be thrown. On such occasions a little chin music may be in order.

Pitchers also get irritated when runners on second base attempt to steal their signs and relay them to the batter. Will describes one occasion when Roger Clemens, the Red Sox pitcher, went into his stretch, looked back at second base, and saw the runner giving the location of the pitch to the batter. He stepped off the mound, walked over to the runner, and said, "If I ever see that again from you or anybody on your team I'm going to bury the guy at the plate." The runner on second base gave Clemens some backtalk. After the next pitch, the batter had to climb out of the hole he had dug to avoid Clemens's fastball honing in on his throat.

Some pitchers have a reputation for throwing at batters. Early Wynn was reputed to have said that he would throw at his grandmother, "if she was digging in." Bob Gibson was also known for his lack of compassion for batters. Even after going into coaching, he wouldn't take any guff while on the mound. Will tells the story of the time when Gibson was pitching batting practice. A young player wasn't quite quick enough into the batting cage, and Gibson yelled, "Eddie, you're in there." The player didn't like the name Eddie, and responded insolently, "The name is Ed." A Hall of Fame pitcher, Gibson merely said, "All right, *Ed*, get in there." He then plugged the ball into the guy's ribs with the first pitch.

The element of fear means that potentially negative outcomes are highly salient to decision makers. In fact, researchers have found that simply being in a bad mood causes people to retrieve from their memories more negative thoughts. The fear of lawsuits causes medical doctors to order unnecessary tests. Even though the probability of a serious illness is low, the threat of a lawsuit causes the careful physician to order it anyway. Similarly, when the stock market metamorphoses from bull to bear, suddenly investors focus only on negative news. Each new bit of negative information causes more selling; positive information is ignored, and inevitably the market becomes oversold. Fear drives the market too low. Those who maintain control of their emotions can make their fortune in such circumstances. Of course, the converse will also occur. During bull markets, investors become optimistic, they focus on positive news, and their estimates of the probability of good things happening is biased upward. Their misplaced hope causes them to buy, the price of stocks is driven higher, and a bubble occurs.

Anger is the obverse of fear. While fear impedes action, anger encourages it. When a decision maker faces the judgment call of whether to shoot or not to shoot, anger biases him or her to action. Of course, some people are quicker to anger than others. While he was writing his book on baseball, managers kept telling George Will to be careful what he said about Roger Clemens; opponents knew that Clemens became really tough when riled, and it made no sense to unnecessarily ruffle his feathers. When angry, individuals focus on the importance of getting even—on punishing the transgressor. The possibility of negative outcomes resulting from the action are ignored. A classic example of anger leading to a decision debacle occurred in World War II. Hitler became enraged when Yugoslavian leaders threatened to withdraw from their alliance with Germany. In order to punish the country, Hitler kept his armies in the nation for an extra month, raising havoc with the populace. As a result, the invasion of Russia was delayed. Months later, the advances on Moscow and Leningrad would fail because winter intervened on the side of the Russian military. That crucial extra month in Yugoslavia could have made the difference in the Russian campaign.

Intuition and Decision Making

When rational decision makers discern a problem, they identify alternative courses of action, the outcomes of each possibility, the positive or negative values of those outcomes, and the likelihood of each occurring. They then combine the information to determine the best course of action. Emotion enters the process to short-circuit the search for alternatives, to distort the estimation of the probabilities of outcomes, and to bias the perception of the positive or negative value of the outcomes. The rational decision maker, then, attempts to avoid having emotion influence his or her analysis of the problem.

Only after the decision has been made does the peerless decision maker allow emotions to assist in the implementation of the action.

The rational approach to decision making, however, has received criticism. In fact, one researcher argued in the *Harvard Business Review* that top executives rarely use a "rational" decision-making analysis. Rather, their approach would come closer to what people call "intuition." Other researchers have found the same phenomenon. The higher up you go in the organization, the more decision making appears to be intuitive rather than rational.

A classic case occurred during John Glenn's historic first orbital flight around the earth in 1962. The risks of the flight were enormous. Glenn rode aboard an Atlas missile, which at the time had the perplexing habit of exploding on lift-off about 25 percent of the time. In addition, none of the control systems for the complex flight had been tested together. The public held the astronauts in awe because they correctly surmised that the men were in mortal danger every time they rode one of the rockets.

But the launch went smoothly, and Glenn was fired into a near-perfect earth orbit. As he headed into his second orbit, a technician noticed that one of the meters was registering that the heat shield had been prematurely released. While it was temporarily held in place by the retro-rocket pack, the heat shield would fall away from the capsule when the retro-rockets were jettisoned after taking the spacecraft out of orbit. Immediately, hearts stopped. If the latches that held the heat shield in place had been released, the capsule would burn up upon its reentry into the atmosphere. To the casual observer watching the events from the visitors' area, the control room appeared perfectly normal. However, as one participant put it at the time, "We are all in a state of shock at the enormity of the situation." If the heat shield was deployed, Glenn would die.

Those in Mission Control recognized that an alternative explanation of the reading was that the instrument had erred. But there was no way to tell for sure. Then, someone thought of the idea of not jettisoning the retro-rocket pack. Could it simply be left on to hold the heat shield in place as the capsule reentered the atmosphere?

Mission Control faced a classic dilemma: If the instrument was correct and nothing was done, America's first astronaut to orbit the earth could be burnt toast. On the other hand, if the retro-rockets were left on to hold the heat shield in place, the aerodynamics of the capsule could be upset. The result might be the same—charcoal-grilled Glenn. Which was the lower-risk alternative?

Time was short. Elaborate models of how air flowed over the

space capsule with retro-rockets attached could not be built in the minutes remaining. No one had ever even thought of testing the flight characteristics of the Mercury capsule with the retro-pack attached. Intuition had to be used. The person with the most experience on the aerodynamic characteristics of the Mercury capsule was Max Faget. So the directors of Mission Control phoned him. Faget and engineers at Mission Control carefully talked through the problem. One of the participants described Faget's thinking in the following way: He had a "first order feel that leaving the retro-pack on wasn't going to be a problem." He understood the engineering gestalt of the situation and could intuit the nature of the pressures and forces that would buffet the capsule. Thus, a "first order feel" was the basis for a decision that controlled the fate of John Glenn. Fortunately, Faget's intuition proved accurate and Glenn returned safely. Later, tests revealed that it was the instrument that had failed. The heat shield had not been deployed prematurely.

Even world-class chess players employ intuition. Gary Kasparov, the world chess champion, is known for his prodigious memory. Countless configurations of positions from previous matches bombard his consciousness as he plays. In fact, the memories frequently serve as an annoyance because they stifle his creativity. A writer who traveled extensively with Kasparov spoke of how he functions:

> His greatest exhilaration, he said, comes from breaking free of traditional constraints, and he claims to find his greatest moves by a sixth sense he cannot explain. He takes risks in chess games, he said, because these moves are beautiful and make him feel alive. "Some positions are so complex that you cannot calculate even two moves ahead. You must use your intuition. Sometimes I play by my hand, by my smell."

Intuition is to chess what "instinct" is to baseball. For those who participate in our national pastime, the use of intuition is placed under the heading of having "baseball instincts." Tony La Russa, manager of the Oakland A's, argued that instincts are much more than mere programmed behavior. Rather, they result from "an accumulation of baseball information. When you trust your gut, you are trusting a lot of stuff that is there from the past."

Indeed, in some instances thinking and the use of rationality are totally disdained by baseball players. George Will told this anecdote about the 1934 World Series: The great pitcher Dizzy Dean heard that the opposing team's manager was holding a series of team meetings. In response, Dean said, "If them guys are thinking, they're as good as licked right now." In a game of split-second reflexes, thinking gets in the way. You have to react. You cannot think your way through hitting a baseball or fielding a sinking line drive. Another baseball great, Branch Rickey, put it simply: "Full head, empty bat." Bill "Spaceman" Lee, a pitcher for the Boston Red Sox, said it yet another way: "When cerebral processes enter into sports, you start screwing up. It's like the Constitution, which says separate church and state. You have to separate mind and body."

One frequently reads that corporate executives should use their intuition to supplement or even to replace rational analysis. In *Business Horizons*, one researcher argued that "top executives have learned through painful experience that analysis by itself is both inappropriate and inadequate." According to this consultant, "The decade of the 1980s may well become known as that period in management history when intuition finally gained acceptance as a powerful brain skill for guiding executive decision making." Another investigator, after interviewing dozens of top executives, concluded that they seldom think in ways that one might simplistically view as rational because they seldom "systematically formulate goals, assess their worth, evaluate the probabilities of alternative ways of reaching them, and choose the path that maximizes expected return." Thus, within the context of high-stakes decision making, it seems that executives bypass rigorous, analytical planning, especially when they face judgment calls involving difficult, novel, or extremely entangled problems. According to that same investigator, "when they do use analysis for a prolonged time, it is always in conjunction with intuition."

While management consultants claim to teach intuitive judgment and provide anecdotes and testimonials of its incredible effects, is there any hard evidence that intuition works? The answer is a resounding no! When people use intuition, they make an overall, or global, evaluation of how they "feel" about a course of action. Those who claim to teach intuitive decision making tell managers to relax, to take their time, to be sensitive, to expand their consciousness, and to be confident enough to approach the problem in a nonjudgmental manner. The problem is that when researchers compare the intuitive judgments of people (including experts) to a standard, the intuitive decision makers invariably do poorly.

In one classic study of intuitive decision making reported in the *New England Journal of Medicine*, a panel of physicians examined a group of 389 boys. The medical doctors identified 45 percent as needing a tonsillectomy. The 214 boys judged to be healthy were then examined by another set of physicians, and 46 percent of these boys were diagnosed as requiring a tonsillectomy. The researchers then took the 116 boys judged to have been healthy in this group and had them seen by a third group of physicians. What do you think happened? Forty-four percent of this group were found to need to have their tonsils out. It seems that no matter what the state of health of the patient, the physicians diagnosed about 45 percent as needing tonsillectomies.

Over one hundred studies have compared intuitive judgments to an objective standard. Not one has found intuitive judgments to be superior. But what is the standard? In some cases, it is the answer obtained from a mathematical formula. In others, the decision is compared to actual outcomes. Finally, intuitive decisions have been compared to subjective expected utility (SEU) models, similar to the one suggested by Benjamin Franklin over two hundred years ago. In many instances the model has been put into a computer, and the computer was used to mechanically grind out an answer. Today, these models are called "expert systems." Of course, the idea that a computer program can outperform an expert drives medical doctors, clinical psychologists, bankers, and stock market gurus crazy. But the data are incontrovertible. As a past president of the American Psychological Association (APA) said, "There is no controversy in social science which shows such a large body of qualitatively diverse studies coming out so uniformly in the same direction as this one." Similarly, other researchers in judgment and decision making have argued that:

> Intuition is fine for small decisions—where to buy groceries, how to organize your filing cabinet . . . but . . . you can develop procedures that will make your decision better than your own unaided intuition. If you follow sound procedures, you'll have a better chance of achieving your goals than if you just make a choice because it "feels right."

Based upon this overwhelming evidence against intuition, is there a place for it in high-stakes decision making? I believe there is. Foremost, sometimes so little time exists that an intuitive judgment *must* be made. The heat shield problem in John Glenn's flight exemplifies just such a situation. In addition, intuition can play another role. Herbert Simon, the Nobel Prize-winning psychologist/economist, argues that intuition is simply the accumulated knowledge of our lifetime applied to a particular problem. (Somehow, it's nice to realize that a Ph.D. economist like Herbert Simon and the manager of a baseball team, Tony La Russa, view intuition similarly.) For Simon, the use of intuition is comparable to thinking of a word or recognizing the face of a friend: people with a good vocabulary can immediately recognize from 50,000 to 100,000 words. Similarly, chess masters can recognize over 50,000 configurations of pieces on a chessboard. Just as we can retrieve immediately any one of the words stored in memory, so can we draw on our thousands of previous experiences to intuit the solution to a problem. As such, intuition can act as a starting point for making a decision. In addition, it can act as a commonsense device to check the results of recommendations that emerge from a computerized expert system.

A third reason exists for using intuition. By the time a decision problem gets to the CEO's level, it has gone through a series of managers who have analyzed it from numerous perspectives. In today's company, filled with MBAs trained in quantitative methods, options have been data-crunched to death. Clearly, inferior action alternatives will have been discarded long before they reach the CEO's level. What is left are the difficult choices. Henry Kissinger has described the situation well; when asked about presidential decision making, he said that "all decisions that get to the President are 51/49 . . . and frequently they must be made quickly." In other words, decisions at the highest levels are judgment calls. A computer will not help. Experts will differ on the solution. In such instances, the peerless decision maker must use his or her accumulated experience to make the choice.

Reason and Emotion in High-Stakes Decision Making

Both reason and emotion are necessary components of high-stakes decision making. The judgment call is when to utilize reason versus when to listen to your emotions. In making a decision, emotion can get in the way to bias how we estimate probabilities and how we value outcomes. Once a decision has been made, however, emotions can add that extra spark to get the task implemented more quickly and efficiently. Indeed, a frequent problem encountered by both individuals and organizations is actually getting decisions implemented. A rational process can be employed to arrive at a decision, and then no steps are taken quickly enough to effect its accomplishment. As we have already seen, a tragic example of the failure to implement a decision occurred in NASA prior to the Challenger disaster.

On January 28, 1986, the Space Shuttle Challenger blew up, killing all seven members of its crew. The terrible image of the explosion overwhelmed Americans, causing immense grief and anger. Those emotions galvanized the country into action and caused a series of investigations to occur, the program to be placed on hold, and the booster rockets to be redesigned. What is important, however, is that prior to the launch of Challenger, decisions had already been made to change its design. The problem was that the plan had simply not been implemented.

The design of the solid rocket booster that caused the Challenger to disintegrate was based upon one used in the Air Force's Titan III rocket, which had shown excellent reliability. The Titan's body was made of steel segments that were joined together and sealed by O-rings. NASA engineers knew that on occasion the O-rings of the Titans had shown some erosion due to the hot gases, so they added a second one to the shuttle's boosters in order to create a safer, redundant system. Problems with the new configuration in the shuttle system became apparent as early as 1977, however, when a test revealed that upon engine ignition, the joints could rotate and decompress the rings, making it more difficult for them to seal properly. As a result of the test, NASA engineers classified the joints as "Crit-1R." That is, a failure could cause a loss of life.

When the shuttle program became operational, engineers examined the O-rings after each flight for evidence of joint problems. In early flights, few problems were found. But engineers were still aware of the potential difficulty, and in 1982, a scientist proposed a new design for the O-ring that used a "capture lip," which would inhibit the rotation of the joint that caused the decompression problem. The difficulty was that it would take over two years to build boosters that had this design, and NASA chose to continue to use the old design while working on the new possibility.

As the shuttle program progressed, increasing evidence began to accumulate that something was seriously wrong with the old design. Beginning in 1983, post-flight inspections after launches and test firings began to reveal a disturbing pattern of erosion of the O-rings. Heat damage to the joints was found in three out of five firings in 1984, in eight out of nine firings in 1985, and again after the flight on January 12, 1986—the one that preceded the Challenger mission. Indeed, after the fifteenth shuttle flight in January 1985, serious heat damage had occurred. Because the flight took place in cold temperatures, the company making the boosters proposed that low temperatures might enhance the probability of "blow-by." These data had also alerted NASA to the problem and more studies were ordered. Meanwhile, the engineers designing a new approach had achieved positive results. In fact, in July 1985, seventy-two new steel case segments for the booster rocket's body that possessed the "capture lip" feature were ordered. The changes were described as a "potential long-term solution," and it was projected that they would be available starting in August 1988.

The problem was that a three-year wait would stop the program, setting it back scientifically, militarily and, most important, politically. Further, NASA suffered from the overconfidence bias that results from repeated successes. As one academician writing in the *Journal of Management Studies* put it, "It had a magical aura. NASA had not only experienced repeated successes, it had achieved the impossible. It had landed men on the moon and returned them safely to earth. Time and again, it had successfully completed missions with hardware that supposedly had very little chance of operating adequately." The presidential commission later investigating the shuttle disaster said that "NASA's attitude historically has selected the position that 'We can do anything.' " This overconfidence caused NASA managers to overestimate the odds of success and to fail to heed the consistent warnings of the O-ring problems. NASA was playing a high-stakes game of Russian roulette, and when the Challenger was launched, the bullet was in the chamber. NASA management did not sufficiently fear the consequences of a failure, and this lack of respect meant that it would not move to halt the program and fix the problem. Only after the Challenger explosion, when anger erupted, did action finally occur.

Postponing the implementation of a choice is a decision just like any other. Unfortunately, sometimes it takes strong feelings to overcome inertia and implement a tough judgment call. Some principles governing the use of reason and emotion in making judgment calls are:

- Keep in mind that in high-stakes decision making, emotions invariably are a factor.

- Use reason to analyze problems and employ emotion to enhance actions.

- Consider the strategy of creating the impression of irrationality in order to gain a power advantage.

- Make rational decisions by identifying all possible outcomes, their probabilities, and their positive/negative values.

- Avoid decision-making egocentrism by recognizing the tendency to assume that others value positive and negative outcomes in the same manner as yourself.

- Your value system influences how you weight various positive and negative outcomes that may occur as a result of a decision.

- Emotion exaggerates and biases perception of the probability of outcomes and perception of the positive/negative values of outcomes.

- Fear increases the belief that negative outcomes will happen and causes people to view bad outcomes more negatively.

- Overconfidence and/or anger decreases the belief that bad things will happen and decreases the perceived negativity of possible bad outcomes.

- Intuitive decisions are best made by experts when time is short, a unique high-stakes decision is required, and a rational analysis has resulted in two or more essentially equivalent options.

10.

THE PEERLESS DECISION MAKER

It was 10:30 P.M. on November 1, 1964, and Bob Swafer, the six-foot-nine star center of Oklahoma State's basketball team, was in the athletic stadium doing his laundry in an industrial clothes washer. This was the time before the Consumer Product Safety Commission, and the washer lacked a safety brake to stop the 2,500 rpm rotation of the drum quickly in the spin cycle when the door opened. Deciding that his jeans were dry enough, Swafer opened the door and reached in with his right hand to take them out, but they were stuck in a pile of laundry spinning at over 100 mph in the large drum. Like a monster in a B-grade horror flick, the flapping jeans legs reached out and wrapped themselves around his arm. Something had to give, and the weakest link in the chain was Swafer's arm. It was ripped off midway between his elbow and his shoulder and joined his laundry in the fast-spinning tub.

Fortunately, Swafer's roommate was there. A premed major, he immediately compressed the wound with a towel to slow the bleeding, then called an ambulance and the team physician. The physician told him to get the arm, wrap it in clean towels, and take it and Swafer to the local hospital emergency room. The doctor at the emergency room knew a medical researcher at the University of Oklahoma Health Sciences Center, Dr. Rainey Williams, who had been experimenting with reattaching the severed legs of dogs. Knowing that speed was of the essence, they called him at home and quickly explained the situation. Williams told them to meet him at the O.U. Medical Center with the arm.

The Stillwater medical team packed the ghostly white arm in ice (the drum rotation had drained all the blood from it), and drove the 65 miles to O.U. at 125 miles an hour. Swafer was in the operating room for over five hours. When he came out of surgery, his fingernails were pink. Soon after surgery, he went into physical therapy, and a year later he could do pushups and pullups. He was one of the first humans to have a limb reattached successfully: His major problem now is sizing his shirt sleeves: his right arm is an inch or so shorter than his left.

Undoubtedly, good luck played a major role in the Bob Swafer miracle. For example, had the blood not been spun out of the detached arm, it would have coagulated and jeopardized the entire procedure. One of the problems in identifying peerless decision makers is that the observer must disentangle simple good luck from sound decision making. Indeed, some argue that they would rather be lucky than talented. When asked what he most sought in his generals, Frederick the Great is reputed to have said, "Lucky ones." Good luck does seem to follow peerless decision makers, but the reason is that they have a "prepared mind" and can take advantage of its occurrence. They can use intuition and experience to make appropriate judgment calls when the stakes are high, such as what to do with Bob Swafer's detached arm lying in a bundle of blood-stained laundry in a washing machine.

Experience and the Peerless Decision Maker

"Don't jump, don't jump!" the flight lead yelled into his microphone. Barely listening, the shaken wingman held tight to his controls, trying to fly his wounded F-105 jet straight and level back to Thailand. In one of his first flights into North Vietnam, a run over "Thud Ridge" into Hanoi, the pilot's plane had been hit by antiaircraft fire. Thud Ridge is a geological formation, fortified with antiaircraft weapons, over which American planes had to fly in order to hit Hanoi during the Vietnam War. It was named for the many F-105s—nicknamed "Thuds"—that smashed into it with a sickening sound after being hit by antiaircraft fire. Now, the pilot's worst fears were real-

ized. His instruments read zero airspeed and no oil pressure. Every
instinct told him to pull the ejection handle and get out of the plane.

Fortunately, his flight leader was experienced. He calmly re-
minded the panicky airman that if his airspeed were indeed zero, he
would be falling like a rock. He then positioned his jet to inspect his
buddy's plane and found no mortal wounds to the aircraft. Meanwhile, the pilot continued to yell: "Where are we, where are we, can
I jump now?" The flight lead kept coaxing him on toward safety in
Thailand. He knew that if the pilot ejected, the best that could be
expected would be life as a POW. Finally, he had him over the run-
way, and that is when he told him: "It's safe to jump now, or you can
land it." Gathering back his faculties, the pilot landed his plane.

Experience saves lives under extreme circumstances, and another
Vietnam story illustrates the point. Cliff Young, a "quant-jock," who
now guides computers through their paces while teaching at the University of Colorado at Denver, once flew Phantoms over Vietnam.
Cliff described to me what he witnessed one day in the clouds over
Hanoi. He was a young, inexperienced pilot flying as wingman for an
old pro. They had just finished their mission of taking out a petroleum storage facility and were heading home when a member of
another flight was hit by antiaircraft artillery fire. Immediately,
warning lights lit up inside the aircraft, indicating a fire in the engine
bays. Outside, smoke and fire streamed from the jet. Another pilot in
the area yelled into his microphone: "Joe Lee, you're on fire! Bail
out! Bail out!" But the old pro didn't say a thing. He just kept flying
and steered his floundering jet toward the Gulf of Tonkin. The airman's strategy was clear: Take the plane as far as it would go over
the water and bail out microseconds before it disintegrated. If he
could fly far enough out to sea, he and his backseater would probably
be saved. Bailing out now could result in death, or worse, becoming
a POW. The risk of going down in flames was better than being captured by the North Vietnamese.

Amazingly, the plane stayed in the air. Finally, it reached the
ocean, but the pro still kept on flying. He had to take it far enough
out so that he could be rescued. Then the Phantom entered a small
cloud and a bright flash could be seen. All that emerged was burning
debris. Everyone was sure the two men had "bought it." All of a
sudden two chutes appeared below the cloud. Within an hour the
airmen were rescued.

When he tells this story, Cliff speaks of the old pro in tones of awe.
They survived the incident because the man was a consummate pilot,

with total command and knowledge of the systems of his plane. He had rehearsed over and over in his mind what he would do if such a situation arose. His strategy was to fly the plane until he felt it pitch up, which would indicate total failure of its hydraulics and imminent disintegration. In that instant he would eject, because a split second later the plane would fall apart. His experience and feel for the plane saved his life as well as that of his buddy.

In high-stakes decisions, experience can be a critical factor. A couple of years ago, I interviewed a number of executives in independent oil firms that had made it through the great oil bust of the 1980s. What I found was a group of mature, older individuals. They averaged well over twenty years each in the oil business. They had seen the good times and the bad. Previous experience had taught them that booms are followed by busts. They had learned that the worst thing that an "oilman" can do is highly leverage his company. Those who lost it all when the boom ended were most frequently the less experienced, who had seen only the good times of the exploding oil prices of the 1970s. They took on massive debt loads in order to expand with the times, and when the plunge occurred, they crashed and burned. It's amazing how many thirty-five- to forty-five-year-old guys you run into in Oklahoma, Texas, and Louisiana who once had a huge house, several expensive cars, a variety of gold watches, and slim, blond wives. Now they are divorced, struggling to make it back into the oil business, significantly older and wiser after losing the shirts off their backs. Similarly, it was the younger, more highly educated and technically sophisticated farmers in the 1970s who went into debt to purchase farmland as prices soared. The older, less well-educated farmers stood back and observed. They were called "too conservative" and "over the hill." But they had also seen land prices rise and fall. They played the game conservatively, and as a result, they were the ones who continued to prosper when farmland prices plunged in the 1980s.

The same ideas hold for manufacturing businesses as well. Don Frey, who now teaches management science and industrial engineering at Northwestern University, was the project manager who brought out the Ford Mustang. He suggests that managers should acquire a broad variety of experiences on their way to the upper echelons. For example, Frey argues that many of the "financial types" who moved to the forefront in so many companies during the 1980s have a restricted range of vision. While these individuals have the best interests of the company at heart, "Their problem is that financial control and measurement is all they know. But important

measures of customer satisfaction or market share are not quantifi-
able before a new product goes to market: too often the financial
types do not realize that beans must be earned before they are
counted."

Frey's remarks emerged from his experiences at Ford and
Chrysler, but similar problems have dogged General Motors. In her
book *Rude Awakening*, Maryann Keller tells of the dominant role
played by finance people in auto companies and the effects of their
lack of real-world experience. While the finance people are responsible for coordinating information and bringing problems to the attention of senior management, they have limited experience. They've
never worked on production lines, sold a car, conducted market research, or attempted to integrate production and engineering. Indeed, because receiving a well-maintained and polished company car
is an executive perk, they even miss the experience of purchasing and
maintaining a car. At the highest levels of the firm, executives have
chauffeurs and drive to work in the back seats of limos. How can they
have empathy for their customers, if they have no experience in the
car-buying process or even driving?

In his many criticisms of General Motors, H. Ross Perot hit hard
at the wall built between GM executives and the buying public. "If I
have a car that gets worked on by mechanics every day," he said, "so
that I never see, feel, or taste reality, and I am driven back and forth
to work, what do I know about the product? I should have to buy a
car from a dealer. I should have to negotiate for it. It should be picked
at random and I should drive it. And when that sucker breaks down,
I ought to have to take it to the dealer and get punched around.
That's reality."

One cannot become a peerless decision maker without that well-
worn coat of experience. Whether in the military, business, medicine,
sports, or law, the bumps and bruises received from making decisions and seeing their outcomes, both good or bad, are the hallmark
of peerless decision makers.

But while experience is necessary, it alone cannot shape a person.
Learning from past events is equally important. In the domain of
baseball, Pete Rose can be called a peerless decision maker. But people live lives-within-lives. Unfortunately, the qualities of analysis
that Pete Rose brought to his baseball life did not extend to his personal life. In baseball, Rose actively sought to learn from experience.
For example, during and after each game he would carefully examine
his bat for the small scuffs that identify where it made contact with
the baseball. He would then work in the batting cage to subtly

change his swing in order to improve contact. After batting practice, he would rub down his bats with alcohol to erase the marks so that he could repeat the process.

The problem was that Rose failed to learn from life's scuffs in the same way. As one observer, who contrasted Rose's scrutiny of his bat with his lack of self-examination, put it: "But if the same sort of examination were possible with human beings, to determine if what they were told had left an impression, Rose would have been unscuffed. People who tried to offer advice were sure they had not left a mark, and they rarely tried again." As a result of his inability to learn from experience, Rose failed to control his gambling habit, went to prison, and lost his chance to enter baseball's Hall of Fame.

One question that I asked all the people I interviewed for this book was: "What are the characteristics of the peerless decision maker?" Answers ranged from "Being lucky" to "Using subjective expected utility theory." One of the most thoughtful responses came from Lola Lopes. Lopes was president of the Society for Judgment and Decision Making at the time, and a chaired professor in the business college at the University of Iowa. She thought for a second, then said: "My answer to that question is different from what most of my colleagues would say. The peerless decision maker would always have a fall-back position. If the first course of action failed, he or she should always have a second option in reserve."

The importance of planning for what to do if a course of action should fail is vital, and experience acts to imprint this lesson. The results of the failure to plan for bad outcomes are illustrated by the Vietnam War embroilment. In his analysis of the Vietnam War, David Halberstam suggested that one cause of the entrapment was that the primary decision makers had "all been partner to so precious little failure in their lives that there was always a sense that no matter what, it could be avoided, deflected. . . ." To take just one incident that occurred in March 1965: A high official from the days of the Eisenhower administration, Emmet Hughes, pushed McGeorge Bundy to consider what would happen if the escalation then occurring were met by a similar escalation by the North Vietnamese. Bundy kept on responding to Hughes's queries with the stock reply, "We simply are not as pessimistic as you are." But Hughes refused to let up, asking what would happen if the North countered the U.S. air escalation with dramatically increased hostile ground activities. Bundy replied with a cool smile: "We just don't think that's going to happen." Hughes pressed on. "Just suppose that it did occur." Bundy could only answer, "We can't assume what we don't believe."

The peerless decision maker has gained experience from living through both success and failure. He or she *always* asks the question, "What happens if we are wrong?" Those of us who went through Vietnam know that failure is an uncompromising teacher.

The Human Imperative

Experience teaches peerless decision makers how to react when the stakes are high. This accumulated wisdom also causes them to consider the emotional and mental limitations of the people whom they lead. At the most basic fundamental level, managers and leaders must even consider people's physiological needs, such as how frequently they urinate.

In May 1961, Alan Shepard was strapped inside the capsule perched atop a Redstone rocket about to become America's first astronaut to go into space. The suborbital trip would last only fifteen minutes, and NASA's experience in launching living things into space had been confined to monkeys. High stakes rested on a successful launch. The Russians had already placed a man in orbit, and American rockets revealed a disturbing tendency to blow up shortly after igniting. A failure would further damage the collective pride of the American public.

If nothing else, Shepard was cool under pressure. One of his favorite activities to relieve anxiety was to imitate the routine of a popular comedian, Jose Jimenez. The day of the flight, he was awakened early and had a large breakfast of steak wrapped in bacon, eggs, and juice. Then, on the way to the launch, he broke into his "Jimenez" prattle with Gus Grissom playing the straightman. Shepard said, "Eef you osk me what make de good astronaut, I tail you dat you got to have de courage and de good blood pressure and de four legs." "Four legs?" Gus asked dutifully. "Weh-ayl, eet ees a dog dey want to send, bot dey theenk dot ees too croo-el."

They arrived at the launch pad, and Shepard was strapped into his seat. A couple of hours passed, and Shepard still sat pointed toward the sky, rooted to a seat that had been molded to conform precisely to the contours of his body. He could barely move his arms or his legs. He sat and waited. The countdown halted. He waited some more. Four hours passed. Then, constrained in one position, he began to feel pressure in his bladder. He had to urinate, and it was getting worse by the second. It seemed that no one had considered

246 · JUDGMENT CALLS

the possibility that while the suborbital flight would last only fifteen minutes, the rocket could sit on its pad for hours with the astronaut strapped into his seat. Bluntly, Shepard had nothing to pee into.

What should he do? Should he urinate into his spacesuit? It had wires everywhere connecting his body to the sensors that monitored all physiological functions. Fortunately, they were low-voltage types unlikely to cause a short that would create real trouble. The second he urinated into his suit, however, the heat sensors would go berserk, and every technician at Mission Control would immediately know what happened. Finally, the sensation became unbearable, and he called to Mission Control for permission to pee. After a moment of silence, they told him, "Do it in the suit." The relief was immediate, but the warm liquid followed the laws of gravity. Because he lay on his back, the urine began running toward his head. It set off sensors all the way up to his chest, and the technicians had a field day. As Shepard reclined in the puddle of urine, he prayed that no electrical shorts would occur and that the call of nature had not ruined the space flight. A couple of minutes passed. When nothing bad happened, Mission Control heard over the closed-loop microphone, "Weh-ayl . . . I'm a wetback now." Shepard took the embarrassing incident and turned it into a joke.

Human beings have basic physiological needs; even astronauts must eat and urinate. Humans also have emotional requirements. They like to feel wanted and to believe that others value them. In addition, they have mental limitations. Our world is exploding with information that demands our attention. Because it takes effort to process all of the messages that we receive, people become unhappy when the amount of information received overloads their cognitive capacity. Peerless decision makers recognize these limitations and attempt to design the environment so as to make it more "user-friendly."

A failure to consider people's information-processing limitations nearly doomed XEROX Corporation when its managers made the high-stakes decision to launch a new office copier in 1980. Technologically, the 8200 office copier was the most advanced available. Packed with computer intelligence, it could collate, enlarge, and reduce. Further, it was reliable and worked efficiently, at least in the lab. In the "real world," however, the market rejected the product. It was the first product failure in XEROX history, and at first no one could figure out why.

After launching a major investigation of the market's tepid reaction, managers discovered that the engineers had failed to look at the human factor. While the technicians spent the better part of their working hours on the machine, users had to walk up to it and within seconds figure out how it worked. As the manager who led the redesign effort explained, "The only problem was no one paid attention to the human interface—to the user. People had to wade through buttons and visual noise and manuals for all features, including the most frequently used one, copying a page or two." As a result, old customers left XEROX and purchased the simpler Japanese models. The redesign took two years. In the end, a machine was produced that was adapted to the needs and cognitive limitations of its human users, and XEROX began to recapture its lost market share.

The Motivation Thing

Peerless decision makers know that people implement decisions, and their plans must include allowances for human needs and limitations. Even the best decisions will fail if the people who must carry them out are pushed beyond their human capacities. Peerless decision makers also recognize that unless those who carry out their plans are properly motivated, the result will likewise be failure. One area in which proper motivation is essential for success is athletics.

Myron Roderick was an Olympic champion wrestler, the coach of NCAA champion wrestling teams, a nationally ranked racquetball player, and the past athletic director of a major university. Myron knows sports, and in his view the most important thing in coaching is "motivation." As he said, the great coaches are able to "convince people they can do more than they realize." Motivation, however, must be controlled. You cannot have yourself or your athletes going through great peaks and valleys. Roderick used as an example a young wrestler named John Smith. I had John in my class in 1988. In street clothes he looked like a normal, skinny undergraduate male who spent some time figuring out how to dress shabbily. Until one of the students told me, I didn't realize that the John Smith in my class was "the John Smith," who was dominating NCAA wrestling. That year John would win a gold medal (at 136.5 pounds) at the Olympic Games, and in 1990 he would win the Sullivan Award as the nation's outstanding amateur athlete.

Why was John Smith the best in the world at what he did? In addition to talent, hard work, and strength, he could control his motivation. As Roderick described it, "John doesn't get too high or too low." He took the matches as they came and avoided emotional roller coasters. At the world level you cannot afford a letdown, which invariably comes if you get too high.

Selecting the personnel to carry out decisions is a vital task for the peerless decision maker. Bringing in people with insufficient motivation will cause a plan of action to fail. As NASA was being built during the early 1960s, a major problem was how to put together the thousands of people required to successfully launch a rocket to the Moon and back. The director of Flight Operations, Chris Kraft, thought long and hard about the type of person he wanted to hire. His strategy quickly evolved into looking for applicants fascinated with space flight. He wanted people who couldn't believe their good fortune in being hired to work for NASA and who would overlook the fact that they would have to work sixty-hour weeks for government salaries.

Kraft also didn't want people strait-jacketed in a standard engineering career path. He wanted those who liked to mess around in a variety of areas. As a result, he avoided straight-A students, and even hired some with C averages. While bright and intelligent, these employees were totally committed to the program and placed its success above all else. They identified with the organization. Part of their self-concept was invested in the knowledge that "I am part of NASA."

Peerless decision makers attempt to create circumstances so that people can be proud of the organization for which they work. If that organizational spirit is lost, so is the commitment. In January 1984, the chief executive officer of General Motors, Roger Smith, announced a gigantic reorganization of his ailing firm. The five automotive divisions were collapsed into two groups: the BOC group, composed of Buick-Oldsmobile-Cadillac; and the CPC group, composed of Chevrolet-Pontiac-GM of Canada. With the change, however, employees also lost their organizational identity. Even the symbols were dismantled. For example, the Cadillac flag was replaced by the BOC flag at plants around the country. The strategy was implemented in order to lower costs by standardizing many of the parts that went into the cars. Unfortunately, one of the results was that GM cars quickly began to look like each other. Buyers could not tell the difference between a Buick, an Oldsmobile, or a Cadillac. The company appeared to have completely forgotten a fundamental rule of marketing: A corporation's brands must be differentiated from each other as well as from the competition. In addition, a second problem—poorly motivated employees—was caused by the reorganization.

The Cadillac Allante project was one example of this. The division brought out the Allante as a competitor to the Mercedes 500SL. It was to be the flagship car. Costing $55,000, it would symbolize the quality and status of Cadillac. What was produced, in fact, was a car that leaked in the rain, had squeaks and rattles everywhere, and possessed distorted windshields. Further, its door locks broke, its interior looked cheap, and its convertible top was nearly impossible to put up or take down. When a senior engineer on the project was asked to explain why the flagship model of GM's flagship division had such problems, his response was, "It takes time to get the bugs out." In reality, the people behind the car were simply unmotivated.

The Allante fiasco woke up the BOC head, and the decision was made to let Cadillac reestablish its brand identity. The division would be allowed to design, market, and build its own cars. When a ceremony took place to commemorate the event, the fifteen hundred employees gathered in a huge warehouse let out an enormous, spontaneous cheer. Then they went outside and took down the BOC flag, replacing it with the yellow-crested Cadillac flag. The strategy worked, and with employees again committed to the brand, quality improved. In 1990, Cadillac was the first auto company to win the much-coveted Malcolm Baldrige Award for Quality.

In addition to a sense of commitment, the peerless decision maker attempts to find the person who is right for the job. In some fields, such as sports, it is easy to understand that talent on the baseball field may not generalize to talent in getting through life—as illustrated by Pete Rose. Similarly, it is apparent that the talents necessary to succeed in wartime may not generalize to peacetime. Winston Churchill was a great leader during World War II—perhaps saving Great Britain from defeat; in peacetime, however, his managerial abilities were average at best. In the Vietnam War, a task force was put together for the purpose of rescuing pilots downed by North Vietnamese antiaircraft fire. These guys would parachute down to the pilot, hook him up to hoists, fight off the enemy, and then hope that they could hang on as they were lifted out. They were the most highly decorated group in the military during the war. One Air Force pilot said, "They had balls as big as this"—and he held up his hands to form a circle the size of a basketball. The peculiar problem of the para-rescue jumpers is that in peacetime they have a hard time staying out of trouble.

It is important to remember that various types of managerial abilities exist. Gary Hart's successes and failures illustrate the point. Hart's difficulties as a presidential candidate are well known. He showed incredibly poor judgment in his romantic escapades with Donna Rice. Despite these lapses, he is currently enjoying great success advising U.S. firms in international business. Hart works for one of the major law firms in Denver—Davis, Graham & Stubbs. His tenure with the firm began while he was still a U.S. senator, prior to his bid for the presidency in 1988, and prior to the Donna Rice affair. At that time he knew that he would be leaving the Senate, and he needed a home base. A senior partner suggested that the firm bring him in because he could attract business due to his connections in Washington. Younger members of the firm fought the idea. Even then, Hart's reputation was blemished. In addition, conservative businessmen in the community did not like his liberal politics. Finally, the senior partners won out, and he came on board.

The goal of the firm in hiring Hart was to differentiate it from other law firms in Denver and to raise its profile. When news of the Donna Rice escapade broke, the decision looked bad. Yet, according to a senior partner in the firm, within about six months after the fiasco ended, Hart "rose from the ashes to act as a counselor to businessmen around the world." What was surprising was the way in which he actually helped the firm. His benefits emerged in completely unexpected areas: instead of greasing the wheels to obtain business with firms having Washington, D.C., connections, Hart went international, creating deals between "U.S. companies and Japan, the Soviet Union, Prague, Spain, and Italy." The senior partner described Gary Hart to me as "very creative, very smart, but with no sense of detail." As a result, the firm hired a handler with an MBA to clean up the "messes that he created." Gary Hart has talent, but it must be monitored and channeled into particular areas. His frailties are incompatible with high political office, where appearance can be more important than substance. In the world of big business, however, one's personal escapades have less relevance. The peerless decision maker recognizes such issues and is able to match the person to the task at hand.

The Planning Imperative

Dwight D. Eisenhower is reputed to have said, "The plan is nothing, but planning is everything." The implicit contradiction says a great deal about peerless decision makers. What are the secrets of planning? They can be summed up in four admonitions: Rehearse; keep it simple; distinguish the strategic from the tactical; and know where you are going.

Rehearse, Rehearse, Rehearse. In an ancient joke, a tourist lost on the streets of New York asked an elderly passer-by, "How do I get to Carnegie Hall?" The old man looked at him and advised: "Practice, practice, practice." So it goes with planning. An effective plan includes large doses of practice. If the players involved aren't sick of the rehearsals, then do more! Until the repetition is so ingrained that it causes boredom, excess capability has not been created. The goal of practice is to move beyond minimum competence levels. Excess capability saves performances, and even lives, when the stakes are high.

Common experience reveals that endless years of practice are required for athletes and musicians to hone their skills. Both must perform complex, coordinated physical actions that can be perfected only through thousands of repetitions. The extra capability gained from the rehearsals pulls them through when their performance begins to falter. (I should hasten to add that good judgment is also critical to high-caliber athletic or musical performances.) Less clear is the importance of practice for tasks that require both coordination and judgment, such as flying an airplane.

Nowhere are the problems that result from a lack of excess capability better demonstrated than in private aviation. The statistics are frightening: private pilots have accidents 200 times more frequently than pilots in commercial aviation. The primary reason for this alarming result is that, while able to fly competently when events are routine, the average private pilot lacks the skills to handle crises. In general, what gets the pilot into trouble is a series of poor decisions. One team of researchers concluded: "Each poor judgment along the way reduces a pilot's alternatives. At the last phase of the sequence, there are no alternatives left." Most private pilots simply lack the skills to fly themselves out of problems frequently created by their own poor judgment.

The difficulties of the average private pilot show up dramatically when they are placed in aircraft simulators. In one research study, the simulator mimicked various in-flight mechanical problems, such as fuel suddenly siphoning off while flying over mountains in heavy clouds. Many of the pilots, even though instrument-rated, could not cope with the problem. "Guys with thousands of hours get in there and hadn't thought about system problems before. They really found themselves loaded and groping for solutions that should have been easy to come by—and I think they were humbled by it." The researchers found that those with "excess capability in time of stress reflected a pattern of good judgment that had been applied throughout their flying lives; they had devoted time to understanding aircraft systems, and were prepared to handle predictable emergencies." In other words, they had practiced, practiced, practiced.

Rehearsal is also vital for purely mental tasks, but this imperative is the hardest for people to follow. Just as practice is required to coordinate the muscles to perform complex physical tasks, so too rehearsal is necessary to prepare the mind in order to perform difficult cognitive feats. One of the reasons for the success of NASA in the Apollo moon program was the attention to such details.

Walt Williams was the person who developed the idea of creating mission rules at NASA and then refining them through rehearsal. At first, the engineers resisted the idea of writing down a set of rules for what would be done whenever something unexpected happened. They argued that you would never know exactly what to expect and that the rules would never work exactly as planned. Williams would respond, "If you'd worked your way through problems, then when you saw a problem, whether you knew exactly what it was or not, you started recognizing the characteristics of it—and understanding the system, you could work your way out of it."

By one estimate, only 10 to 20 percent of the flight simulations at NASA specified techniques used in normal circumstances. Most attention was directed to trying to figure out what to do when abnormal events occurred. For example, if one of a set of redundant systems goes out, how much backup capacity must exist before the flight can continue? In fact, in order to create added pressure when running the simulations, engineers sped up the rate at which Mission Control received the problems. As one of the Mission Control specialists described it, "They always tried to run those [simulations] in double time—or close to it, throwing perhaps two dozen problems at a single controller in the fifteen minutes prior to landing. You had to field the problem, snap out a call, and move on to the next problem almost instantaneously, or you were going to be working on an old problem while a new one had caused the LEM [Lunar Escape Module] to crash." Dwight Eisenhower was right. While plans rarely fit the particular circumstances of a problem precisely, decision makers must develop and then carefully rehearse them.

Keep It Simple, Simple, Simple. A couple of years ago, I heard for the first time an important maxim: "Complex is easy; simple is hard." The pithy sentence packs much wisdom. Consider the problem of forecasting the national economy of the United States. What economists do is build a model in which GNP is the criterion variable (i.e., what is to be predicted) and a series of predictor variables (e.g., interest rates, consumer confidence, layoffs, wholesale prices, etc.) are used as independent variables. The model is built using historical data. Economists run equation after equation to find the best set of predictor variables. The equations are huge—containing dozens of variables. Finally, an optimum fit is produced.

The economist next takes the optimum equation and tries it on a new set of data on the economy, called a "hold-out sample." What happens is that the predictive ability of the equation decreases dramatically. The equation could handle the idiosyncrasies of the first data set, but simply through random fluctuations the second batch of numbers will be different. Then comes the coup de grâce. Can the model forecast future economic activity? As long as no major perturbations strike, the forecast will have some predictive validity —though less than for the hold-out sample. If unexpected events occur, however, the model falls apart completely.

Intelligent people can always develop complex explanations for events. The problem is that the more complex the explanation, the less generality it has. The really difficult task is to identify simple solutions that have generality. The peerless decision maker recognizes the importance of simplicity. Physicists seek it in their explanations of the fundamental basis of matter. Musicians find it in works that stand the test of time. Athletes seek simplicity in their movements. Military generals develop plans based upon the principle. Politicians seek to communicate simple messages to their constituents.

D. F. Hornig spent ten years on the President's Science Advisory Committee. One of the many problems on which he worked concerned the development of air-to-air missiles used to shoot down enemy bombers. A requirement identified by the Air Force for the missile was that it had to be reliable for head-on attack. Bombers had to be shot out of the air quickly, or they could release their payload early and still wreak havoc. The problem with the requirement was that because of the high closing rate of fighter and bomber, the missile had to have a long range and be able to turn extremely quickly in order to hit a maneuvering target. Three missiles were being considered at the time: the Sparrow, the Falcon, and the Sidewinder. On paper, the Sparrow and the Falcon had all the capabilities to perform the mission. But the Sidewinder, because of its heat-seeking nature, could only be used in a tail-attack mode in which the heat from the target's engines would be visible. As a result of the deficiency, it was about to be dropped from consideration when Hornig became involved.

In his investigation, Hornig immediately noticed a major difficulty. Both the Sparrow and the Falcon were enormously complicated, extremely expensive, and didn't work well. The Sidewinder, on the contrary, was cheap and reliable. Hornig recognized that his task was one of changing the requirements in order to make it possible for a simple solution to emerge. His break came when Wally Schirra, who later became an astronaut, noted that in almost all instances airplanes are shot down by tail attack. This legitimized the Sidewinder. As a result, the missile was deployed and for over thirty years has been a successful weapon.

The concept of keeping things simple is one of the reasons for Japan's phenomenal economic success during the 1970s and 1980s. How did Nissan Motor Company come up with its highly reliable automobile engine in the 1950s? You might be surprised to learn that the originator was actually an American who believed in simplicity. After World War II, the company sought to obtain a new, fuel-efficient, water-cooled engine. American engines were too big and fuel-thirsty. Political reasons kept the Japanese from approaching Germany. So, their engineers went to Great Britain and the Austin Motor Company. While awestruck by the size of the plant and the modern equipment it contained, the Japanese were able to come away with the rights to produce a solid, dependable, 1.5-liter Austin engine.

In order to rapidly develop their fledgling auto industry, the Japanese brought over numerous experts from the United States. One such person was David Stone, a retired engineer. In the mid-1950s, he went to Japan and worked in the plants with their engineers to help perfect the cars being developed. While he was there, he was asked to make suggestions on how to build a new 1-liter engine. He told them that they didn't have to build a new engine; they could use the one they had. Incredulous, they demanded to know how. So, Stone worked with them to shorten the stroke of the 1.5-liter engine to reduce its size. In short order, they had a smaller, more fuel-efficient engine that could be produced on the same assembly line as the old engine. Stone's message was to keep it simple and make changes by small degrees. He repeated over and over his basic approach: "Find out what is wrong, try to understand why it had gone wrong, and then break down the corrective process into modest steps." The Japanese learned well from Stone and other Americans. In fact, current estimates indicate that by 1995, three of the five leaders in worldwide car sales will be Japanese.

Toyota calls the process of keeping things simple and of continuously improving designs in small steps *kaizen*. But American companies seem to have moved from the pragmatic approach of the 1950s to one of attempting to make quantum jumps. Rather than keeping things simple, they tend to go for next-generation technology. The Space Shuttle has been identified as a prime example of this fixation. According to NASA's former historian, one explanation for its massive problems in the 1980s is that its managers "seek quantum leaps to new operational technology instead of building up to it incrementally. They want revolution instead of evolution." The pattern is currently repeating itself in the launching of a series of $3 billion weather satellites. The $50 billion plan calls for launching a new satellite every five years over a twenty-five year period; beginning in 1998, the first satellites will be able to monitor the earth's climate—particularly its temperature. But the project has been criticized for being highly risky because its huge size will limit the development of other programs intended to monitor the greenhouse effect.

Dr. James Van Allen described NASA planners as "creating a monster." An oceanographer at MIT said, "It's the shuttle all over again—all of our eggs in one basket." The big question is why NASA should launch a series of huge 29,000-pound satellites when smaller ones could obtain more information, at the same cost, more quickly, and with far less risk. The answer is the fixation on high technology. Just as General Motors jumped headlong into creating robotized factories, but instead got killer robots, NASA shows a propensity for developing highly complex, next-generation space vehicles that may fail too frequently.

High-technology solutions, however, should not be confused with complex solutions. In many instances incorporating high technology into products can increase their simplicity. Developing high-technology products (whether in transportation, medicine, computers, or whatever) is clearly an important task for a nation. One merely had to watch the laser-guided, "smart munitions" honing in on targets in the Gulf war to recognize the value of basic and applied science. Moving to the latest technology, however, is not a panacea. Systems should be proven before being implemented. As a result, an incremental approach of continuous upgrading should be an important goal.

While an incremental approach is recommended for adopting technological change, does such a philosophy hold in all cases? A critical issue facing large organizations today is how to respond to the dramatic shifts that have taken place in the external environment. Corporations, non-profit organizations, and even federal, state, and local governments must deal with an intensely competitive marketplace, slow economic growth, and crises in health care, in the inner cities, and in controlling debt. The potential answers to these problems require individuals to withstand some pain in the short term. The proposed solutions (e.g., raising taxes, lowering governmental handouts, closing factories and military bases, and increasing savings rates) all entail fighting through the individual fence in which pain must be shouldered in the short term in order to create a brighter future. Will an incremental approach of making continuous small adjustments work in such an environment?

I believe that an incremental approach will *not* work when changes must be made that lead to negative short-term outcomes for constituents, whether employees or taxpayers. The reason for this conclusion is found in the "law of decreasing marginal effect" discussed earlier. The law states that each additional unit of a gain or loss has less impact than the preceding one. The net result is the general rule that decision makers should "separate gains" but "aggregate losses"; that is, when a number of positive outcomes occur, people will feel better if they are separated. Thus, when opening presents at Christmas, children and adults alike enjoy the process more if they receive a number of smaller presents to open, rather than simply one big gift. In contrast, if someone owes money to fifteen different creditors, paying is psychologically easier if the bill is aggregated into one large payment. The "bandage" metaphor can be applied to the aggregation of losses rule. That is, most people prefer to have a bandage ripped off in one big tug rather than endure a slow, peeling approach in which all your little hairs are pulled from their roots one at a time.

Employing an incremental change strategy in an environment in which negative outcomes are occurring is tantamount to slowly peeling off a bandage. People naturally resist such a strategy. Under these circumstances, it is best to aggregate the negative outcomes so that they are all taken at once. In other words, discontinuous/revolutionary change is required.

Such a view is advocated by Jack Welch, CEO of General Electric Corporation, and one of the most respected chief executive officers in the United States in the early 1990s. He has run General Electric since 1981, and in that time has transformed it from a slow-moving dinosaur to a dynamic company that is growing stronger in the competitive world marketplace. In an article in *Fortune* magazine, Welch was quoted as saying:

> When I try to summarize what I've learned since 1981, one of the big lessons is that change has no constituency. People like the status quo. They like the way it was. When you start changing things, the good old days look better and better. You've got to be prepared for massive resistance. . . . If your change isn't big enough, revolutionary enough, the bureaucracy can beat you. When you get leaders who confuse popularity with leadership, who just nibble away at things, nothing changes. I think that's true in countries and companies.

Given the ideas of Jack Welch, when is incremental change appropriate? The answer lies in whether one is dealing with technological change or human change. With technology, it seems clear that improvements are best incorporated continuously in small, careful steps. In contrast, when a number of changes in human behavior are required, each of which results in a short-term loss, it is best to make the adjustments in one discontinuous, but painful, effort.

Distinguish the Strategic from the Tactical. Who has the better reputation as a decision maker, CEOs of savings and loans or baseball managers? Until the 1980s, when the S&L crisis struck, I suspect that most of us would have rated the CEOs of financial institutions more highly. Today, attitudes have probably flipped 180 degrees. The calamitous failure of hundreds of S&Ls severely tarnished the reputations of those who run these institutions. What happened? Did older CEOs suddenly become stupid? Was a new class of CEOs hired, the members of which shared a fatal flaw? An alternative explanation for the S&L debacle is that executives confused strategy and tactics, and as a result, they made a series of exceedingly poor judgment calls.

When one studies judgment calls, the focus is on "one-time" decisions that occur infrequently and are "strategic" in nature. Strategic decisions occur prior to tactical decisions, focus on developing larger goals and objectives, and are implemented over the long term. One uses tactics to implement strategy. Problems occur, however, when *tactics* are confused with *strategy*. Tactical decisions are repeated over and over again. By their nature, tactical decisions are amenable to the development of standardized rules for implementation. In baseball, it's given the mythical name of the "book." The "book" doesn't really exist; nonetheless, everyone uses it. The book is a shared consensus of what managers should do in various circumstances in a baseball game. For example, the book says that left-handed hitters are more effective against right-handed pitchers. Similarly, in the business world, tactical decisions are frequently institutionalized in computer programs using expert systems. Thus, most companies use automated systems to determine to which customers they should extend credit. The programs employ various factors that predict whether a person will be a good credit risk, such as type of job, salary, previous credit record, and amount of personal debt.

In some contexts, tactical decisions are replayed thousands of times. As a result, the "law of large numbers" dominates. The law of large numbers says that big samples will be representative of the population from which they are drawn. Thus, if you wish to know how Americans feel about going to war with Iraq (or whomever), pollsters draw a large sample (roughly 2,400 people), which will represent within about 3 percentage points the average view of all Americans. Similarly, if you make small loans to thousands of customers, the law of large numbers ensures that you will make money as long as your basic decision rules for lending are financially sound. Thus, the law of large numbers ensured that banks, S&Ls, and insurance companies remained financially solvent for half a century. These institutions made safe loans to millions of people, and flourished as a result. With deregulation, however, financial institution executives suddenly had to make *strategic* decisions. They had the freedom to invest funds in entirely new ways. In other words, they had to make judgment calls for which they were wholly unprepared, and calamity resulted.

Not all S&Ls have become insolvent. Some, like Golden West Financial, stayed with the known strategy of lending out federally insured deposits to consumers for home mortgages. Run by a husband-and-wife team, the philosophy of Golden West was stated clearly in a recent annual report: "Perhaps we can best characterize Golden West's attitude toward lending by simply saying that your management likes to sleep undisturbed by worries and nightmares." Wall Street likes that approach. As one analyst said, "Golden West is one of the best financial firms in the country, period." In sum, while dull and boring, Golden West's strategy is a winning one because of the law of large numbers.

The difference between strategy and tactics is illustrated by two different types of gambles. First, imagine that I've asked you to flip a "fair" coin and call it. If you are right, I will give you $10,000. If you are wrong, you give me $5,000. When most people are offered such a bet, they will decline it, even though expected-value calculations indicate that it has a positive expected value (for you) of $2,500 (.5 times $10,000 minus .5 times $5,000 equals $2,500). What is happening here? Why do people violate the principles of expected-value analysis? The reason is that people perceive such bets to be risky. So what if they can win $10,000? They have an equal chance of losing $5,000.

Suppose, however, that I change the bet. This time we will toss the coin 100 times and each bet is worth only $100 if you win and $50 if I win. The expected value of this bet is exactly the same as that of the first one—$2,500. Yet almost everyone will play the second gamble. Why? The answer is that the first bet is similar to a strategic decision. It is large (at least for most of us). It is played only once. You can lose your shirt. In contrast, the second bet is similar to tactical decisions. They occur over and over. The law of large numbers operates. In the long run, you will almost certainly win.

The following caveat must be added, however. You will win in the long run as long as the strategy is sound. If a flawed strategy is employed, the law of large numbers ensures that you will fail. For this reason, strategy must be developed slowly, prudently, and with attention to detail. You change strategy only after great deliberation, because if you are wrong, the consequences are dire.

Baseball is to tactics as boxing is to strategy. Baseball is a long-run game. Tony La Russa says that baseball is determined by the "law of cumulation." You win by small achievements done over and over again. A season lasts 162 games; batters come to the plate over 500 times. Under such situations talent shows. As George Will said in *Men At Work:* "Baseball, with its long leveling season, is the severest meritocracy in sports. There is ample time for talent to tell. The ratio of talent to luck is high." On the other hand, boxing at the championship level is a short-run sport. The battles are infrequent and immense stakes rest on the few that occur. So, miracle upsets can happen. For example, a Buster Douglas can defeat a Mike Tyson.

At the international level, warfare has many of the properties of the boxing match. Upsets can occur. Little North Vietnam can defeat two superpowers—France and the U.S.A. For this reason, the long-term strategy of a government should be to take the appropriate small steps to prevent the miscalculations that lead to wars. In order to avoid such calamities, peerless decision makers know where they want to go and monitor their progress along the way to avoid the big mistakes.

Know Where You Are Going. Around age forty most males seem to pass through a stage in which they have to prove that they are still young and virile. At this point, halfway through their expected life span, many guys ask questions like "Where am I going in life?" and "Am I where I wanted to be at this point in my career?" Several years ago, I bumped up against the forty barrier and to my consternation felt the itch. A variety of means exist for soothing the urge—some racier than others. My solution was to go out and buy a four-year-old 911SC Porsche. My wife merely shook her head when I explained that the sleek, fast, maneuverable, polished car was better than a mistress.

The car was great fun. I would drive down the street and nine-year-old boys would give me the "thumbs-up." Looking for a more mature reference group, I joined the local Porsche club and took my car to the Hallett race track near Tulsa. As luck would have it, a professional racing team was also at the track, and I was able to hire one of their instructors to show me how to drive. After giving me a lecture on "the line," what an apex is, and so forth, he put me in the passenger seat and drove my car around the curvy course a couple of times. The smoothness of the ride immediately struck my attention. Nothing jerked, nothing bumped. No great experience of speed was felt as we maneuvered through the tight turns and then accelerated down the long straightaway. The lap time, however, was fast—really fast. Pulling off into the service area, the instructor asked me if I was ready. Full of confidence, I said, "Sure!" and we switched seats.

I checked the rearview mirror, stomped on the accelerator, and we took off like a banshee screaming down the track. We approached the first turn, and I frantically looked for the apex. Thinking that I had it, I braked violently, began the turn, looked up, and noticed that the car was pointed toward a large field filled with old tires. Narrowly staying on the track, I proceeded to take us around the course twice before my instructor suggested that we stop to review the driving lesson. My lap times were slow, really slow. The smooth ride of the instructor was replaced by the jerky movements of the novice. My every instinct was wrong. Consequently, I was always trying to recover from a mistake. Violent changes in speed and direction resulted. It was a miracle that the Porsche, my passenger, and I survived.

I spent a day on the track, and by the end came away with three major impressions: First, driving a car fast takes a great deal of skill. Second, those who drive race cars for a living are athletes. After about twenty-five trips around the two-mile track, I was totally exhausted. Third, smoothness is speed. The key to driving fast is to know where you need to go and to constantly monitor your line. As a result, you can make small corrections early. The longer you wait to correct your driving line, the more violent the maneuver required to get back on course.

Memories of my experience at the Hallett race track came back a couple of years later when I talked with Chuck Gettys about judgment calls. A psychology professor at Oklahoma University, Gettys is one of those rare people who can smile at you while asking a question that destroys an entire line of thought. Because he helped to found behavioral decision theory, I wanted to ask him to describe the attributes of the peerless decision maker. He argued that outstanding decision makers carefully monitor the environment. They catch problems early on and make small mid-course corrections.

Gettys used a supertanker as a metaphor to explain the importance of monitoring in decision making. In order to stop or turn one of these gargantuan beasts, the captain must plan early. If its engines are shut off when cruising at 15 knots, it can take three full miles for the supertanker to stop. The longer the pilot waits to change the course of the vessel, the more violent the maneuver required. The principle of knowing where you are going, monitoring your course, and making changes early applies to piloting supertankers just as it had applied to racing a Porsche. Because peerless decision makers drive their course smoothly, they are hard to identify; emergencies rarely occur—everything rides on an even keel, and little excitement happens once a course of action has been plotted. Peerless decision makers can and will make bold moves. However, once a strategy has been plotted, things tend to go smoothly.

An expression used by pilots, "Stay on top of the power curve," illustrates the importance of monitoring progress. In order to stay in the air, a pilot must maintain enough power to overcome the drag of air passing over the plane. When flying straight and level at cruising speed, few problems occur; more than enough power exists to overcome drag. Problems occur most frequently when landing, because then the pilot would like to be moving as slowly as possible. If the pilot fails to constantly monitor airspeed, descent rate, the plane's angle, and the engine's power setting, catastrophe results.

Thurmon Munson, the great baseball catcher and captain of the New York Yankees in the 1970s, was flying his new Cessna Citation business jet into an airport in 1979. He cut the throttle to reduce airspeed. The plane obeyed the law of gravity and began to sink rapidly. Munson raised the nose to compensate, drag increased dramatically, and the plane began to stall. He then attempted to add power to increase the airspeed, but it was too late. The engines take time to "spool up" and increase power. Munson had failed to carefully monitor his flight path and make small corrections early. He got behind the power curve, and even his last second massive injection of power was insufficient. As a result of inattention, he crashed and burned. The world lost a great athlete.

The peerless decision maker intuitively understands the metaphor of staying on top of the power curve. Whatever the profession, peerless decision makers monitor their environment and make small adjustments early in order to avoid having to make catastrophic corrections at the last moment. But to assess their position and choose the appropriate mid-course corrections, peerless decision makers must also know their destination.

The grizzled sergeant spoke slowly and carefully: "It's nighttime. Pitch black. You can't see your hand in front of your face. You are here"—he pointed to a hill on a map that represented our position, and then to a second hill a couple of kilometers away—"How are you going to get *there*? Are you going to take an azimuth and follow it directly to your objective?" His look told us that anybody who would do that would be dog bait.

The sergeant continued: "When you navigate at night, you follow your feet. When your toes are higher than your heels, you're going uphill. When your left foot is lower than your right foot, you're on the side of a hill. That's all a Ranger needs to know." Traveling at night in mountainous country is a terrible experience. At Ranger School it seemed that our lives consisted of moving from one objective to another at "0-dark-thirty" in the morning. It would be raining, and we would be in a single-file with each of us an arm's length from the guy in front. We had on baseball caps with little pieces of fluorescent tape on the back. You tried your damndest to stay close enough so that you never lost sight of that ghostly glowing piece of tape bobbing up and down in front of you.

Then there were the jokers. When you saw the tape start moving up, you knew to pick up your feet because you would be going uphill. Some thought it really funny to place their hat on their rifle and slowly lift it into the air. They would laugh when the guy behind began cursing as he stumbled around trying to figure out why he wasn't going up the hill. And there was the gambit of suddenly taking off the hat. The guy behind would immediately stop in near panic. The disappearance of the tape meant one of two things: Either he was lost, or the guy in front had just fallen off a cliff.

The sergeant was absolutely correct in describing how to navigate at night. In hilly or mountainous terrain, you cannot take the most direct route. Steep hills turn into cliffs, and gullies tend to have streams and lots of trees and brush that are nearly impossible to get through. What you do is follow ridges. Ridges tend to have gradual slopes, and less vegetation grows on them. Furthermore, you can tell where you are on a ridge. When your left foot is lower than your right, you know that you've gone off course; when your toes are no longer higher than your heels, you've reached the top of a hill. Things become pretty basic at night in the mountains. As a result of these simple ideas, when doing land navigation at night, you plot your path to follow ridgelines. You might take a route that is two or three times longer than going directly from point A to point B. It could take much less time. In addition, you might avoid a broken leg.

Achieving goals is a lot like navigating in the mountains at night. You have a general idea of where you want to go, but you must feel your way toward the objective. In most cases the route is circuitous. You try to select a path that avoids cliffs and the deep brush. At times you must stop and start over. Frequently, you have to get under your poncho and recheck your map.

The story of Soichiro Honda illustrates the importance of setting goals, and shows that the route to achieving them is frequently circuitous. Mr. Honda began his career at a small auto repair shop in Tokyo, where he developed a lifelong passion for building cars. This obsession with automobiles surfaced dramatically during the great earthquake of 1923, when at age sixteen the young Soichiro risked life and limb to drive customers' cars out to safety from under a collapsing building even though he had never driven a car before. After the quake he stayed on and helped the auto shop's owner to recover. Before his twenty-fifth birthday, he had patented cast-metal spokes for wheels and was exporting them all over the Far East.

Honda loved motors, racing, and geisha girls. In the 1930s, he set speed records. At a rally in 1936, however, he had a wreck, and the injuries forced him out of racing. At this point, he decided to begin manufacturing engine parts. He attempted to make piston rings, but knew little about the casting process. He worked night and day for months with no success. Then he enrolled in a technology school and gradually learned to make rings that he sold at the low end of the market. He also developed new automated equipment and orders began to arrive. World War II intervened. Between American bombing raids and another earthquake, his operation was nearly wiped out, and he sold it.

264 · JUDGMENT CALLS

Honda spent a year drinking sake that he made himself, attempting to figure out what to do next. In a country now virtually destroyed by the war, trains were full and gasoline was scarce. His creativity spurred by these inconvenient circumstances, Honda thought of the idea of putting an engine on a bicycle. Using small war-surplus engines made to provide electricity for radios, he began producing motorbikes. When these proved successful, he developed a bigger engine and was soon selling a thousand bikes a month.

Honda made steady improvements in his product line. The brainstorm of creating a motorbike that had a step-through design and could be driven with one hand proved to be a huge seller. Delivery boys could drive while carrying packages. When he hired a finance man to control costs, his company started to become profitable. Then, in the 1950s, the company began racing its motorcycles and winning. In 1959, Honda became the largest motorcycle manufacturer in the world. In 1961, the company won the first five places in two categories at the prestigious Isle of Man races.

It was not until the early 1960s that the company decided to attempt to penetrate the American market. Shunning assistance from the Japanese government, Honda set up shop in California on a shoestring budget. The company's target in the early days was the leather-jacketed motorcycle crowd. Disaster nearly struck, however, when early engines failed on the high-speed American freeways. The company reacted in characteristic fashion by airshipping the cycles back to Japan, where engineers worked night and day to fix the problem. Within a month it was solved. The second difficulty was that the large motorcycles were not selling. In order to save on limited capital, company executives drove around Los Angeles in small 50cc Super Cub bikes. They generated a great deal of attention, and recognizing the marketing possibilities, the managers changed their strategy. They began to focus on signing up dealers to sell the smaller bikes. By 1965, Honda had a 63 percent market share of motorcycles sold in the United States.

Since his childhood, Honda had dreamed of building passenger cars. By the early 1960s, the company was in position to enter the auto market. In 1962, it showed its first vehicles at a Japanese auto show. The vehicles were noteworthy for their small, high-efficiency engines. Again, the company began to race its vehicles, and in 1965, its Formula 1 entry won a Grand Prix victory in Mexico City. In the 1970s, Honda would enter the American market with automobile engines so efficient that they passed the new air-quality standards without catalytic converters.

Soichiro Honda revealed decidedly American characteristics of entrepreneurship, independence, and egalitarianism in running his company. Unlike most Japanese firms, Honda Motor Company developed as an entrepreneurial enterprise. Disavowing the support of the Japanese Ministry of International Trade and Industry (MITI) that controls the political system of Japanese industry, Honda believed that his small firm could outmaneuver the big companies, saying, "We feel that strength is weakness, and weakness is strength." Another characteristic of Honda has been its egalitarian treatment of employees. Soichiro Honda argued that "each individual should work for himself—that's important. People will not sacrifice themselves for the company. They come to work at the company to enjoy themselves. That feeling would lead to innovation." At a Honda plant, workers eat with management and participate in decision-making and problem-solving activities. In an interview with *Inc.* magazine, Honda said, "The most important thing in the world is not diamonds or gold, but humans. In order to do that, we have to have broad contact."

As CEO of Honda Motor Company, Soichiro Honda consistently set a "hair trigger" for action. And he worked by intuition—in part because he rarely had enough funds to conduct market research. Perhaps this was fortunate, because marketing research would never have predicted the huge success of the small motorcycles that gave him his foothold in the United States.

Honda started out with a childhood dream of building a passenger car. The route to his goal was circuitous, but he achieved his dream by always keeping his goal in mind and by sustaining his great love of his work. "I always had a stronger desire for work itself," he said, "than for money—the desire to explore something new that other people haven't done. I don't want to walk on the path that is already created by other people." Because of the decision-making abilities of Soichiro Honda and of the people that he hired, Honda Motor Company has gone on to achieve remarkable success in the United States. In 1982, the company completed the first Japanese auto plant in America; in 1989, the Accord became the largest selling car model in the United States. By the early 1990s, Honda was selling more autos in the United States than any foreign company.

Soichiro Honda possessed many of those extra characteristics held by peerless decision makers. To sum it up, such individuals

- Develop an extensive knowledge base in their field, having experienced both good and bad outcomes in the past.

266 · JUDGMENT CALLS

- Actively seek to learn from their past experience.

- Recognize human needs—from the desire for respect to the need to urinate.

- Create a fall-back position and/or develop a reserve for when plans go awry.

- Develop simple plans and then practice, practice, practice.

- Distinguish strategic from tactical decisions.

- Set goals, monitor their progress, and make early adjustments when they go off course.

Even if we plot carefully, however, we can still follow the wrong path. For each Soichiro Honda, one can find a John DeLorean, whose route to his dream of building an automobile ended in disaster. Things can go wrong for the most skilled decision makers because we live in a perceptual *Wonderland*. Events occur probabilistically; chance influences outcomes. As a result, the best possible decisions can sometimes lead to awful consequences. We need to do better than Alice, though, in making judgment calls. In *Wonderland*, Alice was faced with the choice of two paths. She asked the Cheshire Cat which one she should follow. His response was: "That depends a good deal on where you want to get to." Young, inexperienced, and somewhat rattled, she responded, "I don't much care where—" The Cat wisely replied, "Then it doesn't matter which way you go."

Perhaps above all else peerless decision makers *define their goals*. In order to make a judgment call, they must have a sense of where they want to go. By defining their objectives, they can decide when to shoot or not and when to stay or quit. They can identify the occasions on which they should seek risk or choose security. They have a means for determining when to focus on the present or the future. By knowing their goals, they recognize the importance of determining the cause for events that can help or impede their progress. They recognize that chance influences the outcomes of their actions and that they do not have complete control over the future. They realize that problems can be framed from many perspectives and that true understanding of a problem requires the use of multiple viewpoints. Finally, they understand that both reason and emotion play a role in high-stakes decision making. While the exercise of reason is paramount in analyzing problems, the use of emotion is foremost in moving the implementation forward.

The peerless decision maker described in this book is a fictitious ideal, composed of a blend of chief executive officers, military leaders, U.S. presidents, and other successful individuals who have engaged in high-stakes decision making. Imagine that he, or she, is your mentor, whom you can call upon for help if faced with that tough judgment call when experts disagree and no computer program exists to help you. Consider what steps the peerless decision maker would take to solve the dilemma. As you develop your plan and implement your decision, attempt to relax. Remember that even peerless decision makers can make good decisions that turn out poorly. But also remember that the *process* is the key. By following the fundamentals of high-stakes decision making, over the long haul your decisions will stand the test of time.

SOURCES AND NOTES

1. ON THE NATURE OF JUDGMENT CALLS

page

13–14 Quotations on Cetus and Chiron: Ann Gibbons, "Chiron Buys Cetus: A Tale of Two Companies," *Science*, 253, August 2, 1991, 503–4.

15 Quotation from developer: Kathy Rebello, "A Parched California Could Face an Economic Drought," *USA Today*, March 1, 1991, 8B.

17 April Glaspie quotations: Exactly what April Glaspie said to Saddam Hussein will probably never be known. In testimony before congressional committees, Glaspie stated that her transcript with Hussein had been edited "to the point of inaccuracy." On the other hand, she also said that "a great deal" of the Iraqi record was accurate. Glaspie stated to the committees that she told Hussein the United States would not tolerate the use of force against Kuwait. At best, she appears to have given a mixed message to Saddam Hussein prior to leaving for her vacation.

18 "We know America is very afraid . . .": Tony Horwitz, "Iraq Sending Mixed Signals on Pullback," *The Wall Street Journal*, November 2, 1990, A8.

18 Quotation from General Colin Powell: Craig R. Whitney, "The Empire Srikes Back," *The New York Times Magazine*, March 10, 1991, 34.

19 Unimation VP quotation: Amal Kumar Naj, "How U.S. Robots Lost the Market to Japan in Factory Automation," *The Wall Street Journal*, November 6, 1990, A1, A10.

19–21 Chester Carlson's story: John H. Dessauer, *My Years with XEROX*. New York: Doubleday & Company, 1971.

23 Ford E-coat story: This anecdote is based on a discussion in David Halberstam, *The Reckoning*. New York: Avon Books, 1986, pp. 506–8.

26 U.S.S. *Iowa* material: Richard Halloran, "*Iowa* Captain Doubts Sailor Named by Inquiry Set Blast," *The New York Times*, December 12, 1989, A20.

27 Psychologist's quotation about Hartwig: Susan Moses, "Psychologists Criticize Probe of Blast on *Iowa*," *APA Monitor*, February 1990, 20.

27 Quotation from Captain Fred P. Moosally: Michael R. Gordon, "Navy Reopens *Iowa* Blast Inquiry After Ignition in Gunpowder Test," *The New York Times*, May 1990, A23.

28–29 The "hot-hand" phenomenon: Robert Vallone and Amos Tversky, "The Hot Hand in Basketball: On the Misperception of Random Sequences," *Cognitive Psychology, 17*,1985, 295–314.

29–30 The Casey Stengel story: David Halberstam, *Summer of '49*. New York: Avon Books, 1989, p. 192.

30 Quotation on moral compromises: Robert Grudin, *Time and the Art of Living*. New York: Harper & Row, 1982, p. 80.

31 Yellowstone fire quotation: Scott McMurray, "Yellowstone a Year Later: Surprises Amid the Ashes," *The Wall Street Journal*, August 30, 1989, A8.

32 Webb quotation: Charles Murray and Catherine Bly Cox, *Apollo: The Race to the Moon*. New York: Simon & Schuster, 1989, p. 72.

35 Thomas Jefferson's quotation about George Washington: *The Daily Oklahoman*, February 22, 1991, 10.

36 Honda quotation about Fugisawa: Robert Shook, *Honda: An American Success Story*. New York: Prentice Hall Press, 1988, p. 9.

36 Warthog story: John J. Fialka, "A-10 'Warthog,' a Gulf War Hero, Would Fly to Scrap Heap If Air Force Brass Has Its Way," *The Wall Street Journal*, March 29, 1991, A10.

2. TO SHOOT OR NOT

39 Cadbury Corporation: Thomas Peters and Robert Waterman, *In Search of Excellence*. New York: Harper & Row, 1982, pp. 142–43.

39–40 Storage Technology story: Bro Uttal, "Storage Technology Goes for the Gold," *Fortune*, April 6, 1981, 58.

40 "If you don't know what to do. . . . ": Murray and Cox, *Apollo: The Race to the Moon*, p. 262.

43 Description of Captain Rogers as aggressive and "trigger-happy" and of *Vincennes* as "Robocruiser": John Bary and Roger Charles, "Sea of Lies," *Newsweek*, July 13, 1992, 29–37.

45 "When I was at Oldsmobile": Halberstam, *The Reckoning*, p. 14.

46–47 Vignette on Peoples Bancorp: Ron Suskind, "New England Banker, Sticking to Old Ways, Avoided Rivals' Woes," *The Wall Street Journal*, February 19, 1991, A1, A9.

47 Quotation on realist: J. Edward Russo and Paul J. H. Schoemaker, *Decision Traps: Ten Barriers to Brilliant Decision-Making and How to Overcome Them*. New York: Doubleday, 1989, p. 79. Their quote was in reference to a "business person," but it fits the peerless decision maker as well.

49–50 Material on General Maxwell Taylor: David Halberstam, *The Best and the Brightest*. New York: Penguin Books, 1983, p. 216.

50 Going into Laos: Halberstam, *The Best and the Brightest*, p. 785.

51 Software companies' overconfidence: Buck Brown, "Enterprise," *The Wall Street Journal*, July 7, 1989, B1.

51 Confidence in causes of death: Baruch Fischhoff, Paul Slovic, and Sarah Licthtenstein, "Knowing with Certainty: The Appropriateness of Extreme Confidence," *Journal of Experimental Psychology: Human Perception and Performance, 3,* 1977, (4), 552–64.

51–52 Computer company overconfidence and general discussion of overconfidence bias: Russo and Schoemaker, *Decision Traps*, pp. 70–81.

55–56 The Pearl Harbor discussion is based on Abraham Ben-zvi, "Hindsight and Foresight: A Conceptual Framework for the Analysis of Surprise Attacks," *World Politics*, 381–95.

56 "Mindset" material: Paul A. Gigot, "Iraq Miscues Weren't Just Glaspie's Fault," *The Wall Street Journal*, March 21, 1991, A10.

57 Saudis drinking their oil: Halberstam, *The Reckoning*, p. 463.

58 Judge Jerome Frank quotation: Jerome Frank, *Courts on Trial: Myth and the Reality in American Justice.* New York: Atheneum, 1963, pp. 119–20.

59–60 Algiers Motel trial research: John C. Mowen and Darwyn Linder, "Discretionary Aspects of Jury Decision Making," in L. E. Abt and I. R. Stuart, eds., *Social Psychology and Discretionary Law.* New York: Van Nostrand Reinhold, 1979, pp. 219–39.

62 Identifying alternative solutions: For research on the inability of decision makers to identify all the possible solutions to a problem, see Charles F. Gettys, "Research and Theory on Predecision Processes," prepared for the Office of Naval Research, Engineering and Psychology Programs, Contract Number N00014-80-C-0639, November 1983.

3. TO STAY OR QUIT

65–66 The Jose Gomez story is based on: Martha Brannigan, "Auditor's Downfall Shows a Man Caught in Trap of His Own Making," *The Wall Street Journal*, March 4, 1987, 31.

66 On entrapment "wooden-headedness": Barbara W. Tuchman, *The March of Folly.* New York: Alfred A. Knopf, 1984, pp. 7, 8.

68 University of Ohio theater study and Tenn-Tom Waterway: Hal Arkes and Nancy Blumer, "The Psychology of Sunk Cost," *Organizational Behavior and Human Decision Processes, 35,* 1985, 124–40.

69–71 Penn Square failure: Irvine H. Sprague, *Bailout.* New York: Basic Books, 1986, p. 110.

73–74 Ponzi scheme theory: Benjamin J. Stein, "The Biggest Scam Ever?" *Barron's*, February 19, 1990, 8, 9, and 30–32.

75 "I won't miss Drexel" quotation: "Did Drexel Get What It Deserved?" *Fortune*, March 12, 1990, 81–88.

77 Khrushchev quotation on Vietnam: Halberstam, *The Best and the Brightest*, p. 97.

77 "Butterfly effect": James Gleick, *Chaos.* New York: Penguin Books, 1987, pp. 20–23.

78 Robert Kennedy quotation: Halberstam, *The Best and the Brightest*, p. 98.

81 General Shoup quotation: Barbara Tuchman, *The March of Folly*. New York: Alfred A. Knopf, 1984, p. 341.

83 Benjamin Graham's rules: John Train, *The Money Masters*. New York: Harper & Row, 1980, p. 105.

83 College dropout rate: U.S. Department of Education, *Digest of Educational Statistics*, September 1988, 136.

4. PRESENT VERSUS FUTURE

85–86 Linebacker story: Gerald Eskenazi, "Athlete and Health: Many At Risk," *The New York Times*, Sunday, March 11, 1990, Y25–26.

87 Hank Gathers story: Charles Leerhsen, et al., "Basketball Was His Life," *Newsweek*, March 19, 1990, 52. See also Anne P. Davis, "Gathers' College Career," *USA Today*, March 1, 1991, 12C.

88 University of Arizona study: Jay Christensen-Szalanski and Gregory Northcraft, "Patient Compliance Behavior: The Effects of Time on Patients' Values of Treatment Regimens," *Social Science Medicine, 21*, 1985, 263–73. For more discussion on time and decision making, see John C. and Maryanne M. Mowen, "Time and Outcome Valuation: Implications for Marketing Decision Making," *Journal of Marketing*, October 1991, 54–62. See also Mancur Olson and Martin Bailey, "Positive Time Preference," *Journal of Political Economy, 89*, 1981, 1–25. As a general statement, the desire to take one's gain in the present is an extremely strong finding, but exceptions to the desire to delay losses can be found. For example, many people who know that they must face a bad experience (e.g., having an elective operation) will choose to face it immediately. A factor of dread appears to be operating in some instances to make people speed up the occurrence of certain types of negative outcomes.

88 Estimates of discount rate: Michael Landsberger, "Consumer Discount Rate and the Horizon: New Evidence," *Journal of Political Economy*, November–December 1971, 1346–59.

88–90 The mini-max anecdote: Halberstam, *The Reckoning*, pp. 571–76.

91 Ultralife battery story: Clare Ansberry, "Eastman Kodak Is Pulling Plug on Its Ultralife," *The Wall Street Journal*, April 10, 1990, B1, B12.

91–92 Ray Floyd story: Frederick C. Klein, "On Sports: Another Green Jacket for Faldo," *The Wall Street Journal*, April 10, 1990, A16.

92 "I feel guilty": Carrie Dolan, "Good Intentions Prop Up Fitness Sales," *The Wall Street Journal*, October 31, 1989, B1, 3.

92–93 Iacocca quotation: Halberstam, *The Reckoning*, p. 568.

93–94 Edison story: Summarized from Robert Conot, *A Streak of Luck: The Life and Legend of Thomas Alva Edison*. New York: Seaview Books, 1979. Quote from *Scientific American*, p. 162.

94–95 The Kearns story: Joseph B. White, "How a Detroit Inventor Battled Years to Prove Ford Stole His Ideas," *The Wall Street Journal*, April 8, 1990, 1, 8.

96 For an excellent discussion of time traps, see John Platt, "Social Traps," *Science, 28,* 1973, 641–51.

97 Peter Drucker quotation: Peter F. Drucker, "Marketing 101 for a Fast-Changing Decade," *The Wall Street Journal,* November 20, 1990, A20.

97 Straight commission compensation: Erin Anderson and Richard L. Oliver, "Perspectives on Behavior-Based Versus Outcome-Based Salesforce Control Systems," *Journal of Marketing, 51,* October 1987, 76–88.

98 Investing for the long term: Gary Hector, "Yes, You *Can* Manage Long Term," *Fortune,* November 21, 1988, 63–76.

98 U.S. investments: Louis S. Richman, "How Capital Costs Cripple America," *Fortune,* August 14, 1989, 50–54.

99 3M Corporation's strategy: Russell Mitchell, "Masters of Innovation," *BusinessWeek,* April 10, 1989, 58–63.

99 Lou Harris Poll results: Mark N. Vamos, "How Americans Feel About Their Future," *BusinessWeek,* September 25, 1989, 175.

99 English court ruling: Mary Douglas and Aaron Widowsky, *Risk and Culture.* Berkeley, CA: University of California Press, 1982, p. 23.

99 For a discussion of pollution in the Thames, see P. Casapieri, "Environmental Impact of Pollution Controls on the Thames Estuary, United Kingdom," in *The Estuary As Filter.* Orlando, FL: Academic Press, 1984, pp. 489–504.

100–101 Mississippi River vignette: John McPhee, *The Control of Nature.* New York: Farrar, Straus & Giroux, 1989.

102 The data here on the number of financial institutions per citizen must be interpreted with care. It is difficult to compare across countries because of divergent laws. The statistics are presented to illustrate the general point that the United States has a large number of financial institutions relative to its population.

103–104 Chicago Bulls story: Clifton Brown, "On Fire in Chicago," *The New York Times,* Sunday, March 24, 1991, Y25–26. See also Jack McCallum, "Helping Hands," *Sports Illustrated,* December 17, 1990, 40–45.

5. RISK VERSUS SECURITY

109 Statistics on fluoride: H. W. Lewis, *Technological Risks.* New York: W. W. Norton, pp. 40–41.

110 Boeing quotation: Anthony Ramirez, "Boeing's Happy, Harrowing Times," *Fortune,* July 17, 1989, 40–48.

111 Law of decreasing marginal effect: The idea of decreasing marginal effects can be seen in economics in the concept of decreasing marginal utility. In psychology, it is found in Stevens' power law, and in prospect theory. See Daniel Kahneman and Amos Tversky, "Choices, Values, and Frames," *American Psychologist, 39,* 1984, 341–50.

113 Saving the factory study: Max H. Bazerman, *Judgment in Managerial Decision Making.* New York: John Wiley & Sons, 1990, p. 49.

114 Iraq ambassador's quotation: Ray Betzner, "Students Get Close Look at Mideast Crisis," *William and Mary Alumni Gazette, 58,* October 1990, 1. For an analysis of what caused Iraq to attack Kuwait, see Don Oberdorfer, "The

War No One Saw Coming," *The Washington Post Weekly Edition*, March 18–24, 1991, 6–10.

114 Middle East expert's quotation: Michael Kramer, "The Moment of Truth," *Time*, January 21, 1991, 24.

115 Number of jobs created by small companies in the 1980s: Dana Milbank, "Job Growth Stalls, Despite Recovery, As Many Small Businesses Stop Hiring," *The Wall Street Journal*, February 2, 1993, 2, 4.

115 U.S. Gold Co. quotations: Marj Charlier, "Brothers Bet on Gold Bugs to Hit Pay Dirt," *The Wall Street Journal*, September 20, 1990, B1, B2.

116 Bob Eaton quotation: Maryann Keller, *Rude Awakening: The Rise, Fall and Struggle for Recovery of General Motors*. New York: William Morrow, 1989, p. 177.

116–17 Quotation from Schnellenberger and Tom Osborne story: Michael Janofsky, "Going for 2 Points and Losing No. 1," *The New York Times*, January 4, 1984, B9.

117–18 Pat Jones story: Based on an interview with Pat Jones.

118–19 Paul Kennedy material: Paul Kennedy, *The Rise and Fall of the Great Powers*. New York: Vintage Books, 1987.

119 Paul Kennedy's response to *Wall Street Journal* editorial: Paul Kennedy, "A Declining Empire Goes to War," *The Wall Street Journal*, January 24, 1991, A10.

119 Michael Porter quotation: Michael E. Porter, "The Competitive Advantage of Nations," *Harvard Business Review*, March–April 1990, 73–93.

120 McGeorge Bundy material: In McGeorge Bundy, *Danger and Survival*. New York: Vintage Press, 1988; Kennedy material, pp. 355–56; President Reagan's quotation, p. 571.

120 A principle of opposites: The principle is illustrated by that frustrating game called golf. In golf, to hit the ball high, you must hit down. To hit the ball far, you slow down your swing. To make your ball hook to the left, you swing to the right. It is as though to perform well you must do the opposite of what your instincts tell you.

122 Alternative to Star Wars. Nancy Perry, "The New Case for Star Wars," *Fortune*, December 3, 1990, 121–32.

123 Optimum stimulation level: Marvin Zuckerman, *Sensation Seeking*. New York: Lawrence Erlbaum Associates, 1979.

123 Psychologist's quotation: Daniel Goleman, "Why Do People Crave the Experience?" *The New York Times*, Science Section, August 2, 1988, C1, C13.

124 Dennis Levine story: Dennis B. Levine, "The Inside Story of an Inside Trader," *Fortune*, May 21, 1990, 80–89.

124–25 Stockbroker betting: William Power, "Hottest Commodity in Wall Street Pits? Georgetown Hoyas," *The Wall Street Journal*, March 24, 1989, A1, A4.

125 GM quotation: Keller, *Rude Awakening*, p. 205.

126 Boeing vice-president's quotation: Alan Murray and Urban C. Lehner, "What U.S. Scientists Discover, the Japanese Convert—Into Profit," *The Wall Street Journal*, June 25, 1990, 1, 4.

127-28 Material on bank failures: Sprague, *Bailout.* Quote on diversification, p. 59.

128 Weather satellites quotation: Bob Davis, "U.S. Climate Satellites Weather Criticism," *The Wall Street Journal,* March 22, 1990, 31.

129 Apollo quotations: Murray and Cox, *Apollo: The Race to the Moon,* pp. 261–63.

130 Warren Buffett story: L. J. Davis, "Buffett Takes Stock," *The Business World: The New York Times Magazine,* April 1, 1990, 16–18, 62–64.

132 Quotation on complicated math models: Steven P. Schnaars, *Megamistakes: Forecasting and the Myth of Rapid Technological Change.* New York: The Free Press, 1989, p. 54.

133-34 GE compressor story: Thomas F. O'Boyle, "GE Refrigerator Woes Illustrate the Hazards in Changing a Product," *The Wall Street Journal,* May 7, 1990, A1, A6.

6. FINDING THE CAUSE

137-38 Navy test pilot anecdote: Tom Wolfe, *The Right Stuff.* New York: Bantam Books, 1979, pp. 27–28.

138-39 Bartender story: Robyn M. Dawes, *Rational Choice in an Uncertain World.* New York: Harcourt Brace Jovanovich, 1988, p. 252.

139-140 World Series attributions: Richard Lau and Dan Russell, "Attributions in the Sports Pages," *Journal of Personality and Social Psychology,* 39, 1980, 29–38.

143 The "Heard on the Street" stock scam was widely publicized. For example, see Steve Coll, "A Wall Street Friendship's Crash," *The Washington Post,* November 29, 1987, H1.

143 Experimental stock market study: Paul Andreassen, "On the Social Psychology of the Stock Market: Aggregate Attributional Effects and the Regressiveness of Prediction," *Journal of Personality and Social Psychology,* 53, 1987, 490–96.

144 Information on polygraph tests: Benjamin Kleinmuntz and Julian Szucko, "Lie Detection in Ancient and Modern Times: A Call for Contemporary Scientific Study," *American Psychologist,* 39, July 1984, 766–76.

144 Historians and Nazis: G. Barraclough, "Mandarins and Nazis," *New York Review of Books,* 19, 1972, 37–42.

144 "Historians give an appearance": R. H. Tawney, *The Agrarian Problems in the Sixteenth Century.* New York: Franklin, 1961, quoted in Baruch Fischhoff, "For Those Condemned to Study the Past: Heuristics and Biases in Hindsight," in D. Kahneman, et al., eds., *Judgment Under Uncertainty: Heuristics and Biases.* Cambridge: Cambridge University Press, 1982, pp. 335–51.

144-45 Joe Montana story: Bob Oates, "Montana Made NFC Tops in '80s," *Saturday Oklahoman & Times,* September 22, 1990, 22.

145-47 San Gabriel debris flow: McPhee, *The Control of Nature,* pp. 183–272. Quote found on p. 185.

147-48 These lawsuit examples are described in Judith Hurley, "The $425,000 Beetle and Other Legal Winners," *Medical Economics,* October 1, 1984, 203–12.

148 Berkeley professor's story: Thomas Simmons, "I'll Sue—That's What I'll Do!" *The New York Times,* May 2, 1987, 11.

149 Homelessness and the availability bias: Dawes, *Rational Choice in an Uncertain World,* pp. 93–95.

149 Frequency of death statistics and availability bias. Russo and Schoemaker, *Decision Traps,* p. 83.

150–51 For a discussion of the resemblance criterion, see Richard Nisbett and Lee Ross, *Human Inference: Strategies and Shortcomings of Social Judgment.* Englewood Cliffs, NJ: Prentice-Hall, 1980, pp. 115–18.

151 For a discussion of the "just world" hypothesis, see Melvin Lerner and Dale Miller, "Just World Research and the Attribution Process: Looking Back and Ahead," *Psychological Bulletin, 85,* 1978, 1030–51.

151–52 Rape of twenty-two-year-old woman: "She Asked for It," *Time,* October 16, 1989, 37.

152 One author who has discussed the blaming-the-victim phenomenon extensively is William Ryan, in his *Blaming the Victim.* New York: Vintage Books, 1971.

153 Peter Arnett story: Malcom W. Browne, "The Military vs. The Press," *New York Times Magazine,* March 3, 1991, 27–34.

153 For a discussion of the fundamental attribution error, see Nisbett and Ross, *Human Inference,* pp. 122–27.

154 Annual report study: James Bettman and Barton Weitz, "Attributions in the Board Room: Causal Reasoning in Corporate Annual Reports," *Administrative Science Quarterly, 28,* 1983, 165–83.

155 United Airlines Flight #811: *National Transportation Safety Board: Aircraft Accident Report,* PB92-910402, "Explosive Decompression—Loss of Cargo Door in Flight, United Airlines Flight 811," Washington, DC: U.S. Government Printing Office, March 18, 1992.

155 HUD scandal: Michael Winerip, "HUD Scandal's Lesson: It's a Long Road from Revelation to Resolution," *The New York Times,* July 22, 1990, E20.

156 For a discussion of assigning blame as accident severity increases, see Jerry Burger, "Motivational Biases in the Attribution of Responsibility for an Accident," *Psychological Bulletin, 90,* 1981, 496–512.

158 Owl story and quotation: Ted Gup, "Owl vs. Man," *Time,* June 25, 1990, 61.

7. CHANCE VERSUS CONTROL

161–62 Shukhov story: Alexander Solzhenitsyn, *One Day in the Life of Ivan Denisovich,* translated by Max Hayward and Ronald Hingley. New York: Frederick A. Praeger, 1963. Quote taken from pp. 202–3.

162–63 Harvey Oxenhorn story: Alice Hoffman, "The Book That Wouldn't Die: A Writer's Last and Longest Voyage," *New York Times Book Review,* July 22, 1990, 14.

163 Apollo three-man crew: Murray and Cox, *Apollo: The Race to the Moon,* pp. 106–7.

163–64 London Blitz: W. Feller, *An Introduction to Probability Theory and Its Applications*. 3rd ed. Vol. 1. New York: John Wiley & Sons, 1968, pp. 150–152.

164–65 Las Vegas gambler: McQuaid, *The Gambler's Digest*, 1971, p. 289, cited in Ellen Langer, *The Psychology of Control*. Beverly Hills, CA: Sage Publications, 1983, p. 30.

165–66 Experiments on the illusion of control: Ellen J. Langer, "The Illusion of Control," *Journal of Personality and Social Psychology, 32*, 1975, 311–328.

166 Israeli flight instructor: Reported by K. McKean, "Decisions. Two Eminent Psychologists Disclose the Mental Pitfalls in Which Rational People Find Themselves When They Try to Arrive at Logical Conclusions," *Discover*, 1985, 22–31.

168 Predicting future prices from past prices: Branch, "The Predictive Power of Stock Market Indicators," *Journal of Financial and Quantitative Analysis, 11*, June 1976, 269–85.

168–69 *Consumer Reports* study: "Mutual Funds 1990," *Consumer Reports*, May 1990, 330–41.

169 For a highly readable discussion of technical analysis, see Hersh M. Shefrin and Meir Statman, "How Not to Make Money in the Stock Market," *Psychology Today*, February 1986, 52–56.

170 A highly articulate proponent of contrarian investment strategy is David Dreman, *The New Contrarian Investment Strategy*. New York: Random House, 1982.

170 Peter Lynch quotations: Peter Lynch, "Silly Things People Believe About Stocks," *Medical Economics*, May 1, 1989, 80–91.

172 Dear Abby story: Universal Press Syndicate, June 28, 1974.

173 Insurance president and Hurricane Hugo: Antonio N. Fins, "In Hugo's Wake, a New Storm Kicks Up," *BusinessWeek*, July 9, 1990, 78.

173 Reagan and astrology: George Hackett, "Of Planets and the Presidency," *Newsweek*, May 16, 1988, 20.

174 Statistics on astrology: Nr. Kleinfield, "Seeing Dollar Signs in Searching the Stars," *The New York Times*, May 15, 1990, Section 3, 1, 11.

174 Feng shui material: Michele Galen, "The Chinese Art for Changing Your Fortune," *Newsweek*, August 6, 1990, 86.

176 Paul A. Samuelson and critic: Ronald Bailey, "Them That Can Do, Them That Can't Forecast," *Forbes*, December 26, 1988, 94–98.

177–78 Granada invasion: James M. Perry and John J. Fialka, "As Panama Outcome Is Praised, Details Emerge of Bungling During the 1983 Grenada Invasion," *The Wall Street Journal*, January 15, 1990, A10.

179 Arnauld quote: See Baruch Fischhoff, "For Those Condemned to Study the Past: Heuristics and Biases in Hindsight." This essay also includes an excellent review of research on the hindsight bias.

181 Stress and ethics study: Reported by Amanda Bennett, "Managing," *The Wall Street Journal*, April 11, 1991, B1.

181 Ross Perot material: From Keller, *Rude Awakening*, p. 183.

182 Material on history of gambling and Cicero quote: Dawes, *Rational Choice in an Uncertain World*, pp. 277–78.

182 Ideas for this section on the importance of uncertainty are developed by Robyn Dawes in his *Rational Choice in an Uncertain World*, pp. 182–83 and 268.

8. CHOOSING A FRAME OF REFERENCE

185 General Shoup story: Halberstam, *The Best and the Brightest*, p. 85.

186 Cardiologist material: Ron Winslow and Michael Waldholz, "Agonizing Choices," *The Wall Street Journal*, May 11, 1990, R16–R20.

187–89 Quotations in the Mustang anecdote: Halberstam, *The Reckoning*, pp. 373, 376. Information also obtained from Lee Iacocca, *Iacocca: An Autobiography*. New York: Bantam Books, 1984.

189–91 Quotations on Apollo program: Murray and Cox, *Apollo: The Race to the Moon*, pp. 77, 80, and 83.

191 Material on the space station: William Broad, "How the $8 Billion Space Station Became a $120 Billion Showpiece," *The New York Times*, June 10, 1990, 1, 16.

193–94 Quotations for Space Shuttle section: Joseph Trento, *Prescription for Disaster*. New York: Crown, 1987, pp. 4, 103, 107, 138.

195 Description of 1973 Arab-Israeli War: Dawes, *Rational Choice in an Uncertain World*, pp. 244–46.

196 Quotation from Sadat: T. Dupee, *Elusive Victory: The Arab-Israeli Wars, 1947–1974*. New York: Harper & Row, 1978, as cited in Dawes, *Rational Choice in an Uncertain World*, p. 246.

197–98 The "New Coke" vignette: Adapted from John C. Mowen, *Consumer Behavior*. New York: Macmillan, 1993, pp. 22–23.

199 Quotations from Iacocca: Lee Iacocca, *Lee Iacocca's Talking Straight*. New York: Bantam Books, 1989, pp. 145–46.

200–201 D. F. Hornig material: D. F. Hornig, "Presidential Decision Making," Speech to the Society for Judgment and Decision Making, November 19, 1989.

201–202 Quote from Shea: Murray and Cox, *Apollo: The Race to the Moon*, p. 225.

202 On risk and public fear: Paul Slovic, "Perception of Risk," *Science*, 236, April 17, 1987, 280–85.

203–204 Exxon Valdez clean-up. "Too Much Valdez Clean-Up?" *Fortune*, May 6, 1991, 8.

204–205 Korean War frame for Vietnam: Halberstam, *The Best and the Brightest*, p. 589.

205 Kennedy's sense of history: Robert S. McNamara, *Blundering into Disaster*. New York: Pantheon, 1986, p. 14.

205–206 Cuban missile crisis analysis: Richard E. Neustadt and Ernest R. May, *Thinking in Time*. New York: The Free Press, 1988, p. 5.

207 "It may sound absurd": McNamara, *Blundering into Disaster*, p. 12.

208 Quotations from Don Frey: Donald N. Frey, "The Techies' Challenge to the Bean Counters," *The Wall Street Journal*, July 6, 1990, A10.

9. REASON VERSUS EMOTION

211–13 The Bendix/Martin Marietta story: Roy Rowan and Thomas Moore, "Behind the Lines in the Bendix War," *Fortune*, October 18, 1982, 157–65; John Koten and John Williams, "Bendix–Martin Marietta Battle Pits Resolved Agee Against Shrewd Gray," *The Wall Street Journal*, September 9, 1982, 29, 33; and "Did Main Characters in Big Takeover Saga Let Egos Sway Them?" *The Wall Street Journal*, September 24, 1982, 1, 24.

213 The 1981 chess match: Paul Hoffman, "The Youngest Champ, the Dirtiest Game," *New York Times Book Review*, October 7, 1990, 14.

214 Kasparov quotations: Fred Waitzkin, "Kasparov," *New York Times Magazine*, October 7, 1990, 29–30, 60, 64, 86, and 87.

214–15 The Tom Lasorda story: E. M. Swift, "Back Off," *Sports Illustrated*, August 13, 1990, 34–40.

215 Upton Sinclair: *The Jungle*. New York: Harper and Brothers Publishers, 1951, pp. 98–99.

216 Authority on decision theory, quoted in Dawes, *Rational Choice in an Uncertain World*, p. 10.

221 Curtis LeMay quotation: Steven Kull, *Minds At War: Nuclear Reality and the Inner Conflicts of Defense Policymakers*. New York: Basic Books, 1988, p. 163.

221 Nixon on international relations: Richard Nixon, *The Real War*. New York: Warner Books, 1980, pp. 253, 255.

221–22 Nixon on Vietnam: H. R. Haldeman, *The Ends of Power*. New York: Warner Books, 1980, pp. 253, 255.

225 Saddam Hussein's dream: Thomas L. Friedman, "A Dreamlike Landscape, a Dreamlike Reality," *The New York Times*, October 28, 1990, E3.

225–26 The Tony Cimo story: Art Harris, "Tony Cimo Served Three Years for Avenging His Murdered Parents: He Says the Time Was Well Spent," *People*, April 21, 1986, 34–37.

226 Eliyahu Zeira quotations: Aloup Hareven, "Disturbed Hierarchies: Israeli Intelligence in 1954 and 1973," *Jerusalem Quarterly 9* (Fall), 1978, 12, cited in Eliot Cohen and John Gooch, *Military Misfortunes: The Anatomy of Failure in War*. New York: The Free Press, 1990, pp. 113, 114.

227 *Thinking Man's Guide to Baseball*. This material was found in George F. Will, *Men At Work*. New York: Macmillan, 1990, p. 176.

228 "Chin music" quotations: George F. Will, *Men At Work*. New York: Macmillan, 1990, p. 53. The Bob Gibson story is found on p. 98.

229 Hitler in Yugoslavia: M. J. Horowitz, *Stress Response Syndromes*. 2nd ed. New York: Aronson Publishing Company, 1980, cited in Dawes, *Rational Choice in an Uncertain World*, p.15.

230 Intuition among executives: Daniel Isenberg, "How Senior Managers Think," *Harvard Business Review, 62*, 1984, 81–90. See also Weston H. Agor, "How Top Executives Use Their Intuition to Make Important Decisions," *Business Horizons*, January–February 1986, 49–53.

230–31 John Glenn story: Murray and Cox, *Apollo: The Race to the Moon*, pp. 267, 269.

231 "His greatest exhilaration": Waitzkin, "Kasparov," 62.

231 Tony La Russa quotation: Will, *Men At Work*, p. 30.

231 Thinking in baseball: Will, *Men At Work*, pp. 3, 210–11.

232 Quotation on top executives: Agor, "How Top Executives Use Their Intuition . . . ," *Business Horizons*, 21.

232 Quotations on the way executives think: Isenberg, "How Senior Managers Think," 82.

232 Tonsillectomy example: Russo and Schoemaker, *Decision Traps*, p. 122.

233 APA president: Paul Meehl, "Causes and Effects of My Disturbing Little Book," *Journal of Personality Assessment, 50,* 1986, 370–75.

233 Quotation on decision making: Russo and Schoemaker, *Decision Traps*, p. 119.

233 Herbert Simon material: Herbert Simon, *Reason in Human Affairs*. Stanford, CA: Stanford University Press, 1983, pp. 7–35.

235–36 Challenger story. William Starbuck and Frances Milliken, "Challenger: Fine-Tuning the Odds Until Something Breaks," *Journal of Management Studies,* July 1988, 319–40.

10. THE PEERLESS DECISION MAKER

239 Bob Swafer story: Told to me by Don Cooper, the Oklahoma State University team physician who helped take Mr. Swafer in the ambulance to Oklahoma City.

240–41 Thud Ridge story: Told to me by Colonel (Retired) Glenn Nemenchek.

242–43 Don Frey material: Frey, "The Techies' Challenge to the Bean Counters," *The Wall Street Journal,* July 16, 1990, A10.

243 Role of finance at GM: Keller, *Rude Awakening*, p. 23. Also Ross Perot quote, p. 185.

244 Pete Rose observer's quotation: Michael Y. Sokolove, *The Myth, Life, and Lies of Pete Rose*, New York: Simon and Schuster, 1990, quoted in Florence King, "Born to Win—and to Lose," *The New York Times Book Review,* November 11, 1990, 9.

244 Vietnam decision making. Halberstam, *The Best and the Brightest*, p. 640.

245–46 Alan Shepard story: Wolfe, *The Right Stuff*, pp. 200–212.

246–47 XEROX copier story: Bruce Nussbaum and Robert Neff, "I Can't Work This Thing," *BusinessWeek,* April 29, 1991, 58–66.

248 Hiring at NASA: Murray and Cox, *Apollo: The Race to the Moon*, p. 263.

248–49 The Cadillac Allante project: Keller, *Rude Awakening*, pp. 215–18.

251 Statistics on private aviation accidents: J. Mac McClellan, "We're Better Pilots," *Flying,* April 1990, 37. See also James Ott, "10 Fatal Crashes Spark Call for New Safety Measures," *Aviation Week & Space Technology,* October 9, 1989, 28–30.

251–52 Study on pilot judgment: Berl Brechner, "A Question of Judgment," *Flying*, May 1981, 48–52.

252 Simulations for Mission Control: Murray and Cox, *Apollo: The Race to the Moon*, pp. 261–262 and 303.

252 The maxim "Complex is easy; simple is hard" to my knowledge was first stated by Glenn Shafer, a statistician/philosopher at the University of Kansas.

253–54 D. F. Hornig material: D. F. Hornig, "Presidential Decision Making," Speech to the Society for Judgment and Decision Making, November 19, 1989.

254 Nissan engine story: Halberstam, *The Reckoning*, p. 269.

255 Toyota and *kaizen:* Alex Taylor III, "Why Toyota Keeps Getting Better and Better, and Better," *Fortune*, November 19, 1990, 66–79.

255 NASA weather satellites: William J. Broad, "Troubles Raising Questions About Space Agency," *The New York Times*, July 1, 1990, 14. See also Bob Davis, "U.S. Climate Satellites Weather Criticism," *The Wall Street Journal*, March 22, 1990, B1.

256–57 Jack Welch material: Noel M. Tichy and Stratford Sherman, "Jack Welch's Lessons for Success," *Fortune*, January 25, 1993, 86–93.

258 Golden West Financial: Richard W. Stevenson, "Inside the Nation's Best-Run S&L," *The New York Times*, Business Section, Sunday, September 9, 1990, 3-1, 3-6.

258–59 Coin-flipping example: For a discussion of the issues involving long-run versus short-run decision making, see Lola L. Lopes, "Notes, Comments, and New Findings: Decision Making in the Short Run," *Journal of Experimental Psychology, Human Learning and Memory*, 7, 1981, 377–85. See also Shreekant Joag, John Mowen, and James Gentry, "Risk Perception in a Simulated Industrial Purchase Task: The Effects of Single versus Multi-Play Decisions," *Journal of Behavioral Decision Making*, 3, 1990, 91–108.

259 Tony La Russa story: Will, *Men At Work*, p. 85.

263–66 Soichiro Honda story: Joel Kotkin, "Mr. Iacocca, Meet Mr. Honda," *Inc.* magazine, November 1986, 37–38. See also Shook, *Honda: An American Success Story*, p. 13.

ACKNOWLEDGMENTS

I would like to thank a number of people who contributed to this book. Foremost, Maryanne Myers Mowen must be recognized as my best critic and morale booster. Thanks go to the many colleagues who have made comments on various drafts of the book. They include: Vance Fried, Gary Gaeth, James Gentry, Chuck Gettys, David Holtgrave, Leonard Leff, Irwin Levin, Bob McCormick, Lieutenant Colonel Michael Milam, Michael Minor, Richard Myers, Colonel Glen Nemenchek, Kent Olson, Odell Walker, Robert Weber, and Cliff Young. Also appreciated are the efforts of Deanna Carney, Kerri Lane, Christy Mayberry, Bret Nickel, Rosheen Reynolds, Annette Scott, and JoHelen Wilson—research assistants who were frequently sent on perilous missions to the library to find articles and illustrative examples. My Spring 1991 and Summer 1992 Tulsa MBA classes also deserve thanks for critically analyzing with me drafts of the manuscript. My deep gratitude goes to the many people whom I interviewed for the book: thanks for your assistance and patience. My appreciation is extended to Burton Beals and Ursula Obst at Simon & Schuster for their superb guidance in the craft of writing. Most importantly, I would like to thank my editor, Fred Hills, and my agent, Nat Sobel, for their confidence in me and for making the publication of this book possible.

INDEX

Finland, Russian forces in, 95
fires, natural burn policy for, 31
First Pennsylvania, 127
Fish and Wildlife Service, U.S.,
157
Fisher, Philip, 106
Fitzwater, Marlin, 225
flight simulations, 251–53
floods, 173, 178–79
Floyd, Raymond, 91–92
fluoridated water, 109
Food and Drug Administration
(FDA), 13, 215
football, 98, 116–18, 144–45, 213
Ford, Henry, 23, 187
Ford, Henry, II, 89, 90, 187, 188–89
Ford Motor Company:
E-coat process developed by, 23–
24, 132–33
executive backgrounds at, 208, 243
intermittent windshield wiper
used by, 94–95
management frames of reference
at, 187–89, 205, 208
mini-van project discontinued by,
88–90, 102
new lines introduced by, 89, 90–
91, 187–89, 205, 242
Pinto tank explosion and, 200
short-term focus at, 23–24
forest fires, 31
forest preservation, 157–58
Forest Service, U.S., 31
Fortuna, 174
Fortune, 13, 75, 124, 212, 257
frame(s) of reference, 10, 185–209
in business, 187–89, 197–200, 208
guidelines for, 208–9
historical, 204–6, 209
of individual rights vs. group
welfare, 32–33
legalistic, 198–200
in medicine, 186–87
of metaphors as mini-frames, 191,
208
for military decisions, 185–86,
195–97, 204–6, 207
multiple, 206–8, 209
for NASA programs, 32, 189–92
political, 189–97

professional specialization and,
186–200, 206
in risk perception, 200–204, 209
technological vs. political, 189–94
France, Indochinese involvement of,
205
Frank, Jerome, 58
Franklin, Benjamin, 216, 233
Frederick II (the Great), King of
Prussia, 240
Freedom of Information Act, 177
Freud, Sigmund, 223
Frey, Don, 187–88, 208, 242–43
Friedman, Thomas, 225
friendly fire, 61
front-wheel drive, 89
Fujisawa, Takeo, 35–36
Fulbright, J. William, 80
fundamental attribution error,
151–53
fur trade, 158
future:
optimism about, 99–101, 107
unpredictability of, 176
see also present vs. future
judgment call

Gagarin, Yuri, 189, 190
"Gambler, The" (Rogers), 66
gambler's fallacy, 29–30, 170–73,
183
gambling:
decreasing marginal effect applied in, 114–15
illusion of control in, 164–66
by professional athletes, 244
religious views on, 182
strategic vs. tactical, 258–59
Gathers, Hank, 86–87
Gatling guns, 37
Genentech, 98
General Electric (GE) Corporation,
19, 98, 133–35, 256
General Motors (GM):
Corvette produced by, 140, 188
designs standardized at, 248–49
executive backgrounds at, 243
Ford E-coat process used by, 23
labor issues at, 181, 248–49
Lotus purchased by, 115–16

Los Angeles, Calif.:
  1992 riots in, 119
  San Gabriel Mountains above,
    145–47
Los Angeles Lakers, 104, 172
Los Angeles Times, 145
lotteries, 165
Lotus PLC, 115–16
Louisiana State University, 101
Low, George, 193
Loyola Marymount University, 86–
  87
LT-5 engine, 140
Lundy, Ed, 89
Lusitania, 78
Lynch, Peter, 170, 171

MacArthur, Douglas, 56
McCloskey, Pete, 51
McCormick, Bob, 180–81
McHale, Kevin, 172
McNamara, Robert, 23, 50, 133, 207
McPhee, John, 100
MACV (Military Advisory Corps
  Vietnam), 50, 51
MAD (Mutually Assured Destruc-
  tion), 120, 222
Maddox, 79
madman phenomenon, 222, 226
Magellan Fund, 170
MAGIC, 55
Maine, 78
male chauvinism, 222
managerial ability, 249, 250
Mantle, Mickey, 227–28
March of Folly, The (Tuchman), 66
Marine Corps, U.S., 49, 185
Mars, space travel to, 191
Martin, Billy, 140
Martin Marietta, 211–13, 222
Masters golf tournament, 91–92
Mayer, Martin, 102–3
Maynard, Buster, 214–15
means vs. ends debate, 30, 181
meat-packing industry, federal
  regulation of, 215
medical care:
  frames of reference for, 186–87
  individual rights vs. group welfare
    in, 32–33

for limb reattachment, 239–40
over-confidence bias in, 52
peerless decision maker and, 239–
  240
reason vs. emotion and, 228, 232–
  233
resemblance criterion in, 150–51
shoot/no-shoot decisions in, 44–45,
  61
threat of litigation and, 228
Meir, Golda, 195, 227
Men at Work (Will), 228, 259
Mercedes, 94, 249
Merck, 170
Mercury space program, 32, 200–
  201, 230–31
Miami, University of, 116–17
military:
  causality attribution and, 26–28,
    140, 154
  cultural values and, 224–25
  entrapment situations in, 66, 76–
    81
  faulty assumptions in, 55–56
  frames of reference for, 185–86,
    195–97, 204–6, 207
  friendly fire casualties and, 61
  hindsight evaluations of, 177–78
  overoptimistic assessments for,
    49–51
  peerless decision makers and, 240–
    242
  personnel requirements in, 249
  pilots' judgment calls in, 240–42
  present vs. future decisions in,
    104–5
  and reason vs. emotion, 216–19,
    220–22, 224, 225, 226–27, 229
  risk vs. security decisions in, 24–
    25, 109, 110, 114, 196
  SEU analysis applied to, 216–19
  shoot/no-shoot calls in, 17–19, 41–
    44, 49–51, 55–56, 61
  socioeconomic issues vs., 118–20
  *see also specific armed services and
    wars*
Military Advisory Corps Vietnam
  (MACV), 50, 51
Milken, Michael, 72, 73–74, 124, 127
Mill, John Stuart, 150